RECONSTRUCTING THE
SHIELD OF ACHILLES

An Artistic Reconstruction and Exploration of the Ingenious
Ancient Greek Weapon Immortalized by Homer in Book 18 of the Iliad

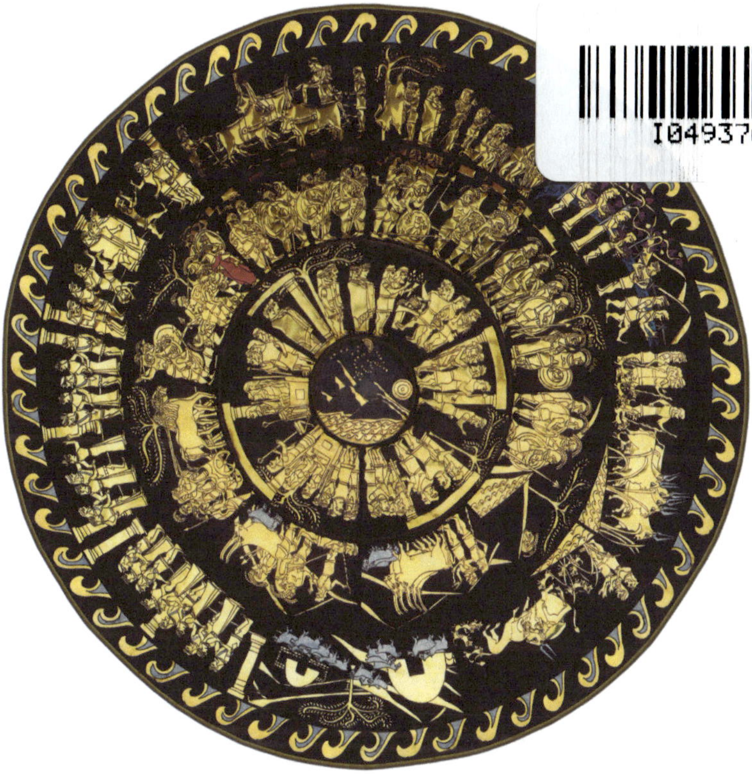

KATHLEEN VAIL

STORY MERCHANT BOOKS
LOS ANGELES
2018

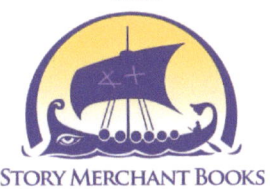

STORY MERCHANT BOOKS

Copyright

Reconstructing the Shield of Achilles

First in the Series – *Makers Take On: The Classics*

Copyright © 2018 by Kathleen Vail. All rights reserved.

Story Merchant Books
400 S. Burnside Avenue #11B
Los Angeles, CA 90036

www.storymerchantbooks.com

ISBN: 978-0-9991621-8-7

Cover Design and Artwork by Kathleen Vail
http://theShieldofAchilles.net

Acknowledgments

"I know, well I know
I am destined to die here, far from my dear father,
far from mother. But all the same I will never stop
till I drive the Trojans to their bloody fill of war!"
A high stabbing cry -
and out in the front ranks he drove his plunging stallions.

[Homer's Iliad, Book 19, lines 420-424, Fagles' translation]

Acknowledging Homer's captivating power over the human imagination lays the foundation of my work. Honorably serving to transmit Homer's legacy, writers throughout the ages have provided me with so much inspiration that without which this work would not have been possible.

As the inheritors of Western Civilization, we are all recipients of Homer's legacy, delightfully passing his legendary traditions on to our children and grandchildren, forming an unbroken chain of transmission spanning countless generations.

Powerfully firing imaginations since the very first telling, Homer's ancient narrative of Hephaistos forging the ageless and invincible weapons of Achilles, with which he heroically brings the Trojan War to a close, has relentlessly resounded throughout the course of history.

Thanks to the earliest audiences inspired by Homer, subsequent generations have grown into ardent lovers of the heroic legends of bygone days, perpetuating the epic glory – the unfading *kleos* – of Achilles.

Germinating in the resourceful soil of Homer's Ancient Greece, human dreams and endeavors blossomed, cross-pollinating poetry with drama, written literature with staged performances and elaborately painted pottery. Soon, state-sponsored statuary and monumental architecture rose with the steady acceleration of science and mathematics, organized athletics and military training, moral governance and political stability. Giving rise to a celebrated way of life unequaled anywhere else in the world, these are the prime components of Western Democracy.

In reality, we have a multitude of artists, writers, scholars, and scientists, famous and unknown alike, to thank for our rich heritage of Western culture. We must appreciate the dreams and endeavors of all our forebears for sustaining, even until today, those ancient seeds of Democracy.

Of course, the ultimate thanks for the preservation of our heritage must, in my mind, go to God, the Immortal Sustainer, Owner of my soul, and Author of my fate. From dreams to endeavors, both successes and failures, I acknowledge that life starts and rests only with God, and agree with Hektor when he tells Andromache in Homer's *Iliad*, Book 6:484-489:

> *No man will hurl me down to Death, against my fate. And fate?*
>
> *No one alive has ever escaped it, neither brave man nor coward,*
>
> *I tell you - it's born with us the day that we are born.*

The late Dr. Bernard Knox, founding director of Harvard's Center for Hellenic Studies in Washington, D.C., was an early supporter of my reconstruction of the shield of Achilles. I owe him an undying debt of gratitude for his confidence in my work and encouraging me to persevere.

Dr. Gregory Nagy of Harvard University's Department of Classics and the current director of the Harvard Center for Hellenic Studies is an indefatigable hero of Homeric proportions. I wish to express my deep thanks for his prolific endeavors contributing to the scholarly pursuit of the Classics. His generosity seems boundless as he has made his wealth of knowledge freely available, making the Classics accessible to scholars and non-scholars, alike. I am especially indebted to Dr. Nagy for his books, *Homer the Preclassic*, and *Homeric Responses*, but nearly everything I have learned about Homer is due to Dr. Nagy's scholarship and generosity.

Dr. Cynthia Shelmerdine of the Department of Classics at the University of Texas at Austin facilitated my meetings with Dr. Elizabeth Fisher of the Classics Department at Randolph-Macon College, and Dr. James A. Arieti of the Classics Department at Hampden-Sydney College. To all three, I wish to express my highest respect for their amazing contributions to the Classics and my deepest thanks for their support.

I offer an extra special portion of gratitude to Dr. Arieti for his generous devotion of time and attention to my manuscript, the foreword he wrote for this publication, and presentations which he facilitated. Dr. Arieti's generosity and support is unforgettable and my thanks to him are endless.

To Dr. Kenneth Atchity I offer my profound thanks, not only for managing the publication of this book, but for all the time and effort he generously and wholeheartedly devotes to every project he takes on. My respect for his work is, I am sure, shared by everyone who knows him, but no one knows the lovely impact his book, *Homer's Iliad: The Shield of Memory* has had on my heart. While reading it, I feel like Penelope, spellbound by an eloquent bard telling the same tales she is weaving on her loom. I am deeply honored to see my reconstruction of Achilles' shield on the cover of Dr. Ken's digital version of *Homer's Iliad: The Shield of Memory*, and my thanks to him are immeasurable for all the support he has given me.

Finally, to my beloved husband and best friend, Mohamed, I give all my love, as well as my eternal thanks and deepest gratitude for loving who I am, as I am, and always supporting my dreams and endeavors with lots of patience and recurring bad jokes about Achilles. When we met, you told me "sometimes reality is better than any dream," and then you succeeded in proving it. You are my hero.

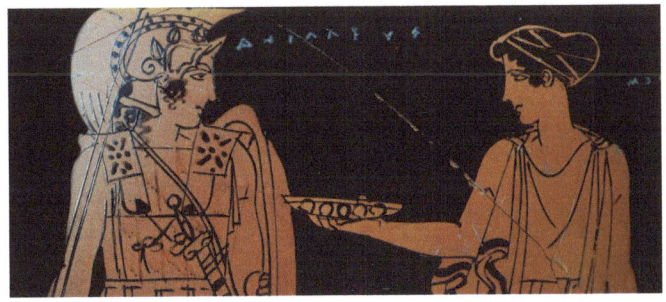

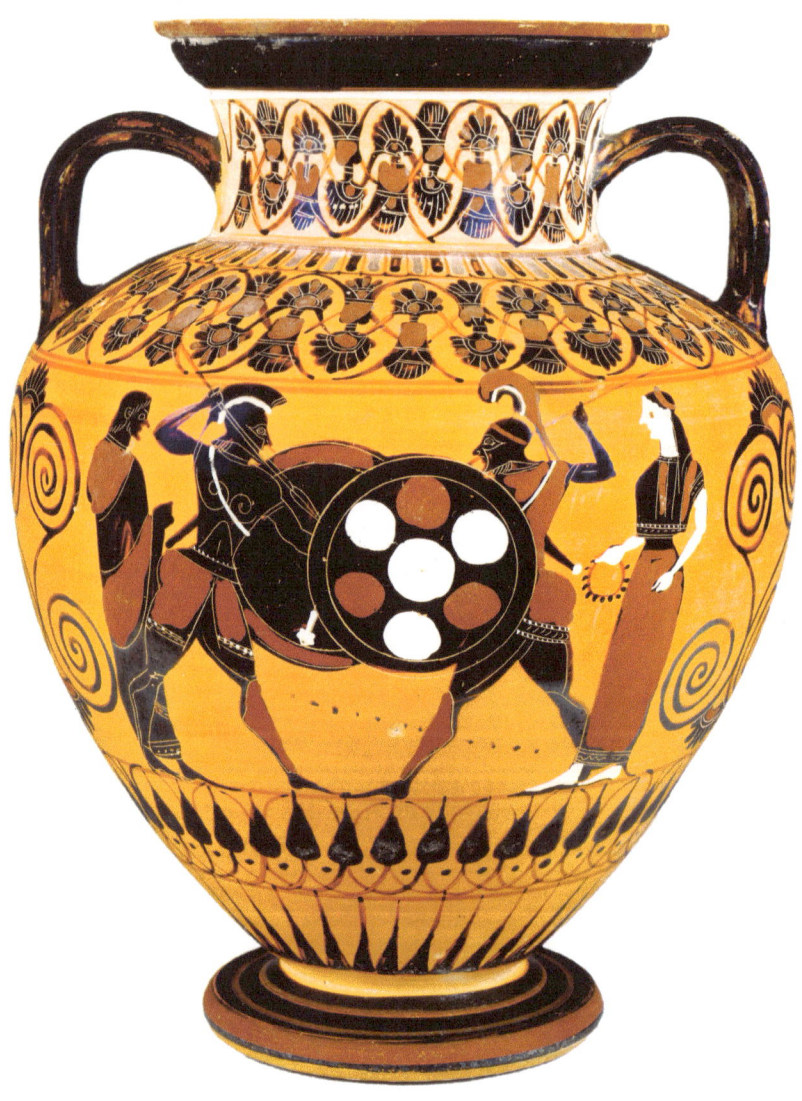

Illustration 1: Attic Black-figure Neck Amphora, ca 550 BCE.
Source: CC0 image from Getty Open Content/Vail via Wikimedia Commons

Table of Contents

Foreword

Achilles does not seem to care at all

about his new shield;[1] Hephaestus has promised Thetis fine armor for her son, armor all will marvel to look upon. Yet it makes no impression on Achilles. In his frenzy to get back into the battle, to meet Hector and his own ineluctable end, all Achilles can think about is the fighting.

The whole world is on the shield, peace, war, life, death, weddings, farming, dancing, courtrooms; we who read the mere description of it are swept into the vividness of each image. Achilles, having the actual shield in his hands, would surely have been dazzled by its beauty, were he able only to stand back from his immediate crisis and see things in their proper proportion.

In Achilles' lack of art appreciation Homer depicts the intensity of the hero's passion: nothing interests him – not food, not sex, not the handiwork of the god Hephaestus – nothing except hastening on the death of Hector and himself.

Fortunately, we are not in the same disordered state

as the hero, so we can pause in our reading of the poem to admire and reflect on the beauties of his armor. It has been pointed out that the shield portrays the kind of long but obscure and inglorious life which Achilles had earlier seemed to choose. [2] But the figures depicted on the shield have, despite their anonymity, achieved an ageless immortality.

The so-called glory of warfare appears on the shield with nameless soldiers besieging nameless cities for nameless motives. Glaucus had told

Diomedes that the generations of men are like the generations of leaves: [3] here we see how. Each leaf has its blaze of splendor in the springtime sun, but it perishes and is forgotten in the huge waste of autumn shedding.

On the shield we see the lives led by these anonymous generations; and from a distance we see mere figures whose individuality we cannot discern. So too human life: when we look at it from afar we see indistinct figures mulling about, all personality and distinctions lost.

How many unfinished stories the shield holds! The marriage of the bride and bridegroom – how will it turn out? The dispute between the litigants over a blood price for a man who has been killed – how will the elders decide? The armies fighting and ambushing each other – why are they fighting and who will win, and does it matter?

The scenes show the parts of life that go unsung, unremembered, the ordinary events which in their ordinariness matter only to the ones involved.

The innermost and outermost parts of the shield depict the elements of nature which order human life: sun, moon, stars, and sea. [4] That the sea should surround all reflects of course the sea-faring life and geography of Greece.

Next we see two cities, one at peace and one at war. In the peaceful city there is a marriage and a lawsuit; in the city at war there are a siege, an ambush, and a bloody battle.

The themes of the *Iliad* are conspicuous:

in peace the way to get a woman is to marry her, not steal her; the way to settle a dispute is to bring it before judges, not resort to violence, even if violence were at the heart of the dispute. In the next band, the themes of war are present too: the death of sons and husbands, the privation of hunger, the vain hopes of easy victory.

That the description of war is much longer than the description of peace is – alas – perhaps reflective of the proportionate time spent in each.

The fourth and most varied band is that devoted to agriculture. Here a field is being plowed with teams going back and forth. As each turned a man would give the ploughman a cup of wine, and he would resume his work.

Homer pauses to tell us that the soil on the shield looks like soil, even though made of gold – so fine was the craft. There is a king's field where laborers reap and bind sheaves of grain; children help, while the king looks on gladly. A feast is in preparation, and women scatter barley for the sacrifice.

There is also a vineyard, and young girls and young men carry away the fruit, and a youth sings to a lyre the beautiful song for Linus, and the youths follow to the music. There is also a herd of cattle, and herdsmen made of gold. Again Homer interrupts the smiles and peace to add two terrifying lions, who have caught hold of a bull and drag him away while the young men with their dogs pursue the bull. The lions break open the skin of the ox and begin to eat him. Dogs and men keep their distance.

Even in the midst of the longest stretch of calm happiness we find this note of fright, this note of the always lurking dangers. Peace has its terrors to limit human happiness. There is also a meadow for sheep in a lovely valley. Finally, there is a scene of a great festival, where men and women dressed in their best clothing meet and dance.

One can suppose that after the harvest and the celebration and the dance will come the wedding, and the cycle of scenes on the shield will repeat: like the generations of leaves, so the generations of bridegrooms and brides, of litigants, of warriors, of farmers. In nameless progression 'neath the sun, moon, and stars, confined by the boundaries of sea, the course of human life goes ceaselessly on.

Hephaestus has said that the shield will be a wonder

for all who see it to marvel at. But who is to do the looking and the marveling? The shield will be seen in its intended purpose by those with whom Achilles enters combat. Now the usual subject matter for shields is what stirs up fright, Gorgon heads, serpents, and fierce battles. [5] Several possibilities present themselves to explain the extraordinary subject matter of the new armor Hephaestus makes.

Fearsome creatures are not necessary to terrorize Achilles' combatants: The Myrmidon is himself so awful that the shield could display benign subjects without any diminution of fear on the combatant's part. And such is what we see throughout the battle scenes in Books 20 to 22. [6]

Secondly, there will be the opportunity for a pathos similar to the kind generated when Homer reminds us in the midst of battle of the dying warrior's life in peace. We can imagine the one about to die seeing on Achilles' shield scenes reminiscent of his own life. He falls carrying into Hades the memory of those pleasant scenes; what in his dying moments will he think the value of glory?

Finally, and most importantly, as Homer displays a new kind of hero in Achilles, a hero who, in discovering guilt, influences the moral consciousness of the West in such a way as to define the civilization, so too he is avoiding the stereotyped construction of the warrior's shield. The difference between the shield we might expect and the one which Hephaestus actually makes forces us to reflect on peace and war and on the value of each.

Patroclus had worn Achilles' first set of arms into battle during his *aristeia*, his greatest moment of glorious activity. He had worn the arms so that the Trojans would think him Achilles and the panic they felt at fighting Achilles would help defeat them. While Achilles watched his friend – his *alter ego*, his other self – depart he must have felt that he himself was departing; after all, the armor did give Patroclus the physical aspect of Achilles.

When Patroclus fell to the might of Hector, Hector stripped the body and donned the armor himself. When, in the final combat with Achilles, Hector engaged Achilles it must have seemed to Achilles that he was fighting against himself, in slaying Hector, slaying himself.

Given Thetis' prophecy, that Achilles' own death would follow upon the heels of Hector's, the appearance of suicide was the virtual reality. For Achilles, it was a way to expiate his guilt in causing the deaths of Patroclus and so many of his comrades.

Through the motif of the armor, Homer depicts the inner struggle of Achilles to cope with the new set of feelings he experiences. [7]

The armor has a history even after the action

of the poem. If, as I have suggested, the armor is *symbolic* of Achilles' wish to commit suicide, it is the *occasion* for the suicide of Ajax, the second greatest Greek warrior at Troy. The products of the gods, when they fall into human hands, come at a high price.

After the death of Achilles, there is a contest for his arms, and, by the aid of Athena, they are awarded to Odysseus. Ajax feels that he cannot live well, and since he believes that a man of noble birth must either live well or die well (Sophocles, *Ajax* 479-480), he chooses suicide. As Ortega remarks, suicide is the most desperate form of adaptation, but it is a form of adaptation.

The arms are presumably lost, but fortunately for us, Kathleen Vail has reconstructed it.

Using her Homer the way Schliemann used his, she has excavated from the text the shape and composition of the shield. In so doing she has confounded some of the critics, who claimed it could never be done.

"Detailed reconstruction of the shield is impossible," writes Webster.

"...nothing so comprehensive and detailed as this could ever have been seen by Homer or his audience," says Hogan.

"It is not to be supposed that the poet had ever seen such a shield as he describes," claims Gardner. [8]

Finding art works of roughly contemporary handiwork, she documents the illustrations and shows that indeed they could have been found on a shield such as Homer describes. It took a god one night to construct the shield; it has taken Ms. Vail – a mere mortal – five years of work and study to complete hers.

Reading Homer's description of the shield while looking at the illustrations will compel one to read slowly, savoring the details. The reader will have to overcome any impulse to rush on and return to the plot as he looks for the correspondence between word and image.

A humorless Platonist – the kind who took Plato literally and failed to see the smile behind the dialogues – might think that these images take us even further away from the reality of the ideas. Homer, the Platonist would say, imitated in words the shield Achilles used; Ms. Vail altered the medium and put the words into pictures, moving still more distant from the original idea of a shield.

What does the dour Platonist know? She has changed the words back into gold and silver; she has revivified the text. She supplies the modern reader with an image for his mind's eye to grasp on to. She has provided for us a glimpse of the world of archaic Greece.

Scholarship has found many uses for the shield. Literary critics have delighted in finding the themes of the *Iliad* in the various vignettes; archaeologists have found the shield a quarry for reconstructing life in Homeric times, about agricultural techniques, legal procedures, festive practices. The illustrations in the text will provide an incentive to all these researches.

Perhaps, however, the best use for this representation of the shield is to stimulate the imagination.

Reading the text while gazing on the illustrations, it is possible Alice-like to be swallowed up into the ancient scenes and to imagine oneself dancing and falling in love or, in my case, as one of the elders adjudicating a controversy.

James A. Arieti
Department of Classics
Hampden-Sydney College
Virginia, USA

FOOTNOTES:

(**1**). Achilles' indifference to the shield is noted by W. Marg, *Homer uber die Dichtung* (Munster, 1957), 32.

(**2**). M. Edwards, *Homer: Poet of the Iliad* (Baltimore: The Johns Hopkins University Press, 1987), 284.

(**3**). Homer's *Iliad,* Book 6:140.

(**4**). Cf. Jaeger, *Paideia: The Ideals of Greek Culture* vol. 1 (New York: Oxford University Press, 1945) p. 50.

(**5**). Edwards, 278; Also T.B.L. Webster, *From Mycenae to Homer* (London: Methuen, 1958), pg. 213.

(**6**). E.g., 20.463-72; 21.73-96, etc.

(**7**). See my article, "Achilles' Guilt," *Classical Journal* 80(1985): 193-203.

(**8**). Webster, 214; Hogan, *A Guide to the Iliad* (New York: Anchor Books, 1979) pp. 239-240; Gardner, *Poet and Artist in Greece* (London: Duckworth, 1933) pg. 27.

Introduction: A Pre-War Prologue

Why is the Trojan War still so popular?

Quite unsurprisingly, the Trojan War did not significantly differ from any other war in the long history of human combatants. It is, however, one of the earliest wars in the long history of recorded combat. Homer's Trojan War saga, the *Iliad*, together with its "sequel," the *Odyssey*, are among the oldest extant works of Western literature.

Although previously documented by Vidal-Naquet to be dated generally around the eighth century BCE, [1] recent analysis by Altschuler dates the composition of Homer's *Iliad* more closely to 760-710 BCE.[2]

Enjoying the advantage of so many ages of storytellers and scholarly study may be one of the bigger reasons why the Trojan War is among the great legends of both human history and recorded words. But time alone does not fully explain the popularity of this epic war between the Achaeans of Ancient Greece and the inhabitants of Ilios, popularly known as Trojans. The uniquely compelling narration of spectacular deeds, both heroic and treacherous, certainly also accounts for the fame of this epic legend.

Homer's brilliant ability to portray legendary deeds

from the perspective of an enlightened, reasonably neutral narrator allows us to examine the events from each participant's perspective. He provides a rich and complex view of human behavior that is timelessly fascinating – creatively blending a narration of ancient history with political analysis, psychoanalysis, and philosophical enlightenment – all with a respectful nod to the religious faith of his time.

Through Homer's eyes we see that the roads leading to war are neither short nor straight. Long and winding paths crisscross each other, back and forth repeatedly. The travelers on these paths jostle each other threateningly, muddying the way with drizzling tears and torrential outbursts of rage. Soon the arrival of war can be blamed on every interested participant, with no one singularly guilty, and no one without dirt on their feet.

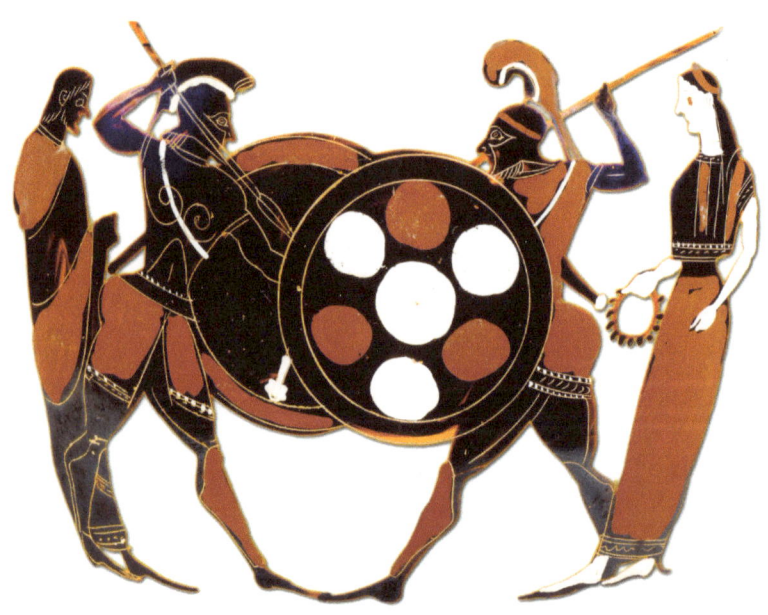

FOOTNOTES:

(1). Vidal-Naquet, Pierre. *Le monde d'Homère (The World of Homer)*, Perrin, 2000

(2). Altschuler, Eric Lewin. *"Linguistic evidence supports date for Homeric epics"* – Altschuler – 2013 – BioEssays – Wiley Online Library. 2013-02-18. Retrieved 2015-12-07, 2017-03-02.

I. The Timeless Roots of the Trojan War

With a history stretching into the earliest roots

of time, the Trojan War consumes a long time in the making. Although commonly blamed on the legendary beauty of Helen, daughter of the union between Zeus and Leda, it is an even more legendary beauty whose earlier union plays the seminal role in instigating the Trojan War.

Ascending to such fame by the occasion of her legendary wedding celebration, it is the sea nymph goddess Thetis, daughter of Nereus and granddaughter of the Sea, who sits on the throne at the timeless root of the Trojan War.

Prior to his rise to Olympian preeminence, Zeus plays only a subservient role in the primordial realm ruled by his Titan father, Kronos. Produced by the union of Uranos (the Sky) and Gaia (Mother Earth), Kronos is the earliest ruler and youngest of the first generation of Titans. Union, it turns out, is a very creative concept throughout Greek mythology.

As the ancestral mother of the Titans, Gaia populates the ancient Greek celestial realm with and without the benefit of union with mates. Hesiod relates in the *Theogony,* for example, that Gaia also gives birth to Pontus (the Sea), *"without sweet union of love."*

It is Pontus, primordial ancestor of the watery realm, who in turn fathers the shape-shifting Titan, Nereus. The maternal grandfather of Achilles, Nereus is also known in the Homeric legends as "the Old Man of the Sea."

The Old Man of the Sea

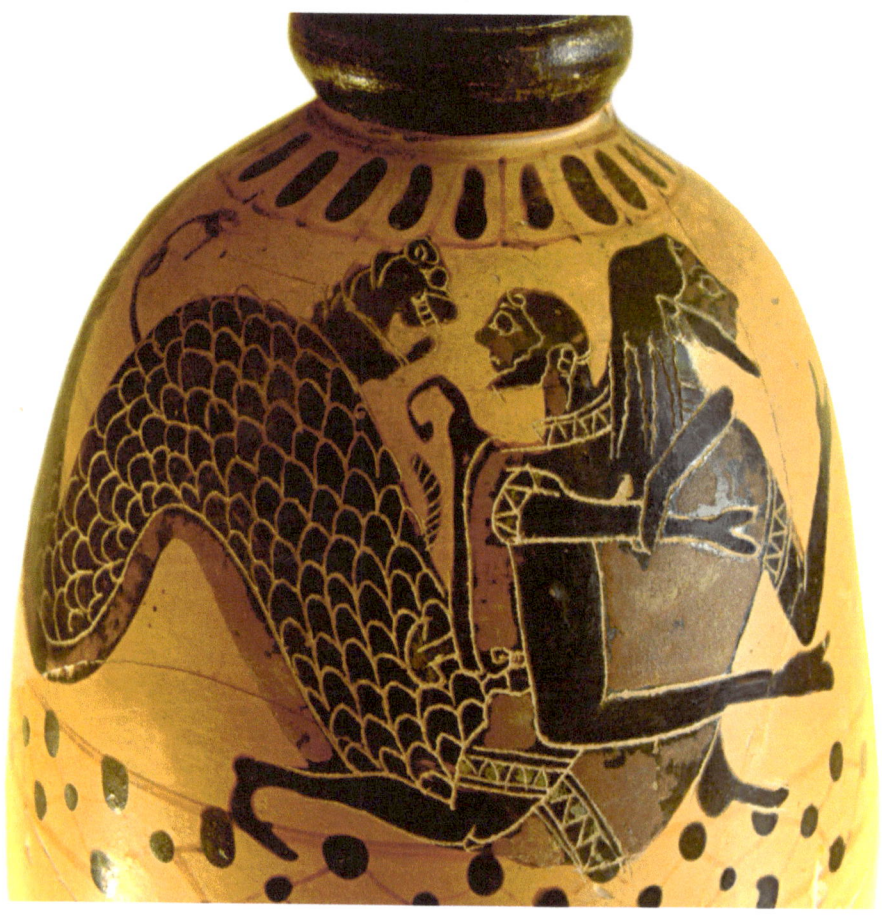

*Illustration 2: Black-figure Lekythos, ca. 590-580 BCE, depicting Herakles
astride the Old Man of the Sea (Nereus).
Source: CC0 image by Bibi Saint-Pol/Vail via Wikimedia Commons*

I. A. The Old Man of the Sea

Residing in the depths of the Mediterranean Sea,

the beautiful Thetis is one of fifty daughters, or Nereids, born to Nereus and his wife Doris. Pursuing the hand of Thetis in marriage, both Zeus and his brother Poseidon compete for the beautiful sea nymph's affection until they learn that the future son of Thetis is prophesied to be greater than both of these formidable suitors.

Thus Achilles' fate is predestined before he is even conceived. Upon hearing this prophecy, the Old Man of the Sea orders his daughter to marry a mortal human, choosing Peleus Aiakides.

Peleus and his brother, Telamon, are comrades in arms with Jason and Herakles in the quest for the Golden Fleece. Sons of King Aiakos of Aegina Island, Peleus and Telamon escape their father's kingdom in their youth, after killing their half-brother, Phocis.

Settling in Thessaly, Peleus overcomes the local ruler and assumes control as king. Setting his sights next on a wife to grace his new kingdom, he pursues the beautiful daughter of Nereus, the Old Man of the Sea.

Thetis, however, is violently opposed to marriage with a mere mortal. Struggling to escape the heroic grip of Peleus, she changes her shape into water, animals, and even fire. But his grip does not fail and, after dominating her shape-shifting ways, Peleus subdues Thetis and they plan a magnificent wedding ceremony.

Hoping to avoid trouble, Nereus invites all the gods and goddesses to his daughter's wedding, except the goddess of strife, Eris. Angry at being unwelcome, Eris sneaks in and tosses among the crowd the legendary golden apple inscribed, *"To the Most Fair."* Provoking a monumental rivalry between Zeus' wife, Hera, and his daughters, Athena and Aphrodite, Eris sows the black seed of the Trojan War.

Paris of Troy

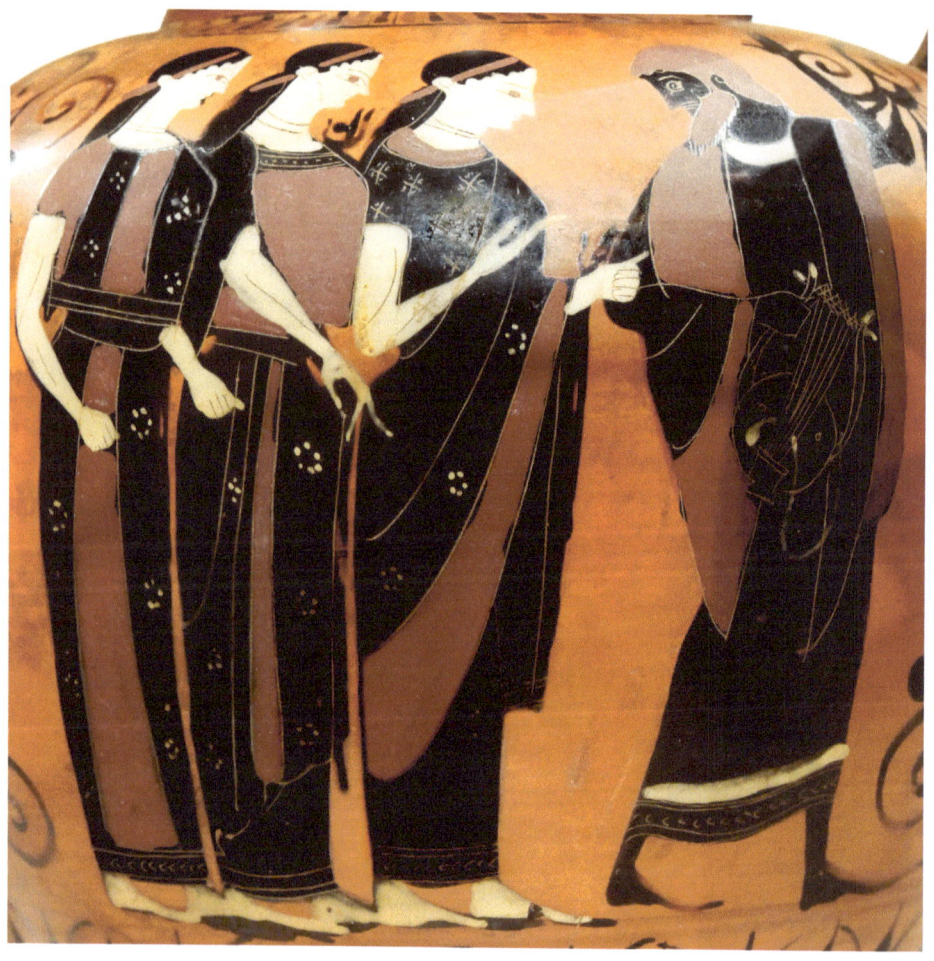

Illustration 3: Attic Black-figure Neck Amphora by the Swing Painter, ca. 540-530 BCE, depicting the legendary "Judgement of Paris."
Source: CCA 2.5 image by Marie-Lan Nguyen/Vail via Wikimedia Commons

I. B. **Paris of Troy**

Prophesied at birth to bring fire to Troy,

King Priam orders his newborn prince to be abandoned on a hillside immediately. Queen Hecuba complies, surrendering baby Paris to a servant, hoping to escape calamity. However, shepherds find the abandoned baby, rescue him and raise him in the countryside. As he grows to manhood, Prince Paris loves and marries the mountain nymph Oenone, a granddaughter of Kronos and Gaia through Rhea.

Oenone receives an invitation to the grand wedding party of Peleus and Thetis and attends with Paris. Mingling with the celestial guests, Paris finds himself at the center of strife over Eris' golden apple inscribed, "*To the Most Fair.*" Appointed by Hermes to select the winner, Paris is asked to choose between the goddesses Hera, Athena, and Aphrodite.

During the judgement, Hera offers Paris a royal kingdom and wealth, and Athena offers him success as a warrior. But when Aphrodite promises him the most beautiful woman alive, he gladly gives her the golden apple. Revealing to him that the most beautiful mortal woman is Helen of Sparta, Aphrodite solemnly swears that Helen will leave her husband, Menelaus, to become Paris' wife.

Learning that athletic games with rich prizes for the winners are being hosted by his father, King Priam, Paris goes down to the city, enters the competitions and takes first place. During the award ceremony, Cassandra recognizes him and announces that the identity of the winning champion is her brother, Prince Paris, long ago abandoned at birth.

After reconciling with his son, the king unwittingly awards Paris a ship and crew for his athletic prize. Triumphantly setting sail to claim his next prize, the beautiful Helen of Sparta, Paris plots to deliver her fiery beauty to his rightful bed in the palace of Troy.

Helen of Sparta

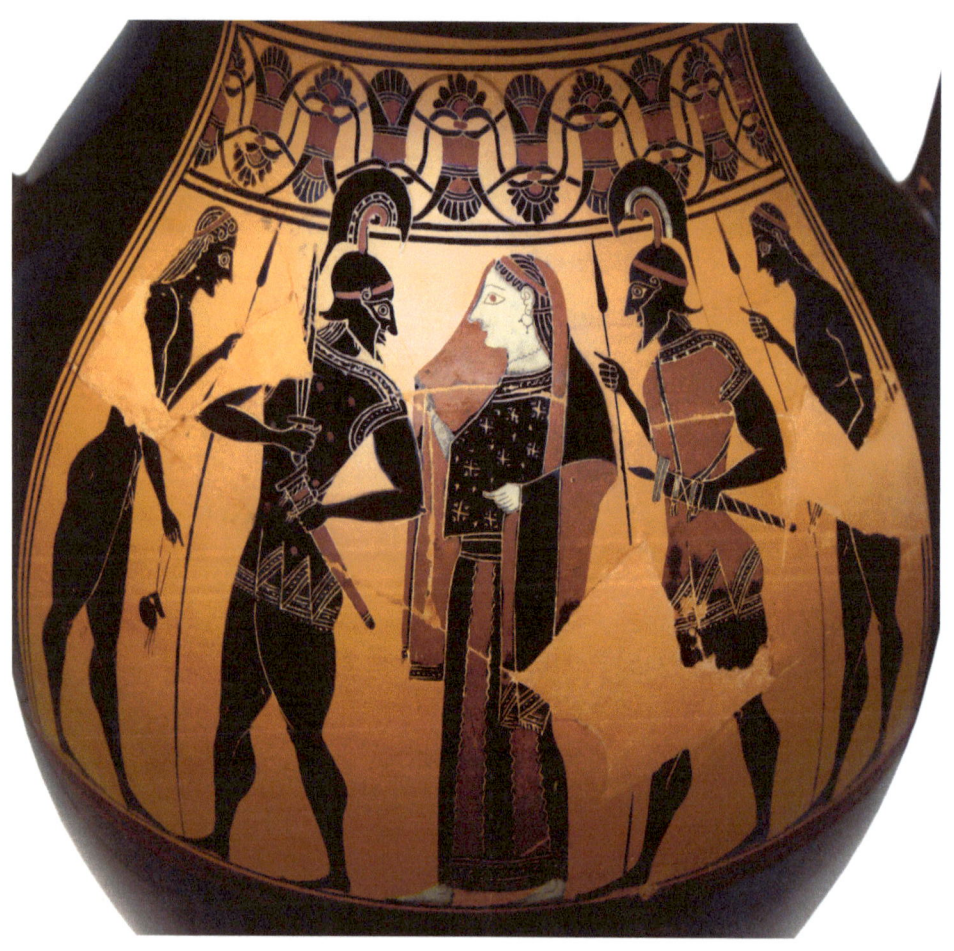

**Illustration 4: Attic Black-figure Amphora, ca. 550 BCE, depicting Helen and Menelaus.
Source: CC0 image by Bibi Saint-Pol/Vail via Wikimedia Commons**

I. C. Helen of Sparta

Famous for her beauty even as a child,

Helen is born of the union between Olympian Zeus and the lovely but mortal Leda. The semi-divine daughter quickly achieves legendary status throughout the region. Her stunning beauty attracts the attention of heroes far and wide and she is abducted at a young age by Theseus, the founding father of the Athenians and slayer of the Minotaur on the island of Crete.

Fresh from their journeys with Jason and the Argonauts, however, Helen's equally legendary brothers, Castor and Pollux, attack Theseus' palace, take brutal revenge, and return their beautiful little sister home unharmed.

As she comes of age, Helen is pressed by a multitude of suitors to choose a husband from among them. Recognizing a dangerous jealousy and rivalry among the suitors, Helen's foster father, Tyndareos, demands that they all swear to defend the winner before Helen will choose her man.

The suitors agree, solemnly swearing loyalty to Helen and her future husband. Helen chooses Menelaus, King of Sparta, as her spouse. Helen's sister, Clytemnestra, soon marries Menelaus' brother, Agamemnon, High King of Mycenae, and Odysseus marries Helen's cousin, Penelope.

Soon Greek and Trojan fates converge, with the unwelcome arrival of Paris in Sparta while Menelaus is in Egypt. Upon returning, he learns Paris has taken Helen to Troy. Summoning all the suitors who swore loyalty to himself and Helen, they quickly convene a council of war.

Assembling an army under the command of Agamemnon, logistics and planning consume ten years in the lead up to war. Finally, the Greeks launch their legendary "thousand ships," and invade the Trojan shores. It takes another ten years of waging war against Troy before Helen is restored to her rightful home and husband, but it is a war that will be remembered forever.

Shining Prince Achilles

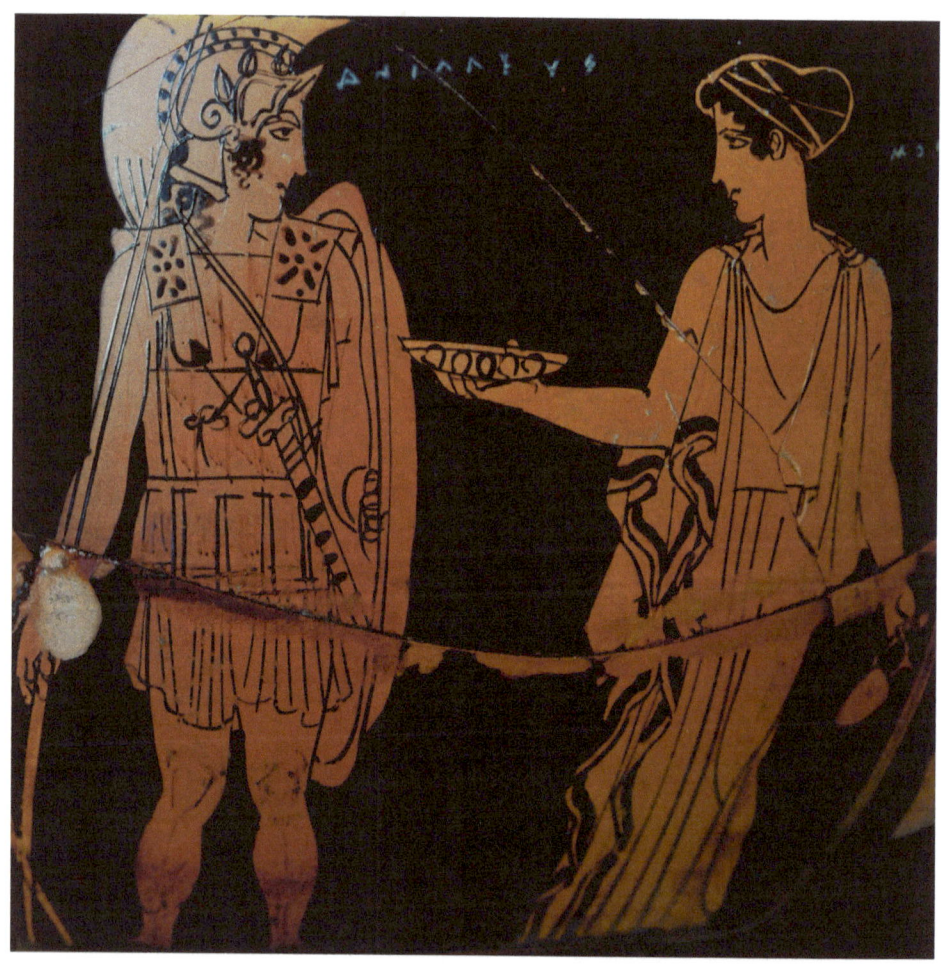

Illustration 5: Attic Red-figure Kantharos, ca. 450-400 BCE, depicting the captivating gaze of Achilles as he is visited by a sea nymph.
Source: CCA 2.5 image by Marie-Lan Nguyen/Vail via Wikimedia Commons

I. D. Shining Prince Achilles

Fated either to die after a short life full of glory,

or after a long but uneventful life, the son of Thetis and Peleus is born with a heavy destiny. Nevertheless, Thetis plans an exceptionally long life for her newborn baby and, holding him by the ankle, she dips him into the river Styx. In this way, she hopes to thwart any early disaster by making him immortal.

Full of warrior's prowess, Achilles is a strapping young man with a band of soldiers known as Myrmidons under his command when Agamemnon assembles his army for the war against Troy. Upon learning news of the war, however, his mother strips Achilles of his command.

Hoping this new expedition will pass him by, Thetis disguises her son as a girl and orders him into hiding among the women at the court of King Lykomedes on the island of Skyros. Once there, Achilles secretly reveals himself to Deidameia, one of the King's daughters. They fall in love and soon she gives birth to Achilles' son, Neoptolemos.

Thus, Achilles escapes the war draft of Agamemnon. However, the war goes poorly for both Greeks and Trojans. As the years drag on, each side gains and loses ground, like the ebb and flow of the ceaseless tide oozing under the aging, beached ships of the homesick Greeks.

Insisting that only Achilles can turn the tide

in favor of the Greeks, Odysseus departs in search of the draft-dodging hero. Learning of Thetis' ruse to hide her son at the court of King Lykomedes, the clever Odysseus devises a plan to unmask the young prince from among the princesses. Inviting all the young ladies to pick presents of jewelry and finery from the cart he arrives on, Odysseus watches as someone's eye lands on a full set of fine armor also in the cart.

Instantly he recognizes Achilles, takes him aside and explains why he has come. Abandoning his hiding place immediately, Achilles returns to his home with Odysseus where he resumes command of his men and they set sail for Troy.

Not merely prized possessions, women

are tangible assets to tired soldiers at the end of a long day on the battlefield. As booty is plundered in the course of the war, prizes are awarded to the warriors, and slave women are the most valuable prizes.

Achilles is soon awarded a female trophy to adorn his personal war tent and she succumbs to his captivating charm. In the lovely and loving Briseis, Achilles finds his food well-cooked, his clothes freshly washed, someone tender to care for his wounds, a loving soul to warm his bed, and a face much nicer to look at than those of his burly companions.

All goes well for Achilles until Agamemnon captures Chryseis, the daughter of a Trojan priest of Apollo, and takes her as his personal war prize. When Chryseis' father arrives to ransom her from a life of slavery, Agamemnon staunchly refuses.

Soon the Greeks are inflicted with plagues of death and dysentery in their camp and they blame Agamemnon for offending Apollo. Achilles boldly declares that Agamemnon must return the daughter of Apollo's priest to her father. In this way, Achilles announces, Apollo would relinquish his curse and the plagues would leave the Greeks' war camp.

Agamemnon complies, but to punish Achilles for insubordination, he orders Achilles to give him his girl prize, Briseis, to replace Chryseis. Achilles angrily surrenders his beloved Briseis but, in retaliation, he gives Agamemnon his oath that he will no longer participate in the war.

At Achilles' command, his Myrmidons sit idle in their camp, day after day, shining their armor and exercising to keep their bodies strong. Achilles spends his days likewise, heartlessly ignoring the fate of the Greeks. But the tide of war turns once again, and soon the Greeks are hard pressed by Trojans beating them back to the shoreline and threatening to set fire to their ships.

Critically in need of Achilles and his soldiers, Agamemnon expediently forgives his outspoken but heroic captain. Forming an embassy of officers, the high king sends them to persuade Achilles of the king's petition. Entertaining them generously in his tent, Achilles listens politely as the officers speak, one by one.

Hoping to spark the fire of compassion in Achilles,

the embassy lists the wonderful gifts that Agamemnon offers if only Achilles will take back his oath and re-enter the battle. With competition burning fiercely in the heart of Achilles, he finds no room for compassion. However, no officer knows Achilles as well as his beloved and best friend since childhood, Patroklos. He points to Achilles' armor hanging on the wall of his tent, gleaming brightly from its daily shining.

Patroklos states what a waste it is, Achilles' armor, shining brightly but finding no battle to shine in. No argument has the power to persuade Achilles like the powerful argument of ungained glory. Patroklos uses Achilles' love of competition in battle to beat his obstinate rivalry with Agamemnon. The strategy is successful, but not entirely.

Achilles allows Patroklos to command the Myrmidons in his stead, wearing Achilles' shining armor into battle. Not wanting any harm to befall his beloved companion, Achilles firmly commands that Patroklos must return to camp after he reaches the Trojan walls.

Fresh ranks of shining warriors burst forth

with the rising sun, powerful Achaeans hungry for Trojan blood. At the front of the ranks, the Trojans see Achilles, recognizing his armor, his horses, and his chariot. Lightning bolts of fear strike and stagger the Trojans. Taking the advantage, Patroklos leads the charge, flashing in Achilles' armor.

Reeling from the shock of fresh soldiers and fierce battle, the Trojans are pressed back to their walls and many retreat through the gates. But Hektor, eldest son of King Priam and the bravest hero of the Trojans, enters the battle at just this moment, encouraging his men's fighting spirits.

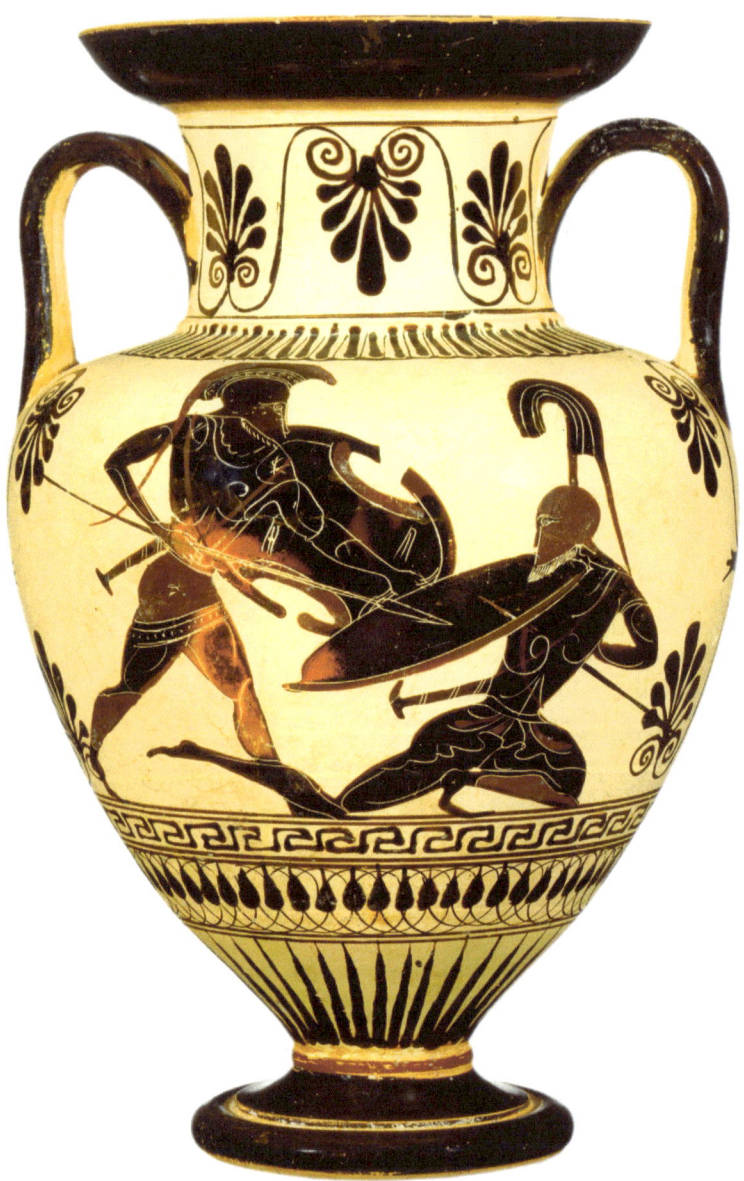

Illustration 6: Attic Black-figure Neck Amphora, ca. 500-480 BCE.
Source: CC0 image by Getty Open Content/Vail via Wikimedia Commons

Racing to engage the fearsome Greek hero, Hektor believes he is approaching Achilles. It is, however, Patroklos, shining in the glory of near victory, and in this moment he forsakes Achilles' final advice. Although safety lies in that direction, he is unable to return back to camp in the face of Hektor's approach. It is Patroklos' fate, instead, to bravely face Hektor in battle.

Although attacking heroically, Patroklos is no match against the Trojan prince. Heartlessly slaying Patroklos, Hektor then grievously strips Achilles' armor from the slain soldier's body. Quickly changing, Hektor puts on Achilles' armor, proudly displaying his blazing battle trophies. Towering thus over the pitiful body of Patroklos, Hektor faces the terrible onslaught of Greek warriors battling to reclaim the beloved lifelong friend of Achilles.

When Achilles learns Patroklos is slain,

his grief and rage are overwhelming. Echoing loudly throughout the camp, his terrifying cries of grief and anguish are heart-wrenching to every soul. Even the sea nymphs under the ocean hear his cries. His mother, screeching in reply, flies from the watery depths to quickly reach his side.

Taking Achilles' face in her hands, Thetis holds her son and consoles him, crying uncontrollably beside him. Relinquishing hope for her son's long and uneventful life, she embraces his fate as she embraces his body. With tears mingling, Thetis kisses her son and offers him some hope. Telling him her plan, she promises to petition Hephaistos for new armor. As she expects, she feels Achilles' spirit start to revive.

Seeing the spark of fire return to her beloved son's eyes, Thetis sets off for Olympos. Only with new armor can he re-enter the battle, avenge the death of Patroklos, and face the fate her shining son was born to achieve.

Prophesied before his birth, before even her wedding to Achilles' father, Thetis was informed that her son would rise to greater fame than even Zeus or Poseidon. And so it has come to pass. Long after the demise of the entire Olympian pantheon, we are still celebrating the heroic son of Thetis.

Singing to succeeding generations, singing throughout the ages, we are still celebrating the great and unfading glory of Shining Prince Achilles.

Thetis Receives Achilles' New Armor

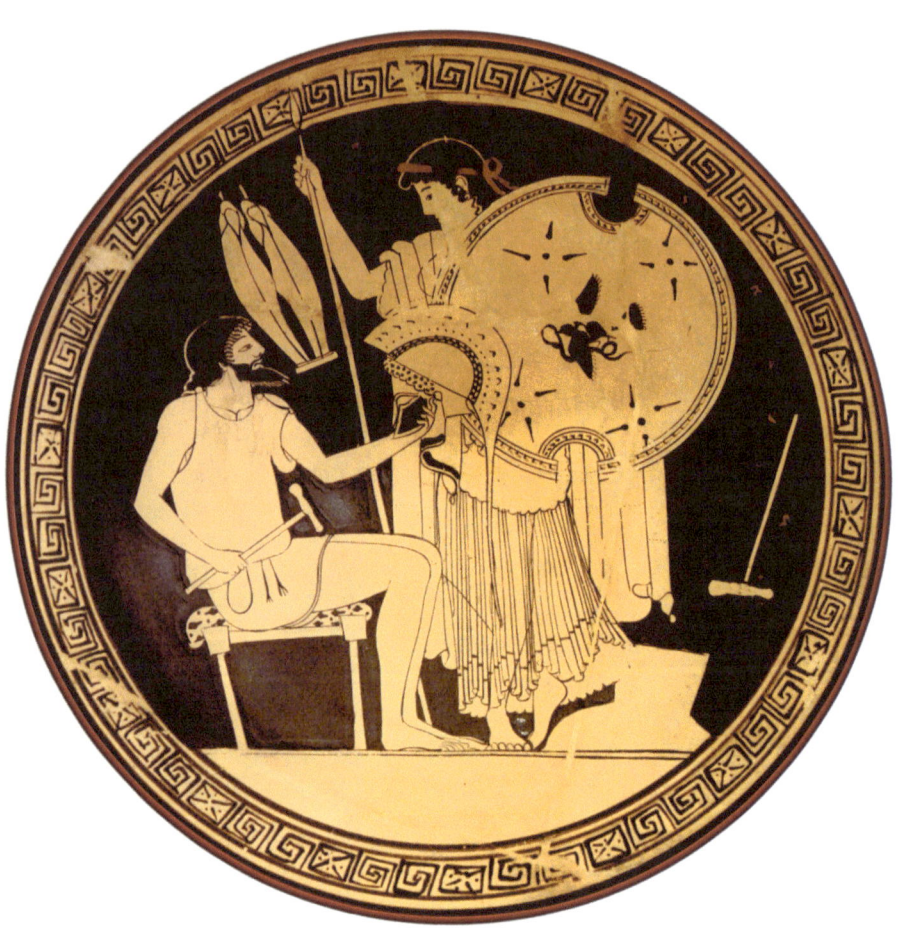

***Illustration 7: Attic Red-figure Kylix by the Foundry Painter, ca. 490-480 BCE,
depicting Thetis receiving Achilles' new armor from Hephaistos.
Source: CC0 image by Bibi Saint-Pol/Vail via Wikimedia Commons***

II. A Mother's Sad Request for Her Son

Rising up to aid Hephaistos, maids of gold moved like lively young girls;
perfectly made, they had speech, wit, and motion,
and other skills immortal.
Briskly surrounding their lord for support, he made his way to Thetis,
gracefully waiting for him to join her upon a silver throne.
Taking her hand, he greeted her warmly,
"Sweet Goddess, we are honored;
but are you in need, my dearest Thetis? Your visits are so seldom.
Please tell me if I may be of help, for I will if I am able -
if it is a thing allowed to be done, not known to be forbidden."

"Hephaistos," Thetis softly said, with tears on her lashes and cheek,
"Never has another Olympian goddess suffered such sorrow and pain.
No mortal before Peleus Aiakides, my husband chosen by Zeus,
had ever been given a sea nymph to wed, nor gave her a cheerless bed.
But there I accepted my wifely duty, endured without desire,
and though my man is constrained now by age,
pain continues to mock me.
I nursed and raised the son gifted to me; he became a man above men.
Quickly he grew, and I nurtured him

better than blossoming orchard trees.
All this did I do just to see him off, in a ship bound for war with Trojans,
and I shall not see him in Peleus' hall, his family home, again.
Yet even while sunlight still kisses his eyes, my son is destined to suffer
and I do not have the power to help him,
though I stand nearby for comfort.

"The girl-prize given him by the Greeks,
Agamemnon took back for his own.
Hot burned the heart of my son at this deed,
and he yearned for the girl intensely.
Trojan warriors beat them back to their ships,
and the Greeks could not escape.
Agamemnon's officers begged my son's help,
and offered him incentives.
He did not deem them worthy of aid, nor helped delay the disaster,
but armed Patroklos in his own gear, and sent him into battle.
Fiercely they fought at the Gate all day, and nearly took the city,
but Apollo spied Menoitios' great son slaying many Trojans.

Killing him in battle, he then gave Hektor a hero's reward for the deed.
It is for this I have come to call: now my ill-fated son needs a shield.
A breastplate, too, and a crested helmet,
and a pair of tight-clasping greaves.
Hektor stripped the armor from his slain foe,
the courageous hero Patroklos,
and now my son lies numb on the ground,
in his tent, overcome by grief."

Enheartening her, the Great GameLegs said,
"Have courage, my Lady! Please trust me!
Good gear I can make, but to hide him from death?
Now, that is another matter...
I only wish I could help him with that, as I can with the making of arms,
for I am an expert - no eyes have beheld
such gear as I shall provide him!"

Leaving her then, and going to his shop, he swiftly set about working.
Twenty smart bellows he aimed at the fire, stirring the coals up fiercely.
Huge bursts they would blow if the toil was tough,
and delicate breaths as needed.
He spoke his commands and the bellows obeyed,
fully used to the work required.
Molten gold and silver boiled in the blaze,
and tin, and Olympian bronze.
With a powerful hammer in his right hand,
and tongs in his dexterous left,
Hephaistos mounted the great iron block, knowing that all was in order.

His first task fulfilled was a well-fashioned shield;
very strong, wide, and shining.
Triple-ply was the sparkling rim around it,
and the shoulder strap was silver.
The shield was skillfully crafted together, formed of five welded layers,
and Hephaistos surpassed himself with his art
and his brilliant decoration...

[From Homer's Iliad, Book 18, Lines 417-482, Vail's Translation]

Kathleen Vail

What Does the Shield of Achilles Look Like?

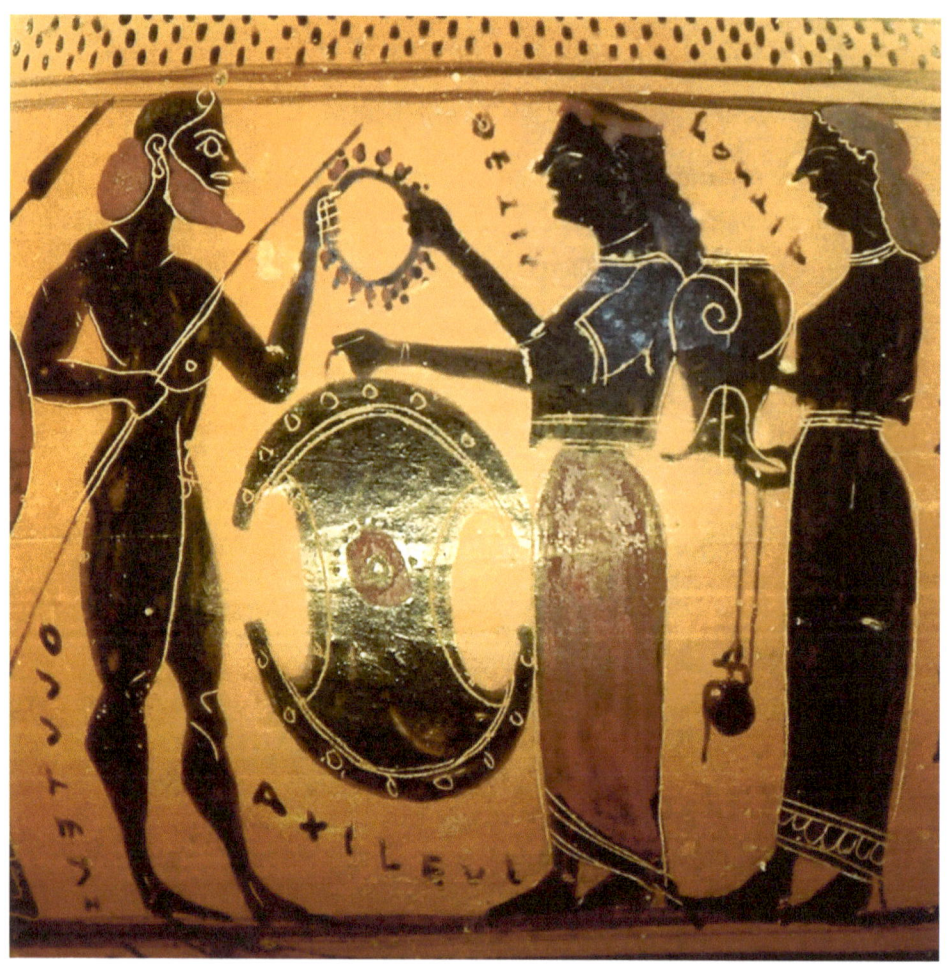

Illustration 8: Detail of an Attic Black-figure Hydria, ca. 575-550 BCE, depicting Thetis giving Achilles his weapons newly forged by Hephaistos. Source: CC0 image by Marie-Lan Nguyen/Vail via Wikimedia Commons

III. Reconstructing the Appearance of Achilles' Shield

The appearance of Achilles' new shield

is an ancient mystery, a wonderful topic of debate fascinating the imaginations of Homer's audiences from its first recital. Clearly relishing the interlude between Achilles' grief over the loss of Patroklos, and the re-entry of Achilles into battle, Homer intensifies the dramatic buildup by lingering to elaborate on the dazzling shield as Hephaistos is forging it.

"In a larger sense," writes Atchity, "the shield of Achilles is a suspension of the narrative momentum, a respite from the brutal reality of the battle (between Hektor's slaying of Patroklos and Achilles' of Hektor). In this sense the shield's appearance is... a kind of respite, a time of re-creative detachment, from the pressures of reality."[1]

Atchity notes, "The image of the shield widens the perspective of the poem, universalizing its visionary scope." He adds, "Including many individuals and several collectives but refusing to give them specific names, the shield expresses the essentially – or typically, or ideally – human."[2]

As the pivotal device ensuring Achilles' immortality, it is this universality depicted on Achilles' shield that accounts for the shield's immortality, as well. Emblazoned in human memory from Homer's first narration forward, this glorious creation is, as prophesied by its creator, Hephaistos, "a wonder to behold."

Historical Reconstructions of Achilles' Shield

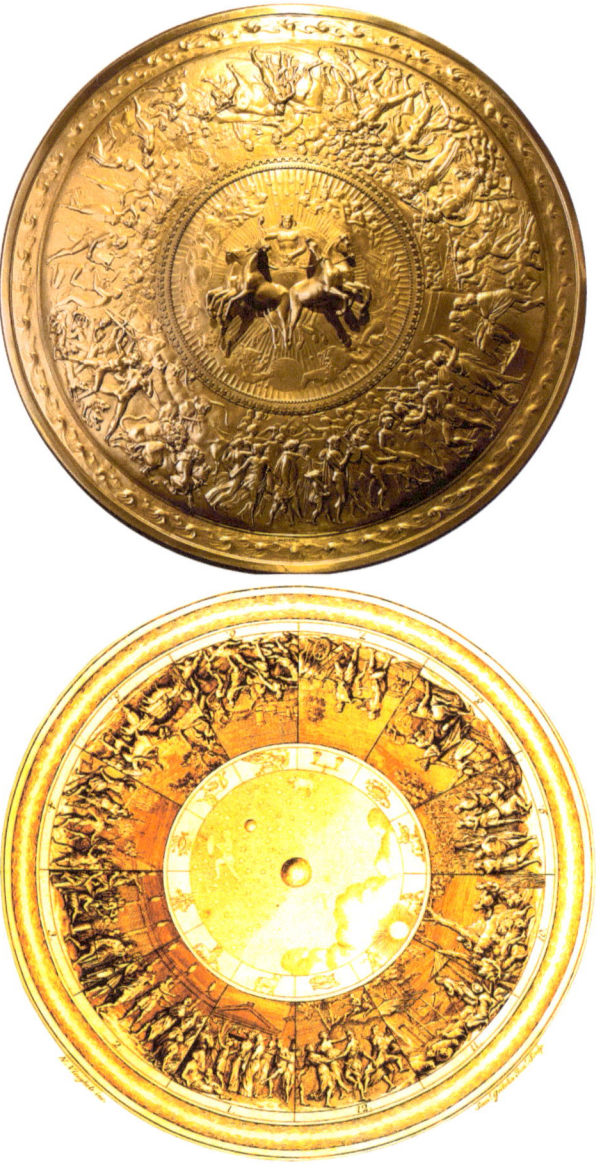

Illustration 9: Top: 1821 Reconstruction of the Shield of Achilles by John Flaxman.
Bottom: 1715 illustration in Pope's Iliad by Gribelin after Vleughels, colorized by Vail.
Source: CC0 image by Vail via Wikimedia Commons

However, perhaps considering the shield of Achilles impossible "to behold," Atchity maintains, "Excavations and reconstructions will never give us more than we have now of Homer's masterful shield. Anything more than the words would be too weak." [3]

Although "to behold" Hephaistos' wondrous creation may be interpreted figuratively, there is no compelling reason for constraining our creative imaginations to thoughts and words only. Atchity, in good company with Gardner, Hogan, and Webster, may be forgiven for imagining that a literal, artistic reconstruction of Achilles' shield is impossible, yet many renowned artists throughout history have offered wondrous works of art inspired by Homer's masterpiece.

Historical reconstructions of Achilles' Shield

include the beautiful masterpiece created by John Flaxman in 1821. Commissioned by Philip Rundell, it was presented to King George IV on the occasion of the king's coronation banquet. According to Great Britain's Royal Collection, additional silver-gilt versions of Flaxman's shield were produced between 1821 and 1822. One of which, originally presented to the Duke of York, is now exhibited in the Huntington Collection in San Marino, California.

The Royal Collection considers it likely that Flaxman, a notably "keen Greek scholar," relied on the description of Achilles' shield in Pope's translation of Homer's *Iliad* published in 1715.

Interestingly, Volume 5 of Pope's *Iliad* also contains a beautiful illustration of Achilles' shield entitled, *The Shield of Achilles as described in Homers 18th Ilias in Twelve Tables.* This is an engraving by Samuel Gribelin based on a drawing by French painter Nicolas Vleughels (1668-1737). David Coster likewise produced an acclaimed engraving of the shield of Achilles in 1715, based on the drawing by Vleughels. [4]

FOOTNOTES:

(1), (2), (3). Atchity, Kenneth. *Homer's Iliad: The Shield of Memory* (Amazon Kindle, 2014), Chapter 8, location 3782; Chapter 4, location 2207; Introduction, location 114.

(4). see also: *Bouclier d'Achille*, plate VII, pg 322, engraving by David Coster after Nicolas Vleughels. *Apologie d'Homere et bouclier d'Achille*, Paris, 1715.

The Shield of Achilles by Kathleen Vail

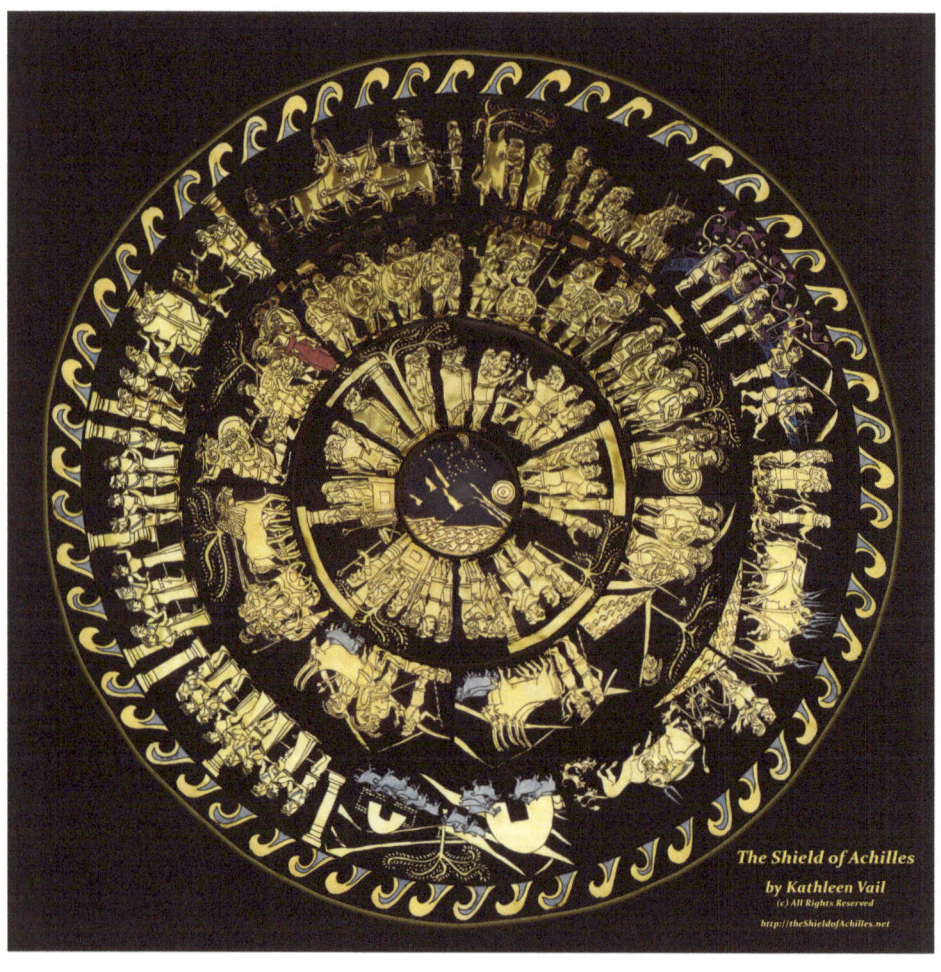

Illustration 10: The Shield of Achilles by Kathleen Vail © All Rights Reserved

IV. Vail's Reconstruction of Achilles' Shield

Exploring a more literal Homeric representation

for my reconstruction of Achilles' shield has resulted in, perhaps, a slightly more historically and artistically relevant design. Starting with a mathematical assumption of my own height (5'5") as representative of Achilles' height, the life-size diameter of the shield was based on covering the body from shoulder to thigh, as depicted in ancient Greek vases. Then, the individual ring heights were derived from the diameter and the space devoted to individual scenes within each ring was divided up equally.

After inscribing the scene images with a stylus on individual thin sheets of brass, they were painted with enamels to match, as literally as possible, the original descriptions in Homer's Greek. Bronze, silver, and tin, as well as specifically mentioned colors, e.g. red and blue, are represented with colored enamels, and unpainted brass represents inlaid gold.

The finished brass sheets were then trimmed and assembled on a convex, multiple-ply sturdy board base covered with a lightweight suede. Finally, according to Homer's specification, I attached to the back of the finished shield a shoulder strap of silver chain links.

Filled with intimate glimpses of ancient Greek life, accompanied by my personal translation of Homer's original description, the following is an in-depth exploration of each scene on the legendary shield of Achilles.

IV. A. Epicenter: CREATION

[Homer's Iliad, Book 18, Lines 483-489, Vail's Translation]

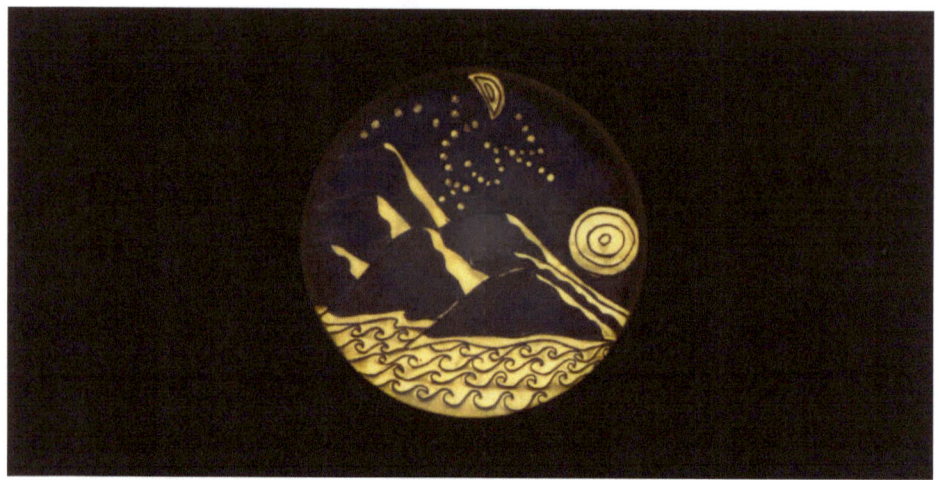

Illustration 11: Epicenter: Creation. From the Shield of Achilles
by Kathleen Vail © All Rights Reserved

Earth, heaven, and sea he made with an unwearied sun,
and moon waxing.
All the stars, too, which crown the night sky:
Pleiades, Hyades, Orion.
The Great Bear, too, also known as the Wain
attended the mighty hunter,
and she pivoted there, unable ever to swim in the ocean current.

IV. B. Inner Ring: CIVIL LIFE

IV. B. 1. Wedding Procession

[Homer's Iliad, Book 18, Lines 490-495, Vail's Translation]

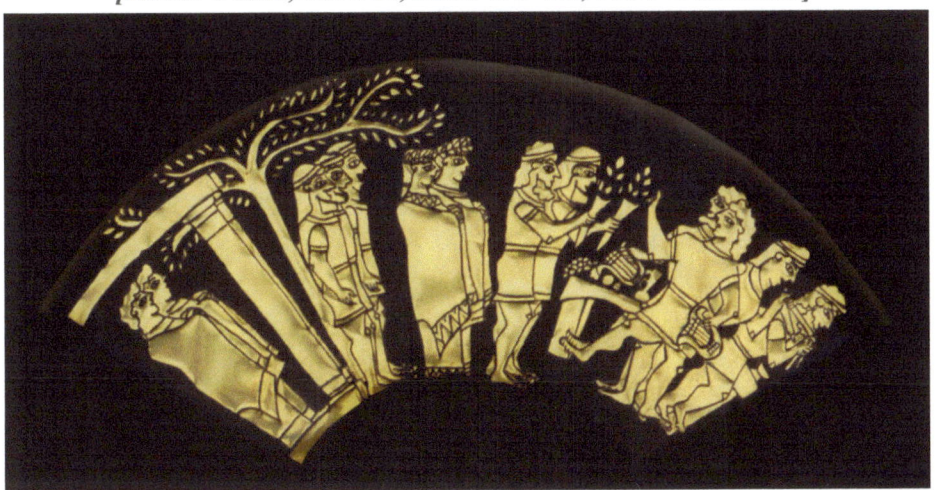

Illustration 12: Inner Ring: Wedding Procession. From the Shield of Achilles
by Kathleen Vail © All Rights Reserved

Two cities he pictured, of eloquent men, each in well-rendered scenes;
with weddings in one, and feasts awaiting
as torchmen led brides from their homes.
In front and behind the procession was growing,
with townsmen singing in choir,
and others played lyres or piped on their flutes,
and dancing 'round to the tune.
Women stood still as the brides passed by
and gazed in awe at the sight.

IV. B. Inner Ring: CIVIL LIFE

IV. B. 2. Conflict in the Market

[Homer's Iliad, Book 18, Lines 496-504, Vail's Translation]

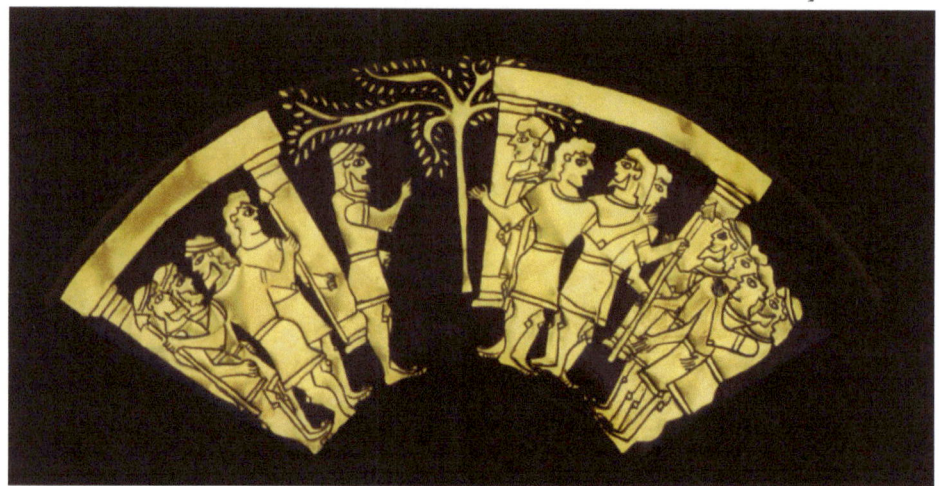

Illustration 13: Inner Ring: Conflict in the Market. From the Shield of Achilles by Kathleen Vail © All Rights Reserved

Then in the market, surrounded by men,
two argued the blood-price for murder.
The guilty man loudly claimed he would pay,
but the other quickly decried him.
They both demanded a verdict by judges,
and crowds had to be restrained
from yelling encouragement to the men
and adding to the tumult.

IV. B. Inner Ring: CIVIL LIFE

IV. B. 3. Judgement of the Elders

[Homer's Iliad, Book 18, Lines 505-508, Vail's Translation]

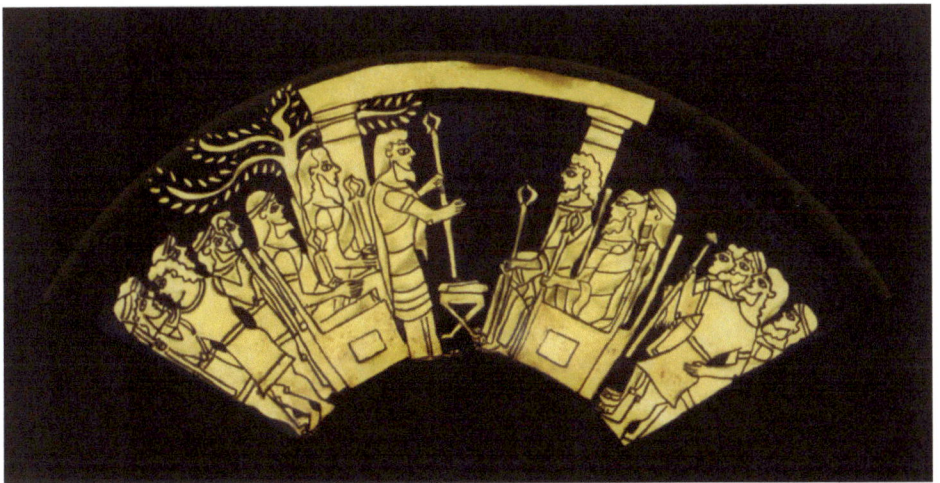

Illustration 14: Inner Ring: Judgement of the Elders. From the Shield of Achilles by Kathleen Vail © All Rights Reserved

**The Elders each sat in the sacred circle
on seats of smooth-polished marble.
The honored staff of the clear-speaking Herald
each carried in his hand,
and using it both for support and oration,
each stood and spoke in turn.
Placed in the center were two bars of gold
as a prize for the straightforward judge
who would best decide how to solve the issue,
and speak most righteously.**

IV. C. Middle Ring: WARTIME

IV. C. 1. City Under Siege

[Homer's Iliad, Book 18, Lines 509-512, Vail's Translation]

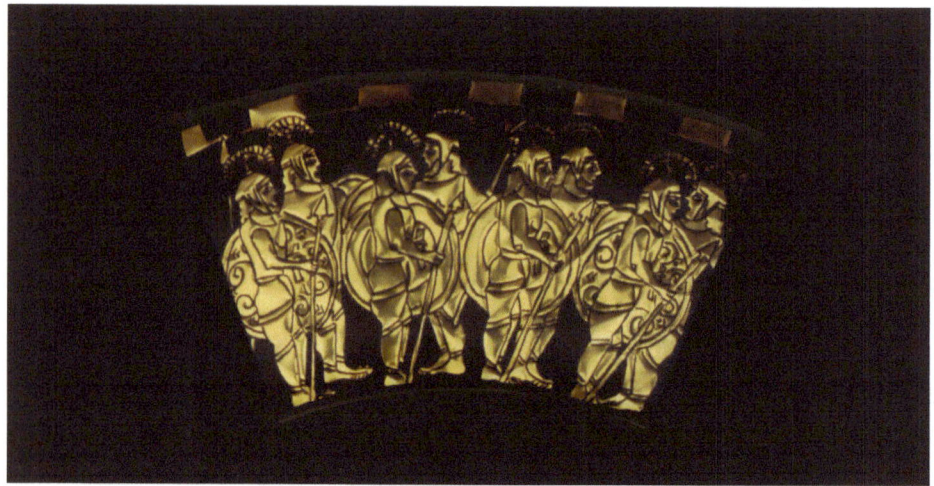

Illustration 15: Middle Ring: City Under Siege. From the Shield of Achilles
by Kathleen Vail © All Rights Reserved

Wartime, next, in the other city, displayed in preparations:
Two columns of well-armed troops surrounded
the walls of a city for sieging.
But they disagreed on the plan of action;
some wished to conquer completely,
while others wished to negotiate peace
and set terms for half the town's treasure.

IV. C. Middle Ring: WARTIME

IV. C. 2. Arming for a Raid

[Homer's Iliad, Book 18, Lines 513-515, Vail's Translation]

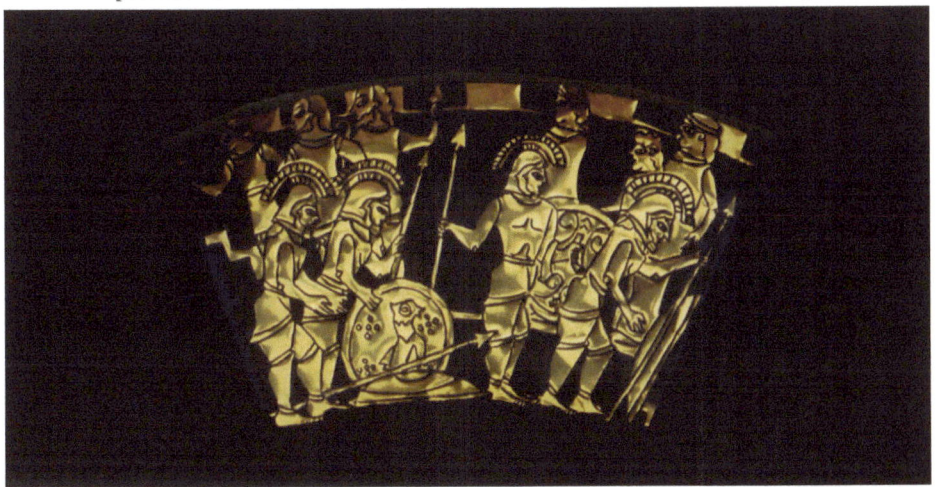

Illustration 16: Middle Ring: Arming for a Raid. From the Shield of Achilles by Kathleen Vail © All Rights Reserved

The townsmen were hungry, but bowing to neither,
they quickly armed for a raid.
Women and children kept watch from the walls,
with men too old or disabled.

IV. C. Middle Ring: WARTIME

IV. C. 3. Ares and Athena Lead the Raid

[Homer's Iliad, Book 18, Lines 516-519, Vail's Translation]

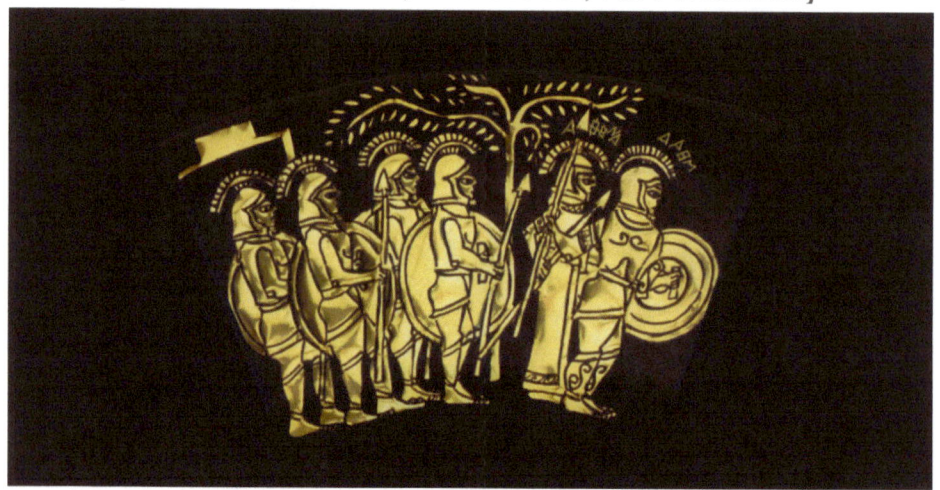

Illustration 17: Middle Ring: Ares & Athena Lead the Raid. From the Shield of Achilles
by Kathleen Vail © All Rights Reserved

The men filed out through a secret gate
led by Ares and Athena.
So splendidly armed were these glorious two,
ornate in immortal gold,
that men were small in comparison
and humbly marched behind them.

IV. C. Middle Ring: WARTIME

IV. C. 4. Warriors Hiding

[Homer's Iliad, Book 18, Lines 520-524, Vail's Translation]

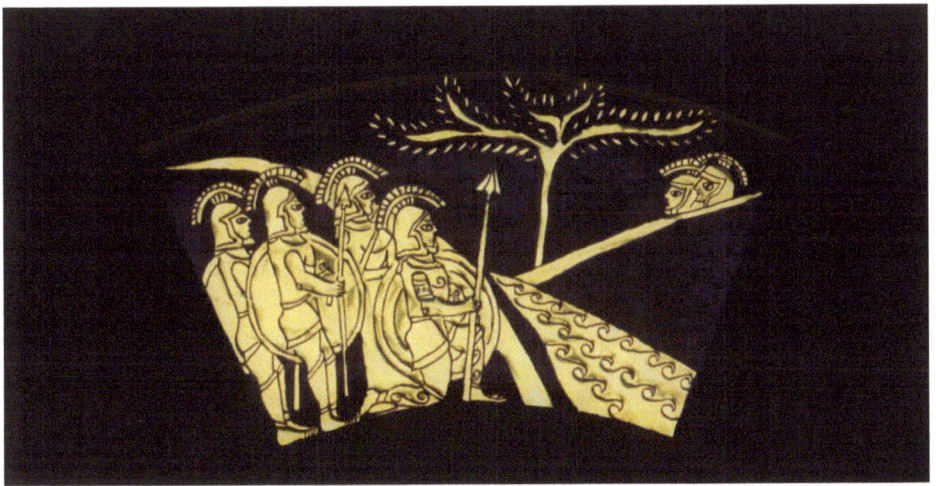

Illustration 18: Middle Ring: Warriors Hiding. From the Shield of Achilles by Kathleen Vail © All Rights Reserved

When the warriors came to their ambush point,
a stream where flocks were watered,
They hid together among bronze hills
and stationed two lookouts at hand.
There the two hid, awaiting the sight
of the sheep and the curving-horned cattle.

IV. C. Middle Ring: WARTIME

IV. C. 5. Peaceful Herdsmen

[Homer's Iliad, Book 18, Lines 525-526, Vail's Translation]

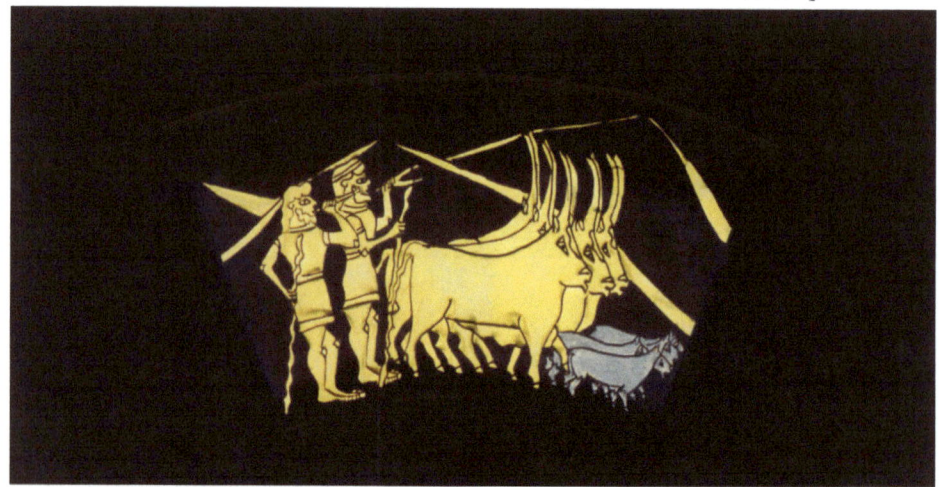

Illustration 19: Middle Ring: Peaceful Herdsmen. From the Shield of Achilles
by Kathleen Vail © All Rights Reserved

Then the flocks and herds both came in view,
followed by two men piping.
In peace they trailed behind their beasts,
with no hint of the imminent danger.

IV. C. Middle Ring: WARTIME

IV. C. 6. The Raiding Party Attacks

[Homer's Iliad, Book 18, Lines 527-529, Vail's Translation]

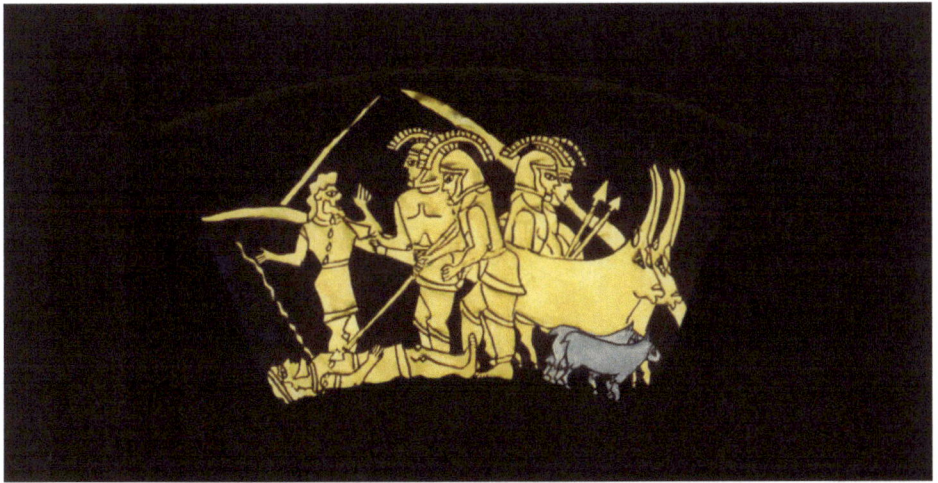

Illustration 20: Middle Ring: The Raiding Party Attacks. From the Shield of Achilles
by Kathleen Vail © All Rights Reserved

In a sudden rush the signal blared
and the raiding troop surprised them.
Quickly they killed both herdsmen at once,
and captured the frightened beasts.
Then guiding the straying silver-grey sheep,
others quickly regrouped the flocks.

IV. C. Middle Ring: WARTIME

IV. C. 7. The Troops Are Alerted

[Homer's Iliad, Book 18, Lines 530-532, Vail's Translation]

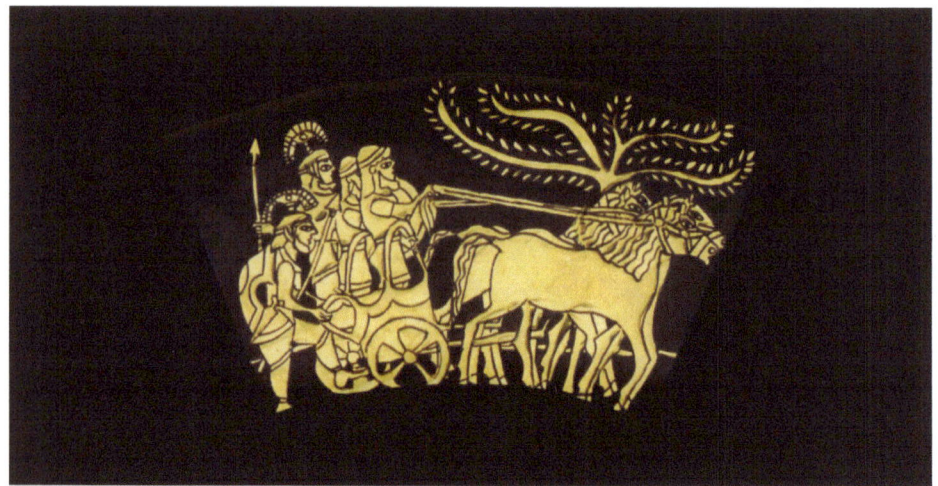

Illustration 21: Middle Ring: The Troops Are Alerted. From the Shield of Achilles by Kathleen Vail © All Rights Reserved

The troops at the city walls heard the sounds
of lowing and stampeding cattle,
so climbing behind their brisk-trotting steeds,
they raced their chariots onward.

IV. C. Middle Ring: WARTIME

IV. C. 8. Battle!

[Homer's Iliad, Book 18, Lines 533-540, Vail's Translation]

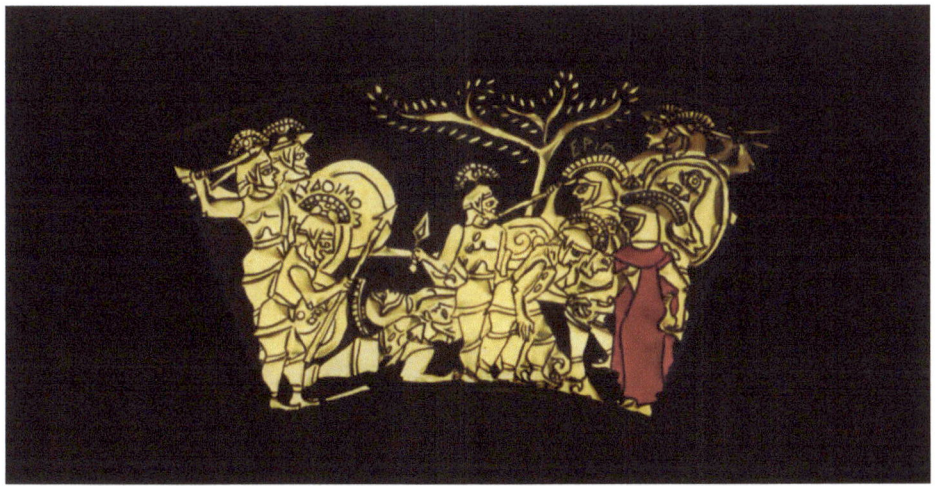

Illustration 22: Middle Ring: Battle! From the Shield of Achilles
by Kathleen Vail © All Rights Reserved

Upon the riverbanks fighting began
as foes threw spears at each other.
Then Strife and Tumult entered the skirmish,
together with terrible Fate,
who kept barely living a man with wounds,
and preserved another unwounded;
and yet another she grasped by the foot
and dragged him to death in the clamor.
Fate wore a cloak fully covered in blood,
and appeared a gruesome figure,
and the warriors fought as in real war
and pulled their dead away.

IV. D. Outer Ring: PEACETIME

IV. D. 1. Plowing the Field

[Homer's Iliad, Book 18, Lines 541-549, Vail's Translation]

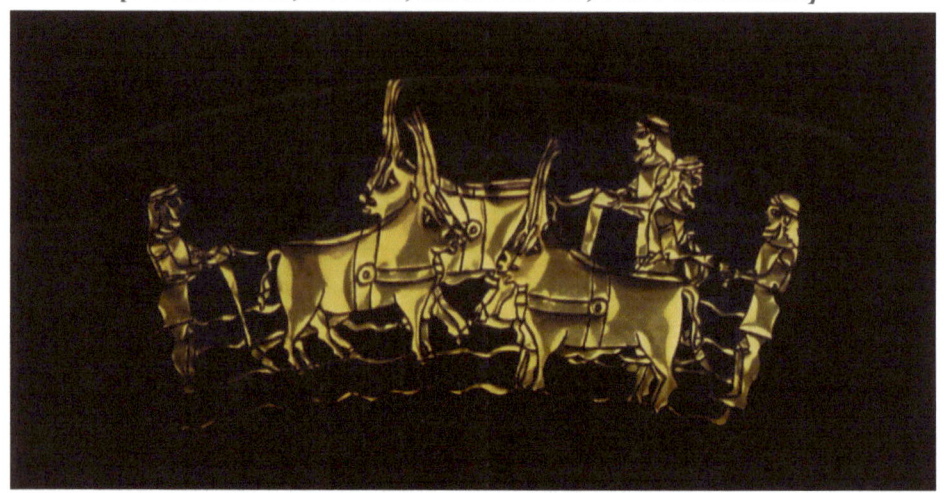

Illustration 23: Outer Ring: Plowing the Field. From the Shield of Achilles by Kathleen Vail © All Rights Reserved

Hephaistos put next a freshly plowed field
with many plowmen upon it.
One guided his ox-team with care through the turn
as he reached the wide field's limit,
and there, awaiting the hard-working man,
was his friend with a sweet cup of wine.
Back along the deep furrows they drove their beasts,
eager to have the work finished,
and the turned-up sod seemed black behind them,
although in truth it was gold.
For this was the fame of the Master Smith's craft:
his handiwork looked real.

IV. D. Outer Ring: PEACETIME

IV. D. 2. Harvesting the Grain

[Homer's Iliad, Book 18, Lines 550-560, Vail's Translation]

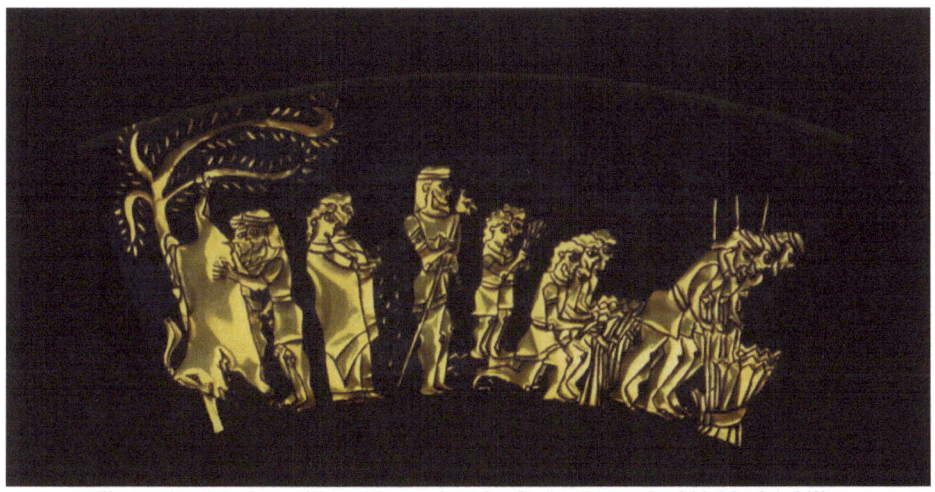

Illustration 24: Outer Ring: Harvesting the Grain. From the Shield of Achilles
by Kathleen Vail © All Rights Reserved

He also placed there a wealthy king's field
where men swung razor-sharp scythes,
for here was pictured the mowing of grain,
and harvesters bent to their tasks.
Golden stalks were falling along the way
and binders tied them in sheaves.
Three binders he pictured, and children gleaning,
offering handfuls of wheat.
Upon a newly-mown swath stood the king,
staff in hand and full of contentment,
while under an oak tree, off to one side, his men prepared a great feast.
Sacrificing an ox, they slaughtered the beast
as women winnowed barley for a meal.

IV. D. Outer Ring: PEACETIME

IV. D. 3. Gathering the Grapes

[Homer's Iliad, Book 18, Lines 561-572, Vail's Translation]

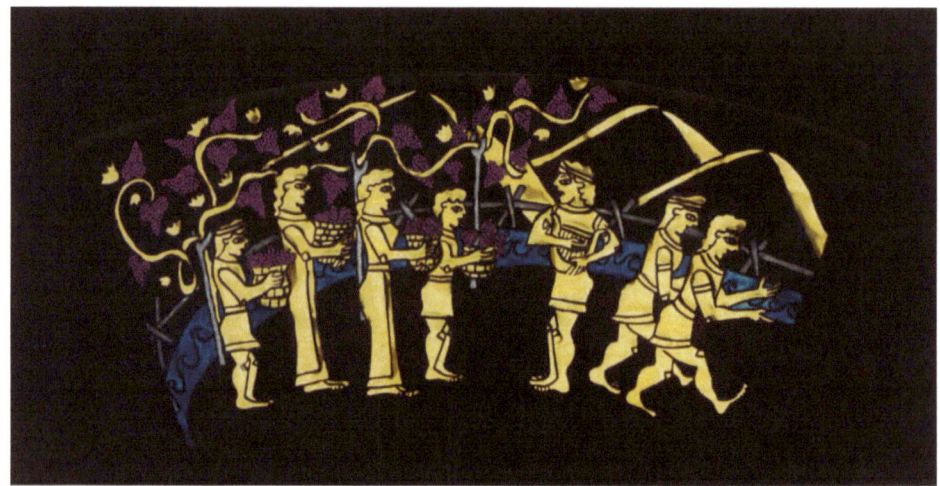

Illustration 25: Outer Ring: Gathering the Grapes. From the Shield of Achilles
by Kathleen Vail © All Rights Reserved

A vineyard in gold he next created, with vines hung heavy with grapes;
yet the hanging clusters appeared deep purple
and draped on silver supports.
The encircling channel appeared clear blue,
and the fence around this was tin;
and there was only one way out for the vintagers with their harvest.
Here were children with well-woven baskets
loaded with honey-sweet fruit;
on a rustic lyre a youth sang sweetly a delicate song of Linos,
while others sang out in unrestrained joy,
keeping time as they skipped together.

IV. D. Outer Ring: PEACETIME

IV. D. 4. Herding the Cattle to Pasture

[Homer's Iliad, Book 18, Lines 573-578, Vail's Translation]

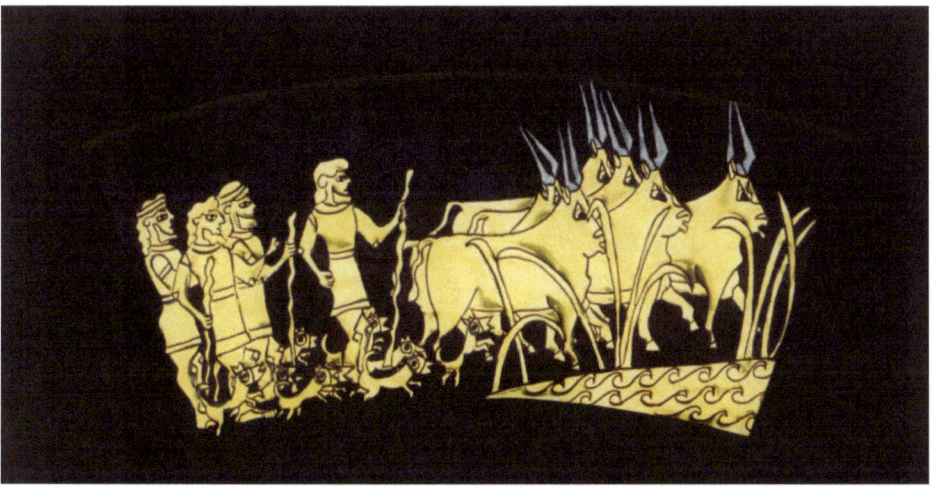

Illustration 26: Outer Ring: Herding Cattle to Pasture. From the Shield of Achilles
by Kathleen Vail © All Rights Reserved

A herd of oxen he next placed there,
with gold bodies and straight horns of tin.
From stable to pasture they lowed and shambled,
alongside a rippling river
with swaying reeds and a sweet murmuring
rising up from the bubbling water.
Four golden cowherds followed slowly behind,
with nine nimble dogs beside them.

IV. D. Outer Ring: PEACETIME

IV. D. 5. Lion Attack

[Homer's Iliad, Book 18, Lines 579-587, Vail's Translation]

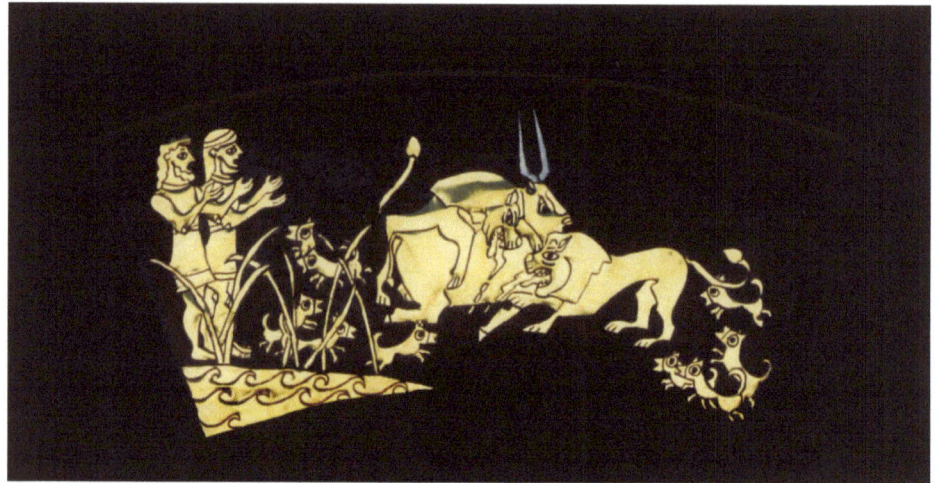

Illustration 27: Outer Ring: Lion Attack. From the Shield of Achilles
by Kathleen Vail © All Rights Reserved

Then a pair of lions charged a bull:
In two huge bounds assaulted,
then dragged him off as he bellowed in fear,
as the dogs and men pursued.
The herdsmen commanded their hunting dogs
as the lions tore into the bull,
but they were no match for lion's teeth,
and they raced back and forth, merely barking.

IV. D. Outer Ring: PEACETIME

IV. D. 6. Valley of Sheep

[Homer's Iliad, Book 18, Lines 588-589, Vail's Translation]

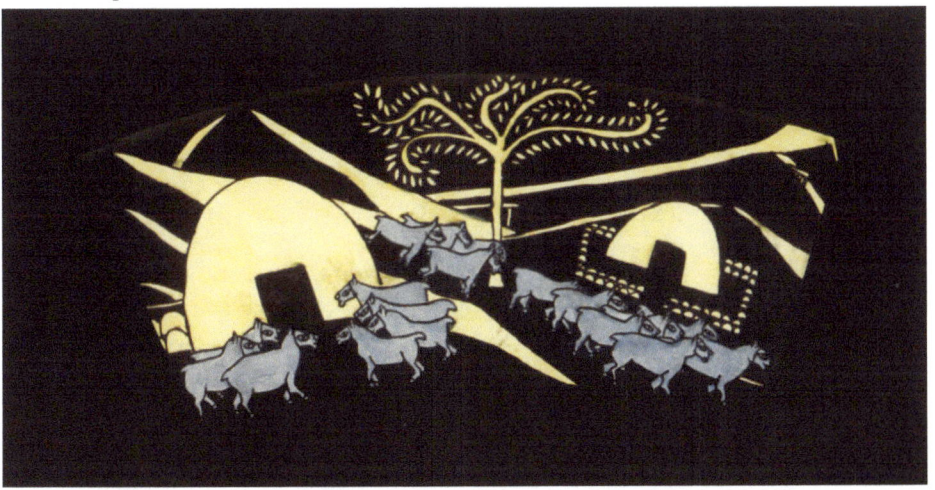

Illustration 28: Outer Ring: Valley of Sheep. From the Shield of Achilles by Kathleen Vail © All Rights Reserved

**The Bandy-legged god put next on the shield
a wide valley with silvery sheep,
a beautiful pasture with huts and sheds,
and tidy sheepfolds fashioned.**

IV. D. Outer Ring: PEACETIME

IV. D. 7. Circle-Dancing

[Homer's Iliad, Book 18, Lines 590-602, Vail's Translation]

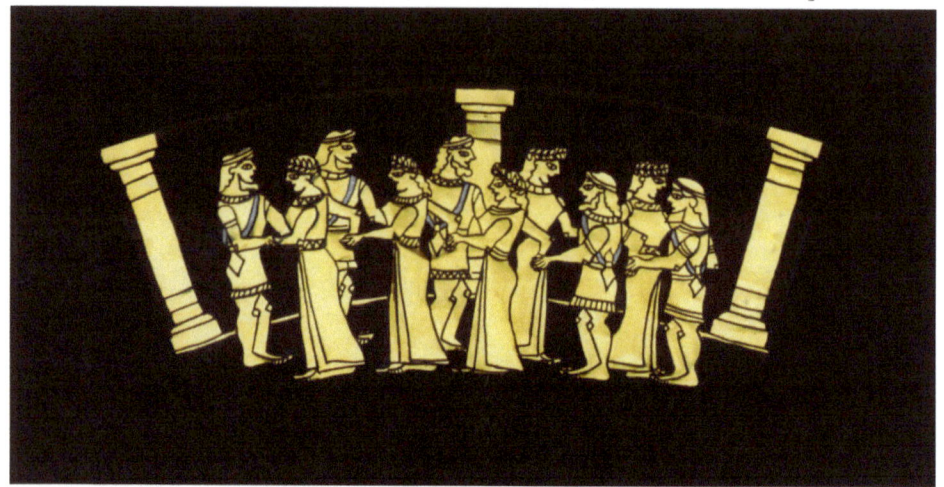

*Illustration 29: Outer Ring: Circle-Dancing. From the Shield of Achilles
by Kathleen Vail © All Rights Reserved*

*He fashioned there, also, a wide dancing floor,
like the one in Knossos' palace
that Daidalos made for King Minos' daughter, the beautiful Ariadne.
Young men he pictured with noble young girls,
all dancing there, hand in hand.
The girls were dressed in the softest of linen,
with wreaths woven for their hair;
the men wore tunics gleaming with oil,
and gold daggers on silver chains.
They danced in a circle, always in step, as a potter gives a spin
to a pot he is making, to see how it runs as it turns upon his wheel.*

IV. D. Outer Ring: PEACETIME

IV. D. 8. Line-Dancing

[Homer's Iliad, Book 18, Line 603, Vail's Translation]

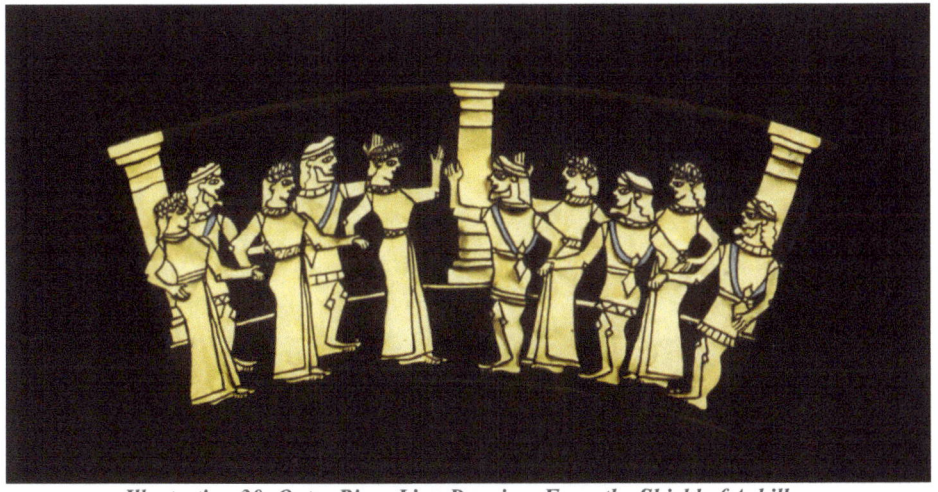

Illustration 30: Outer Ring: Line-Dancing. From the Shield of Achilles
by Kathleen Vail © All Rights Reserved

And also in lines, they appeared as in ranks,
and advanced upon each other.

IV. D. Outer Ring: PEACETIME

IV. D. 9. Acrobats Join the Action

[Homer's Iliad, Book 18, Lines 604-606, Vail's Translation]

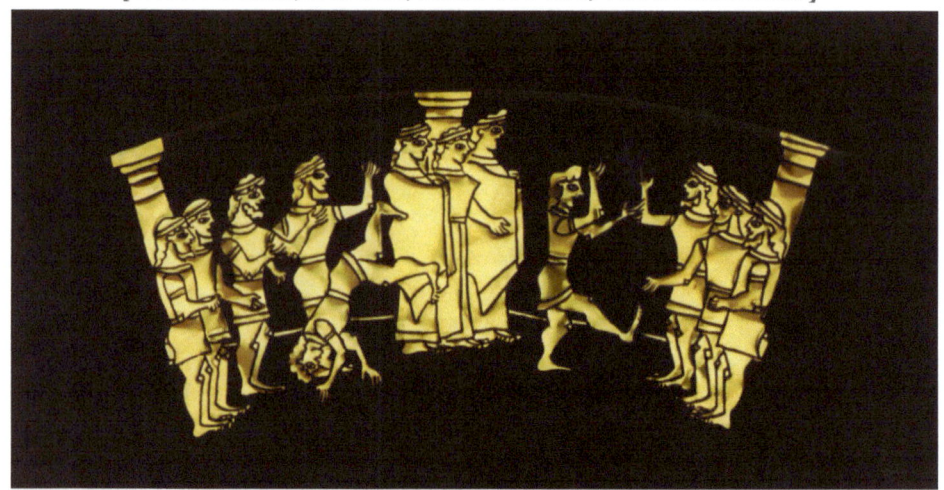

Illustration 31: Outer Ring: Acrobats Join the Action. From the Shield of Achilles by Kathleen Vail © All Rights Reserved

Then with effortless spins and dexterous handsprings,
two tumblers joined the action,
and the wide-eyed company cheered and laughed
at their comical acrobatics.

IV. E. Outer Rim:
MIGHTY OCEAN CURRENT

[Homer's Iliad, Book 18, Lines 607-608, Vail's Translation]

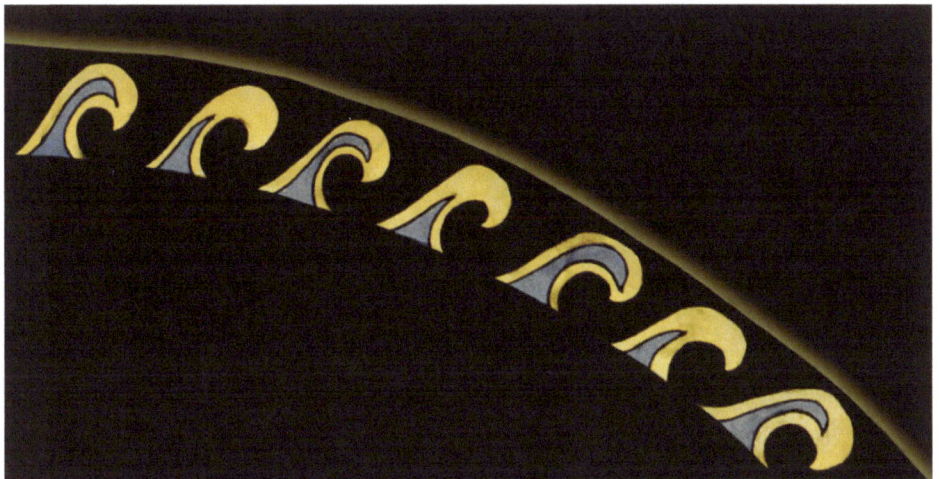

Illustration 32: Outer Rim: Mighty Ocean Current. From the Shield of Achilles by Kathleen Vail © All Rights Reserved

Lastly, encircling the solid shield's rim, power brightly shined
In wave after wave, as Hephaistos made the mighty ocean current.

Kathleen Vail

What Happens to Achilles' Shield When He Dies?

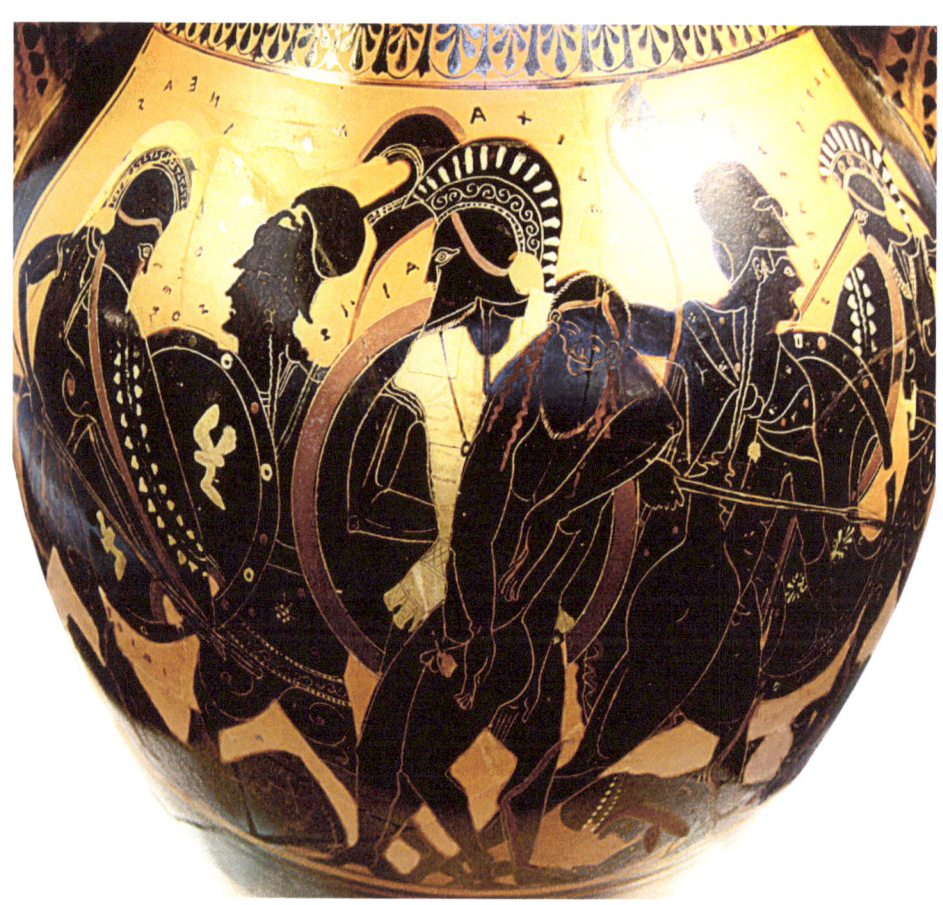

Illustration 33: Attic Black-figure Amphora, ca. 510 BCE,
depicting Aias (Ajax) carrying the body of Achilles out of the battlefield in the midst of other
named warriors, including (l) Aeneas and Neoptolemos, and (r) Menelaos and Paris.
Source: CC0 Image by Bibi Saint-Pol/Vail via Wikimedia Commons

V. The Death of Achilles and Disappearance of His Shield

Enheartening her, the Great GameLegs said,
"Have courage, my Lady! Please trust me!
Good gear I can make, but to hide him from death?
Now, that is another matter…
I only wish I could help him with that,
as I can with the making of arms,
for I am an expert – no eyes have beheld
such gear as I shall provide him!"

[From Homer's Iliad, Book 18, Lines 463 – 466, Vail's translation]

His divine armor, as Hephaistos warns Achilles' mother, will not save her son from his impending death. Nevertheless, Achilles chooses bravery over safety and heroically enters the fray, seeking only the death of Hektor, the murderer of Patroklos and thief of Achilles' armor.

Arieti points out that by avoiding the stereotypical construction of a warrior's shield, "The difference between the shield we might expect and the one which Hephaestus actually makes forces us to reflect on peace and war and on the value of each."

"Homer displays a new kind of hero in Achilles,"

adds Arieti, "a hero who, in discovering guilt, influences the moral consciousness of the West in such a way as to define the civilization." Arieti continues, "When Patroclus fell to the might of Hector, Hector stripped the body and donned the armor himself."

Imagine the psychological impact of Hektor's dazzling appearance on Achilles. His mortal enemy is now standing before him, dressed in Achilles' old armor. He must look like a mirror-image of Achilles. This is a profoundly fascinating perspective.

Finding an interesting semblance of suicide from his perspective, Arieti explains, "When, in the final combat with Achilles, Hector engaged Achilles, it must have seemed to Achilles that he was fighting against himself, in slaying Hector, slaying himself."

"Given Thetis' prophecy that Achilles' own death would follow upon the heels of Hector's," Arieti continues, "the appearance of suicide was the virtual reality. For Achilles, it was a way to expiate his guilt in causing the deaths of Patroclus and so many of his comrades."[1]

From another perspective, Achilles may also be viewed as a martyr, knowingly sacrificing his life in the pursuit of justice. Not only does Achilles avenge the death of the heroic Patroklos, but he also avenges the kidnapping of Helen which was ultimately responsible for bringing on the entire Trojan War.

By single-handedly pursuing the death of Troy's greatest warrior, Achilles effectively brings on the defeat of the Trojan military. Although his death, indeed, follows close on the heels of Hektor's, Achilles' heroism ultimately ends the Trojan war, allows the recovery of Helen, and sets the Greeks on their various courses for home.

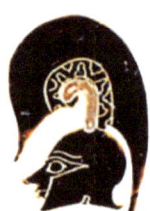

FOOTNOTES:

(1). J. Arieti, "Achilles' Guilt," *Classical Journal* 80(1985): 193-203.

V. A. The Epic Death of Achilles

> *He fashioned, as well, a blazing breastplate,*
> *besides the massive shield;*
> *then a helmet he wrought, close fitting and grand,*
> *of gold with a flashing crest,*
> *and complex designs all wondrously made,*
> *and leg greaves of supple tin.*
> *His work completed, the Famous Smith*
> *bore the arms to Achilles' mother,*
> *who, clutching the armor, flew like a hawk*
> *sweeping down from snowy Olympos,*
> *in haste to deliver the flashing gear*
> *bestowed by Great Hephaistos.*

[From Homer's Iliad, Book 18, Lines 608-616, Vail's translation]

Seething with righteous, passionate anger,

Achilles buckles on his new armor and picks up the shield, hardly glancing at it; he is focusing only on killing Hektor. [1] With a warriors' instinct, Achilles shrugs and flexes, jumping and dodging, pivoting and testing both fit and balance, finding his new armor as light as wings.

Swearing he will not halt this day until he has made all the Trojans sick of war, Achilles races onto the field of battle with a great shout, driving his team of well-bred war horses straight into the front line, in search of Hektor. However, Aineas, who will one day be famous for founding the city of Rome, steps up first to face Achilles. [2] Behind him, every Trojan's knees are trembling at the sight of Achilles flashing like the war god, Ares.

Achilles Fighting Hektor and Aineas

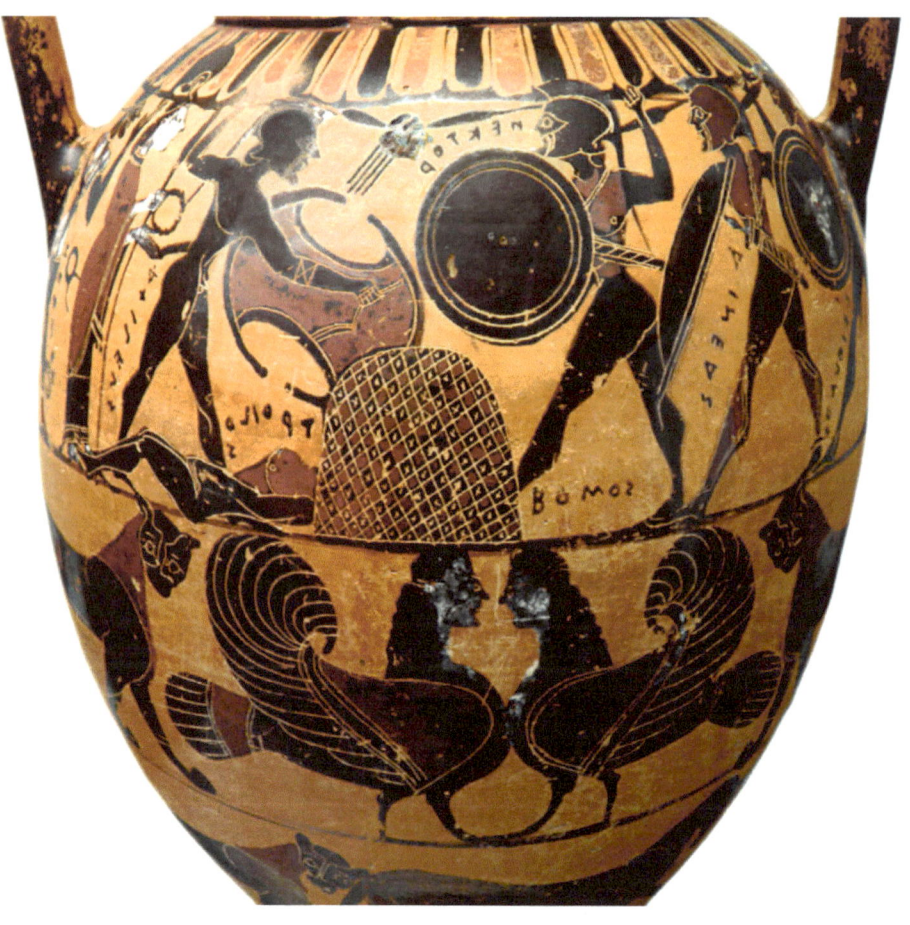

*Illustration 34: Attic Black-figure Amphora, ca. 550 BCE,
depicting Achilles fighting Hektor and Aineas over the slain and decapitated
body of Troilos. To the left of Achilles is Hermes and Athena.
Source: CCSA 2.0 image by Carole Raddato/Vail via Wikimedia Commons*

Exchanging proud words of warning, Achilles and Aineas are each determined to gain honor at the expense of the other. Then, Aineas drives his spear into Achilles' shield and a loud clanging noise resounds upon the impact. Achilles grips his shield strongly, holding it out from his body in case the spear might drive through it, but this is unnecessary. Constructed of five layers, the spear pierces the two outer layers of bronze, but the middle layer of thick gold deflects the ashwood spear of Aineas.

Next, Achilles hurls his spear and hits Aineas' shield where it is thinnest, sending up a sound of screeching as the spearhead strikes the plate. Horrified, Aineas leaps back, deflecting Achilles' spear by squatting low and holding the shield high. Bouncing up and over Aineas' back, the spear buries itself in the battlefield.

Carrying up a huge boulder, Aineas rises to crush

his enemy, as Achilles closes in on him with his glittering sword thirsty for blood. Sometimes miracles are more timely than others, and this is the perfect moment. Ensuring Aineas will survive to achieve a far greater fate, Poseidon blows a battle-haze of confusion into Achilles' eyes, helping Aineas to slip away.

The haze in his eyes dissipates from Achilles when Aineas has safely escaped. Retrieving his spear, Achilles swears resentfully at the lost opportunity. Perceiving that Aineas has been helped by the gods, Achilles swears Aineas to hell and turns his attention once again to the battle.

Goading his men to increase their bravery, Achilles swears that he will fight the whole war by himself. [3] He and his soldiers roar like a pack of lions, charging the Trojans and breaking through their front line at the same moment that Hektor is reentering the fray.

Rushing into the midst of flashing bronze,

flying hooves, and pivoting war carts, Achilles rends the sky with a heart-stopping shout. Swords and spears are thrusting in every direction and blood sprays wildly from beasts and men. The first Trojan to reach Achilles receives his head split in two. Achilles cries out happily, as though singing for joy. [4]

Piercing the second man's skull with Achilles' spear, the Trojan's brains and blood explode from his helmet. A third soldier panics, turning to run away, but Achilles pulls his spear from the skull of his last enemy and boldly drives it into the back of the cowardly Trojan.

Next, Polydoros speeds past Achilles. The young son of Priam is known as the fastest runner of the Trojans, but his speed is not enough to save him today. Achilles casts his spear, hitting the young prince in the back and the hungry spear burrows deeply, piercing through to his navel.

A fateful meeting not yet appointed

presents itself amid the horrific cries of dying Trojans. Hektor spies his young brother dying at the hand of Achilles and, raising his sword while shouting and running, Hektor flies out of control like a raging fire.

Startled by the wild shouting, Achilles sees Hektor approaching and prays to the gods, knowing it is his time, his glorious opportunity for revenge. [5] Yelling at Hektor, he urges him to run straighter, in order to meet his fate sooner. Hektor is unafraid, responding that perhaps he will kill Achilles because fate is decided only by the gods.

Throwing his spear murderously at Achilles, Hektor is astonished to find the spear returned, landing in front of his feet. As well, Achilles lunges three times at Hektor, stabbing powerfully with his spear, but in vain. And, on the fourth lunge, Achilles finds that Hektor has completely vanished!

More enraged than ever, Achilles pushes forward, butchering every Trojan in his path. Flashing and slashing right and left, Achilles tramples the falling soldiers under his horses' hooves as he advances through the enemy lines, inflicting mayhem and bloody slaughter.

Flushing his enemies down the bank of a river,

Achilles leaves his spear beside a tree and wades into the fray, butchering all by his sword until he tires. [6] Then, taking a break from his mad slaughter, Achilles captures twelve Trojan soldiers. He uses their own belts to tie their wrists behind their backs and, reserving them to burn on Patroklos' funeral pyre, he sends them back to camp with one of his men.

Reclaiming his spear from beside the tree, Achilles again throws himself back into battle. Another son of Priam, unarmed and practically naked, is taking a rest after removing his hot and sweaty battle gear. With a gasp, he finds Achilles before him, raising his spear to run him through. [7]

Although the young man begs Achilles to spare him, the beloved of Patroklos swears he will kill every man that heaven puts in front of him. Encouraging him not to be such a coward, Achilles tells the Trojan prince to look at him – Achilles – born of a king and a goddess, but death is awaiting him, too, such is fate.

The time will come and death will be delivered by a spear, or maybe by an arrow, Achilles says, uncannily foretelling his own fate. Then without another word, one more son of Priam slumps to the ground after eating the spearhead of angry Achilles.

His next opponent throws two spears at once at Achilles. [8] The first spear hits his glorious shield, deflecting off the gold. The second spear nicks his right arm, delivering Achilles' first wound and causing his own throw to miss. Drawing his sword without hesitation, Achilles lunges and slashes, opening the man's belly and then stripping the armor off the dead body.

There might have been no end to this carnage,

except that floodwaters suddenly come pouring down the river bed, flooding the plains around Troy and floating the corpses strewn all over the battlefield. Jumping over bodies, chariots, and armor, Achilles prays for help to stay ahead of the waves, running like the wind to escape the sudden flood. [9]

The water's strong currents flow under his feet, surging and pushing Achilles off balance, but he finds the strength to keep running. Then, accompanied by huge blasts of wind from the sea, fire breaks out all around him in roaring gales. Every green thing not yet flooded goes up in flames, and the water begins steaming and boiling.

Then the waters recede, rebuffed by the battling fire, in answer to Achilles' prayer for help. Soon Achilles is once again in hot pursuit behind the Trojan soldiers, but the exhausted warriors stream into Troy as the gatekeepers swing open the city gates.

The hands of Fate hold Hektor outside the walls,

unable to enter the gate as Achilles approaches. The Trojan prince is unwilling to face his people if he runs away from Achilles. [11] Preferring glory, even at the price of death, Hektor ignores the pleas of his mother and father shouting down to him from the towers on the wall.

With Achilles closing in on him, Hektor sprints away at the last moment, bolting like a deer in fear for his life, racing away from the city gates alongside the towering walls. Running light-footed like a chariot horse trained for the races, Achilles' armor flashes brightly as he speeds untiringly toward his fate. Three times around the town they race along the walls, with Achilles never gaining on Hektor, and Hektor never gaining greater speed.

Finally, in the fourth round, Hektor turns and faces Achilles, hoping to end the nightmare of running and running and going nowhere fast. Promising Achilles he will not dishonor Achilles' body if he kills him, Hektor hopes for Achilles to promise the same. But Achilles swears there can be no promises between man and beast, nor between wolves and sheep. He swears he will kill Hektor for all the men that Hektor has killed, and he hurls his spear at Hektor.

Ducking expertly at the moment of Achilles' cast,

Hektor escapes the danger. Planting his feet solidly, Hektor then throws his spear, watching in horror as it bounces off Achilles' shield, far beyond Hektor's reach. Knowing that his end is now nearby, Hektor pulls out his sword, swinging with all his strength, but Achilles draws his shield close. Having retrieved his own spear, Achilles raises it, poised with perfect aim at Hektor's throat. It is the only vulnerable spot in Achilles' old armor, stripped from the slain Patroklos. [12]

Straight through the neck, Achilles drives his spear, and Hektor drops to the dirt. Still able to speak, Hektor begs Achilles to have mercy on his dead body. He prophetically warns Achilles to take care, in case Achilles angers the gods and they allow Paris to bring him down by an arrow from Apollo.

But Achilles tells him to shut up and die, yanking the spear from Hektor's throat. He swears he wants to butcher Hektor and eat his body raw, for all the pain that Hektor has caused him. Then, after Achilles strips the armor off of Hektor and reclaims it for himself, the other Greek warriors step in close to stab the body of the fallen Trojan prince.

With Patroklos' death avenged, now Achilles plans his beloved's burial. Piercing Hektor's tendons between heel and ankle, [13] (an ironic reference to Hektor's Achilles' tendon?) Achilles runs a leather strap through both, tying the body to his chariot.

Achilles' driver shakes the reins and he shouts his team into a run. Rising like flames of fire from the walls of Troy, screams fill the air as his people see the prince's body defiled and dishonored, dragging through the dirt behind Achilles' war cart.

The army pays last respects to Patroklos

upon returning to the ships. Although exhausted, Achilles does not dismiss his men. [14] Instead, they drive their war carts past Patroklos, mourning him one by one, paying their last respects to his body. Three times they drive their teams around the body of Patroklos, with cries of grief rising as though from one voice.

After slaughtering beasts for the funeral feast, the Greeks disperse to disarm and then return to the feast. But not Achilles. Giving orders for the following morning, for the funeral pyre of Patroklos, Achilles then drops in the sand near the water's edge, weeping until he sleeps.

Patroklos visits Achilles all night in his dreams, making requests of Achilles and begging him to bury him quickly. [15] Upon awakening, still weeping, Achilles turns to the task of building the huge pile of wood, that, once burned, will be the site of the burial mound he knows he will share with Patroklos. By nightfall all is ready, and the funeral pyre of Patroklos keeps burning all night long. Achilles, all the while groaning and crying, tends the fire with loving care.

At dawn, the embers stop glowing and Achilles sleeps, exhausted. But voices and trampling footsteps of soldiers soon wake him as they begin mounting stone upon stone for the burial mound. Carefully retrieving

Patroklos' Funeral & the Ransom of Hektor

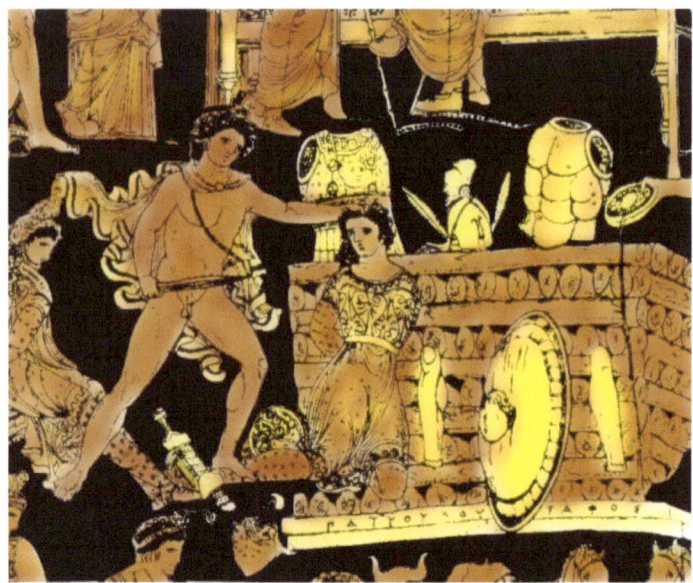

Illustration 35: 1884 Drawing, Apulian Red-figure Volute Krater, ca. 330 BCE. Achilles preparing Patroklos' funeral pyre (colorized by Vail). Source: CC0 Vail via Wikimedia Commons

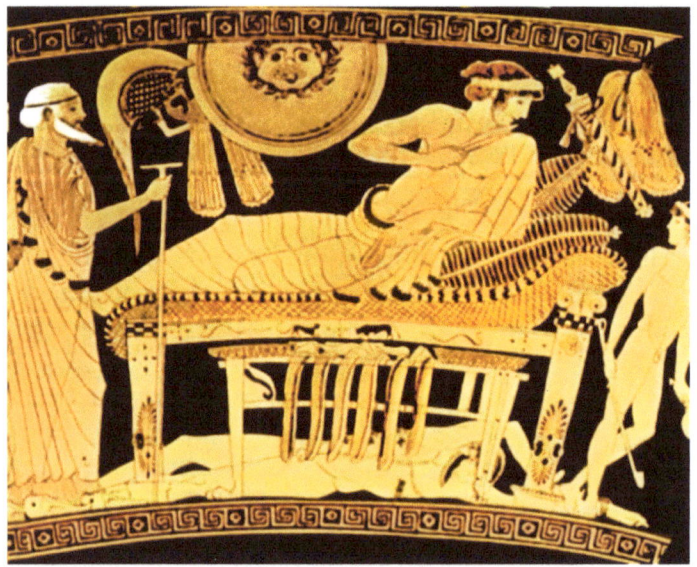

Illustration 36: 1924 Drawing, Athenian Red-figure Skyphos, ca. 480 BCE, Priam ransoming Hektor from Achilles (colorized by Vail). Source: CCSA 3.0 Vail via Wikimedia Commons

Patroklos' bones from the ashes, Achilles stores them in a golden urn provided by his mother, Thetis. Achilles orders that his own bones must share this urn when fate comes to take his life. [16]

Holding funeral games next, Achilles awards the prizes for chariot racing, boxing, wrestling, running, sword fighting, throwing a boulder of iron, and archery marksmanship. For the next twelve days, Achilles sleeps fitfully down by the shore, rising at dawn to drive his chariot three times around the burial mound of Patroklos, still dragging the body of Hektor. The gods protect the dead body from damage, but Achilles' brutal treatment begins to offend them.

Finding the balance of favor slipping from Achilles,

his mother brings him warning from Olympos. [17] Obedient to Thetis' advice, Achilles agrees to give back the body of Hektor to King Priam in return for gifts as ransom.

Visiting Achilles' war hut secretly in the dead of night, Priam is treated by Achilles as his own father. Pitying the old man, Achilles goes to free the body of the prince. He orders Hektor's body to be anointed, dressed, and wrapped in beautiful shrouding. Then, with his own two hands, Achilles lifts the body of Hektor, placing it on a couch and, with help from his men, they place the couch on Priam's wagon. [18] Crying in the darkness to Patroklos, Achilles fears the anger of his best friend and prays for his understanding. Returning back inside, he orders food for the king, and together they share the first meal either has eaten since the death of Hektor. Taking his hand, Achilles promises Priam that he will suspend the war for eleven days, as the king requires, for the proper burial of his son.

Weeping in the darkness, as well, the last mournful voice of the *Iliad* belongs to Helen. The beautiful Greek wife of Paris, whose kidnapping brought all this trouble to Troy, weeps for herself and for her dead brother-in-law, Hektor. In all of Troy, Helen mourns, Hektor was her only friend.

Twenty years have passed since she last saw Greece, she laments, where no one could restrain themselves from staring at her beauty. With the arrival of the war, however, and even more since the death of Hektor, Helen mourns that now no eye will look upon her without revulsion. [19]

The *Iliad* ends, but Achilles still lives

at the end of Homer's epic. The final event narrated is the funeral of Hektor. However, as Priam warns his people, the war is not yet over. With the dawn of the coming twelfth day, Achilles will rise again, delivering fresh fire to Troy with his army of untiring soldiers.

The *Iliad* ends, but blood still beats in Achilles' veins. Achilles' divine armor is still on his body, flashing in the sun and striking terror in the hearts of the Trojans. What is the end of the story, the end of Achilles? Where will we search for his armor?

Fortunately, Homer reveals more details of the Trojan War in the *Odyssey*, his epic poem of the ten years it takes Odysseus to return home. In fact, the details of Achilles' death are revealed to Achilles himself at the same moment when we, the readers, first learn the details, as well. [20]

Homer relates that High King Agamemnon returns home from the war only to be murdered by his wife and his adoptive brother, who has seduced Agamemnon's wife in order to steal the throne. Agamemnon's soul is delivered to Hades, where he meets his greatest captain, Achilles, together with Patroklos and other warriors who died at Troy. Achilles greets Agamemnon, offering compassionate words regarding the king's ill-fated death, so shortly following the time of his greatest victory at Troy. Achilles laments that Agamemnon should have died at Troy, too, thus preserving his great honor as a legacy for his son.

Agamemnon, High King of Mycenae, Commanding Officer of the Trojan War, returns a very beautiful greeting to Achilles:

> *Well-fated hero, Peleus' son, so much like a god full of glory.*
> *Across the ocean from Argos you died, outside of the Trojan town.*
> *Over and around you the soldiers slashed,*
> *fighting to the death for your body.*
>
> *...Finally, a storm forced us back to the ships*
> *and we carried your body with us.*
> *Your well-formed limbs we washed and rinsed*
> *in a bath of fresh warm water.*

Then, after anointing your skin with oil, we laid you upon your bed.
Like torrents fell the hot tears of captains,
who cut off their hair in grief....
We mourned you for seventeen days and nights,
mortal men, goddesses, and nymphs.
Then, slaughtering oxen with great long horns
and slaying fattened sheep,
around your body we laid the pile
and brought flame to your funeral pyre.

...The sea nymphs covered you with fat and honey
and you blazed like the sun in the fire,
turning to ash as captains rode past in their war carts
and wearing full armor.
Every foot soldier followed in rank, single file, saluting your honor.
And, hot as a fire consuming a forest,
the flames burned your flesh away.

...We carefully collected your bones at dawn, to preserve in wine and oil
in the golden urn your mother offered, which you had packed
with the bones of Patroklos.
Just as you ordered, we obeyed and your bones lie now intermingled.

...We piled the mound high to mark the place of your burial
for coming generations,
and your mother gave games in your name for our champions,
awarding great trophies and treasures.

Every man will remember the meaning of honor
by your life, Great Prince Achilles.
Your glory will live in our memory forever;
your name will never die. [21]

The Muses and Sea Nymphs Mourning Achilles

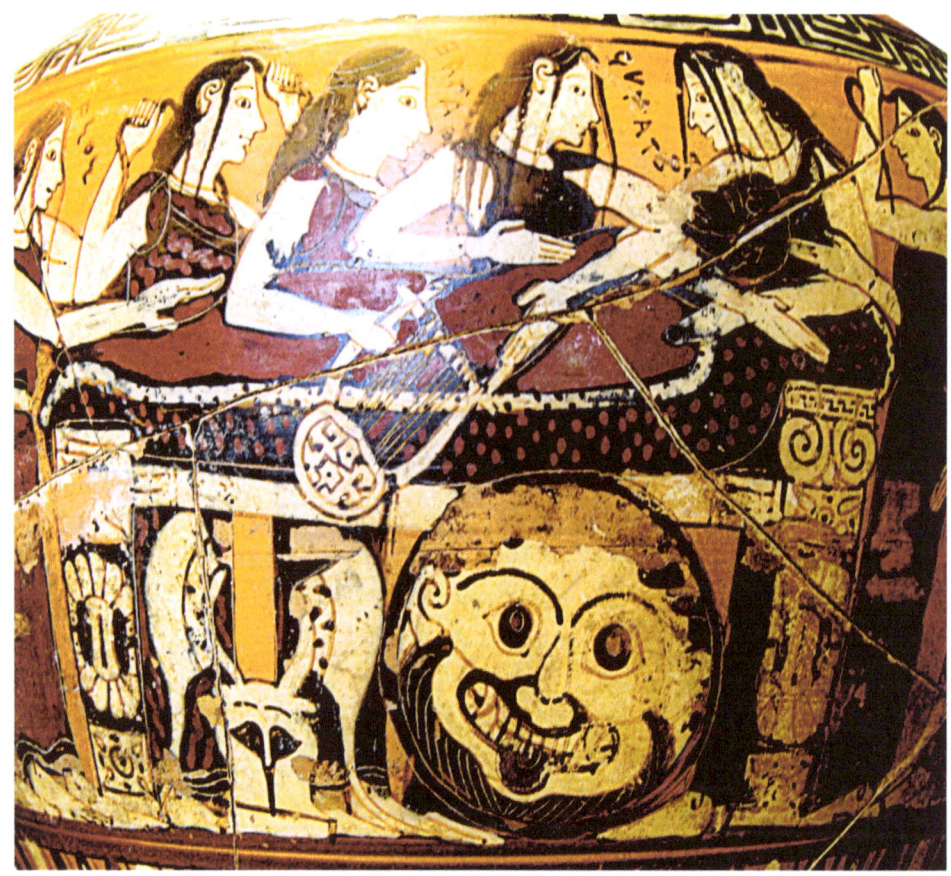

Illustration 37: Corinthian Black-figure Hydria, ca. 560-550 BCE, depicting Thetis, the Sea Nymphs (Nereids) and the Nine Muses mourning the death of Achilles. Source: CC0 image by Bibi Saint-Pol/Vail via Wikimedia Commons

FOOTNOTES:

(1). Homer's *Iliad*, with translation by A.T. Murray, Ph.D. Cambridge, MA, Harvard University Press; London, William Heinemann, 1924. Book 19, line 369

(2). *Iliad*, 20:174; **(3)**. 20:360; **(4)**. 20:385; **(5)**. 20:420; **(6)**. 21:25; **(7)**. 21:65; **(8)**. 21:160; **(9)**. 21:270; **(10)**. 21:600; **(11)**. 22:105; **(12)**. 22:321; **(13)**. 22:395; **(14)**. 23:5; **(15)**. 23:65; **(16)**. 23:244; **(17)**. 24:135; **(18)**. 24:590; **(19)**. 24:775

(20). Homer's *Odyssey*, with translation by Samuel Butler, revised by Timothy Power and Gregory Nagy. London: A.C. Fifield, 1900 Book 24:26; **(21)**. Book 24:36-89

V. B. The Divine Shield of Achilles Disappears

Odysseus stands fighting over the body of Achilles

when the hero goes down, providing cover and protection against any dishonor the Trojans might attempt. [22] Under Odysseus' careful defense, Telamonian Aias heaves the body of Achilles over his shoulder and makes his way off the battlefield.

With a cohort of soldiers providing cover, the loudly grieving men escort Achilles' body back down to the ships. Soon, the entire army prepares for Achilles a funeral of the highest honor.

Achilles' mother and her sister sea nymphs join the funeral, and all nine of the Olympian muses attend, as well. For seventeen days and nights, they mourn Achilles, paying him respect with funeral parades. On the eighteenth day, the men burn Achilles' body on the pyre.

Next, Achilles' bones are placed gently into the golden urn which Thetis had earlier given her grieving son for the bones of Patroklos. Obeying the order which Achilles gave during the funeral of Patroklos, the bones of the two beloved best friends are now joined in death and the urn is placed into the burial mound. [23]

Thetis announces great funeral games in Achilles'

honor, offering prizes of stunning value. The highest prize is Achilles' armor, created by Hephaistos. This magnificent prize is offered to the winner of the title, *the Best of the Achaeans*, and the competition narrows down to Telamonian Aias and Odysseus.

Holding a vote to decide the matter, the Greek captains award the title to Odysseus, but Aias cannot swallow his anguish over losing the spectacular armor of Achilles. Recorded in Homer's *Iliad*, the competition over Achilles' armor is greatly expounded upon by Sophocles in his perennially popular tragedy, *Ajax* (Latinized from Aias). Aias is so certain of victory, that when it goes to Odysseus his sanity escapes him completely. Sophocles tells us that in the night Aias sneaks out to the captain's tents, determining to kill them all.

Diverting Aias, Athena sends confusion to his senses and he kills the army's herds of livestock, slaughtering the animals in his wild rage. Awakening the next day, his senses returning, Aias understands his terrible mistake and knows his ludicrous action will make himself a laughingstock for many generations.

With no way for Aias to recover his honor,

he considers what he must do next. Losing the award of Achilles' armor is bad enough to bring on temporary insanity, but following up with ridiculous behavior on his part is the final atrocity for Aias.

Finding he cannot go home and face his father, Telamon, with this shameful tale of his deeds, he prefers instead to die. Burying the handle of his sword in the dirt, then swearing he will speak no longer to the living, he falls upon his sword, promising he will from here on out speak only to the shades in Hades.

But even in Hades, Aias has little to say. His anguish accompanies him to the grave, though he thought to relieve himself of it by ending his life. Homer tells us of Odysseus' visit to Hades, where he attempts to talk with Aias, but Aias refuses to speak. [24]

Calling softly to Aias, he asks him if he has not yet gotten over his anger at Odysseus over the ill-fated armor of Achilles. He speaks gently, telling Aias all the Greeks mourn his loss as deeply as they mourn Achilles. But Aias gives no reply, turning slowing and walking away.

Odysseus does not die in order to visit Hades,

it is one of the many fantastic places he comes to on his journey. But does he still possess the shield of Achilles at this point? Now that we know he wins the armor in the funeral games for Achilles, can we find what happens next? Perhaps we can. Prior to addressing Aias in Hades, Odysseus and Achilles exchange greetings.

Achilles asks Odysseus for news of his son, Neoptolemos. He tells

Achilles that he himself brought Neoptolemos from the island of Skyros to the battle at Troy and that in battle Achilles' son excelled.

Joining Odysseus and the other captains in the belly of the horse wheeled up into Troy, Odysseus informs Achilles that it was only Neoptolemos who held his nerve until the perfect moment to attack. And, at the victorious end of the Trojan war, Neoptolemos loads a ship with all of his valuable plunder, embarking without having received a single wound from the enemy. [25]

Odysseus never once mentions the divine armor of Achilles being promised or given to Neoptolemos. Despite the existence of alternative legends, notably Sophocles' *Philoctetes*, in which Odysseus presents Achilles' armor to Neoptolemos when they arrive at Troy, nevertheless, Homer himself never narrates this transfer of armor, even at the most perfect moment when Odysseus speaks to Achilles in Hades.

Homer only states that Neoptolemos leaves Troy with lots of plunder and a "noble war prize," considered by Sophocles, Euripides, Hyginus, and others to mean Andromache, the wife of slain Prince Hektor.

Odysseus' son Telemakos also comes to age

in his father's absence and, like Neoptolemos, yearns for news of his father. To follow Odysseus from this point forward, we must join Telemakos on his journey as he searches for his father.

Suitors are eating Penelope out of house and home, pressing her to choose a new husband. Telemakos knows that his mother is running out of patience and time, waiting for Odysseus' return. When news arrives that some soldiers have returned home from Troy, Athena disguises herself as a seafaring captain named, appropriately, Mentor. Mentor advises Telemakos to commission a ship and go find out the fate of his father.

With Mentor's help, the ship is outfitted, a crew is employed, and Telemakos sets out on his journey. Coming in time to the kingdom of Pylos, the wise old King Nestor receives him, recognizing the face of Odysseus in the boy.

Telling Telemakos of arguments that blew up between Menelaus and Agamemnon after the victory at Troy, Nestor explains that one-half of the ships left the next morning with him and the other half stayed behind.

Odysseus' ships were also among Nestor's. But, turning back after another argument split him from Nestor's group, Odysseus preferred sailing back to Agamemnon.

After sailing for four days, Nestor and the first group arrive back home safely and, since then, many others have also returned.

Nestor relates that Neoptolemos has arrived home, leading the Myrmidons, Achilles' fearless soldiers. Notably, Homer makes no mention here of Achilles' armor transferring to his son – Nestor relates only that Neoptolemos is now in command of Achilles' army.

The wise old king of Pylos also informs Odysseus' son that High King Agamemnon has returned home to his unfaithful wife's evil plotting, only to meet his cruel fate at the hand of vile assassins.

Nestor remarks to Telemakos what a good thing it is for a man to leave a brave, strong son behind him. He then relates how Orestes avenged the murder of his father, Agamemnon, by killing his mother and her lover, his scheming uncle Aegisthos. [26]

Traveling next to the Kingdom of Sparta,

Telemakos is graciously received by Menelaus and Helen. Telling stories of the war to the young prince of Ithaka, Menelaus shares his latest news.

Admitting that his information is only secondhand, not having any witness, Menelaus tells Telemakos that his father is marooned and sits crying on the island of the nymph Kalypso. With no ship and no soldiers, and not even an oar, Odysseus has no means of leaving.

Explaining that the source of this news is Proteus, the Ancient of the Sea, Menelaus narrates how he trapped the legendary sea monster into giving information while he and Helen were on their way home from Troy. [27]

Leaving Telemakos at this juncture, we must backtrack to Odysseus' ships, as they are splitting from Nestor's group to return to Agamemnon, still at Troy. Because, if Menelaus is correct, and Odysseus, presently marooned on Kalypso's island, has lost his ship, perhaps he has lost the spectacular shield of Achilles, too.

We must trace Odysseus' travel, to learn if Achilles' shield is still with him, or if something has happened to it along the way.

Turning back to Troy and Agamemnon, Odysseus'

fleet of twelve ships are instead blown off course by a westerly wind to the far coast of Ismaros.

Landing and killing many natives who come out to fight them, Odysseus and his soldiers then disagree on the next plan of action. He orders them all back out to sea, and quickly, but the soldiers defy their captain. Instead, they slaughter cattle and sheep for a feast and spend their time drinking wine and arguing with Odysseus.

Meanwhile, a few men of Ismaros survive the attack, sneak home, and alert their army. Early next morning, the Greeks face a terrible battle, taking casualties until the tide turns. Finally, they escape to their ships, grieving over this new loss of men. [28]

Running low on water, Odysseus picks a landing party and sends them ashore on the coast of the Lotus-eaters. When the three men fail to report back to the ships, Odysseus goes out and finds them already addicted to the lotus flower, no longer interested in their families, friends, or homes. They rail at him as he kicks them all the way back to the ships, where he ties each one to his oar-bench. [29]

Odysseus' crew row strongly and they put back out to sea, sailing next to the land of the one-eyed Cyclops. Across from the Cyclops' mainland, the crew go ashore on a deserted island where they find good water, hunt wild goats, and enjoy a long day of feasting.

The next day, Odysseus and twelve of his men go ashore on the Cyclops' mainland, entering the unattended cave of a giant Cyclops named Polyphemos. Returning home with his sheep, the brutal cannibal Cyclops traps the men inside with the sheep.

Two by two, the giant cannibal picks off Odysseus' men, gruesomely thrashing them to death and eating them. Within 24 hours, Odysseus and only four men are left alive, desperately scheming to avoid being Polyphemos' next meal.

Odysseus Escapes the Cyclops & Circe's Magic

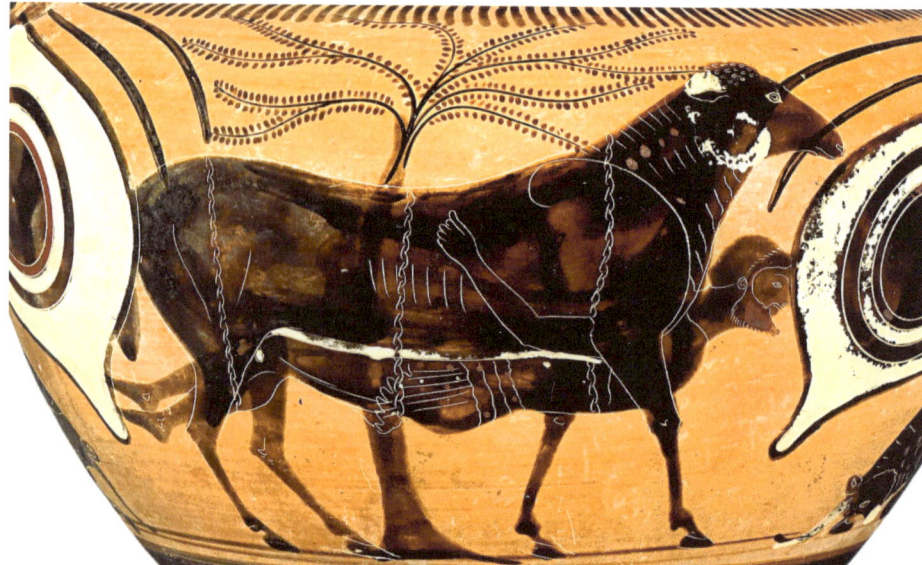

Illustration 38: Attic Black-figure Mixing Vessel, ca. 650 BCE, Odysseus escaping the Cyclops' cave under a ram. Source: CC0 Getty Open Content/Vail via Wikimedia Commons

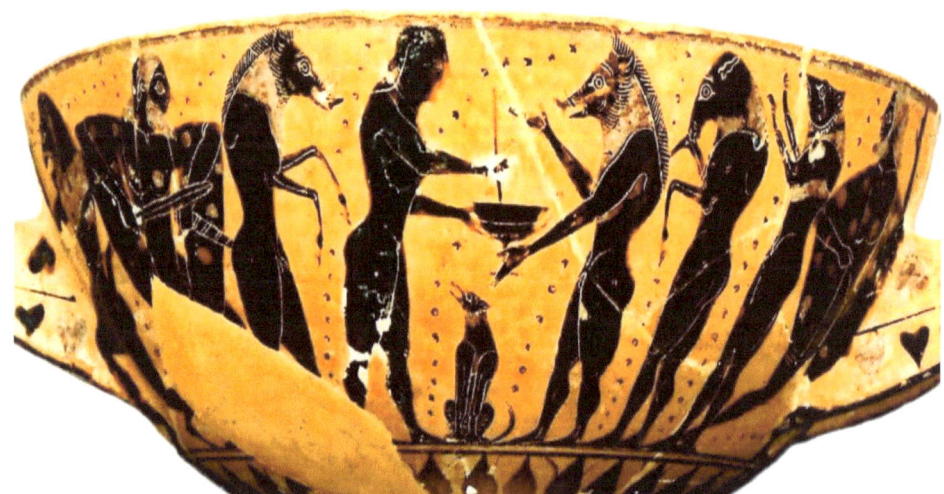

Illustration 39: Attic Black-figure Kylix, ca. 560-550 BCE, Odysseus' men receiving the antidote to Circe's magic spell that had changed them into pigs. Source: CCA 2.0 Lucas/Vail via Wikimedia Commons

Offering brandy to the Cyclops until he passes out, Odysseus and his men poke the Cyclops' eye out with a burning, pointed tree trunk. He opens the cave in blind rage and pain, trying to catch the men escaping. But they tie three sheep together for each man, and fashion slings under the bellies of each middle ram, within which each man hides until they are free.

At the shore, the men quickly load the sheep onto their ship and return to the desert island where the rest of Odysseus' fleet is waiting. [30]

Jumping out of the frying pan straight into the fire,

Odysseus and his men sail their twelve ships from terrible trouble to death and disaster. Visiting Aiolia Island next, Odysseus points his ships in the direction of home shortly after King Aiolos generously provides Odysseus with a bull's hide bag filled with wind for the ship's sails.

This is our first glimmer of hope in our search for Achilles' shield. Jealous of all the treasure their captain is carrying home from Troy, Odysseus' crew want to open the new bag. Certain that it must be filled with gold and silver from King Aiolos, they are nearly home when they finally decide to open the bull's hide bag.

Suddenly, the sky explodes with a horrific hurricane bursting from the bag. Violently tossing their ships on mountainous waves, gale winds blow them all the way back to Aiolia.

Disgusted with Odysseus and his men, King Aiolos banishes the Greeks from his island. They sail next to a land where the day is so long it becomes morning soon after dusk. This land is filled with a tribe of bloodthirsty cannibals who slingshot the ships with huge boulders, sinking all of Odysseus' ships except his own. [31]

Now, with only one ship left, Odysseus lands next

on Aiaia, the island where the mysterious sorceress Circe lives. Dividing themselves into two parties, Eurylokos takes twenty-two men, and Odysseus takes the remainder. Barely escaping the terrible fate of his men, Eurylokos races back to Odysseus, choking out a report that his men are all turned into pigs by Circe's magic!

Luckily, Hermes appears and teaches Odysseus how to foil Circe's magic. Hermes' secret succeeds and Odysseus beaches his ship after seeing his

Kathleen Vail

Odysseus Consults Tiresias in Hades

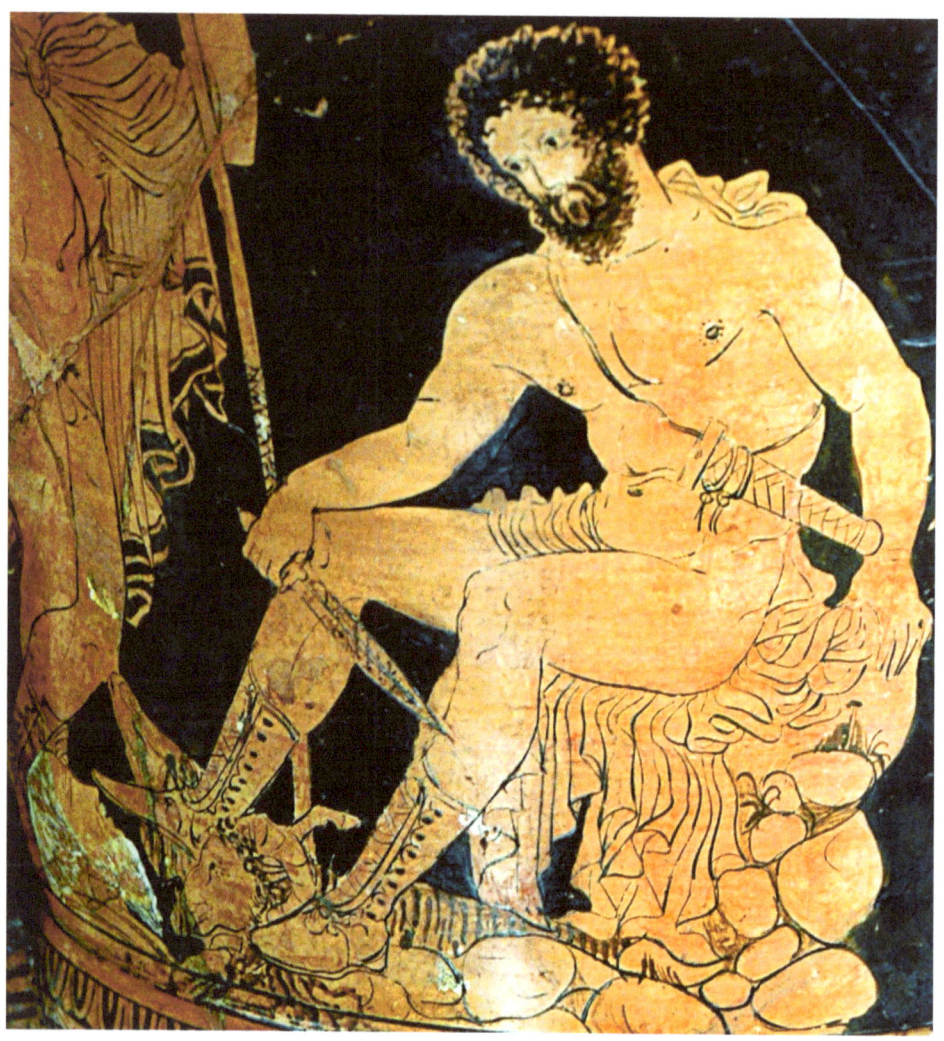

Illustration 40: Detail from a Lucanian Red-figure Calyx Krater by the Dolon Painter, ca. 380 BCE, depicting Odysseus consulting Tiresias in Hades. Source: CC0 image by Marie-Lan Nguyen/Vail via Wikimedia Commons

men regain their human shapes. In return for changing his men back, Odysseus promises to stay with Circe for as long as he can do so willingly, and she swears to use no more magic on him or his men.

After one year, however, Odysseus begs to leave, and Circe informs him that his way home leads next through Hades. She instructs him on what to do, and how to survive in the land of the dead.

Upon his arrival on her island, Circe had recommended to Odysseus that he unload his ship before beaching it, hiding his possessions in hidden holes in the rocks.

It is not recorded that Odysseus obeyed, and neither does he retrieve any hidden goods now, as Odysseus and his men set sail for Hades.

So we have no reason to think the divine shield of Achilles is anywhere else but still among his treasure, still safely stowed away in his ship, at least up until this point in Odysseus' journey. [32]

Following Odysseus' footsteps into Hades,

we recall again his visits with Agamemnon, Achilles, and Aias. He learns here, as well, from the seer Tiresias, how to continue his journey home. Tiresias warns him, also, not to touch the herds of Helios' cattle or sheep, or else Odysseus will find himself the lone survivor of a shipwreck at sea.

While in Hades, Odysseus visits with his mother and sees the shades of many others. But fearing the hand of death may catch him, Odysseus turns back and runs for his ship, embarking and commanding his crew to row away. [33] Returning to Circe, she explains to Odysseus all the strange things Tiresias has told him, clarifying the Seer's instructions.

Soon Odysseus and his crew return to the sea, successfully navigating past the Sirens, Skylla, and Charybdis, enduring a terrifying nightmare of wailing voices, bellowing waves against life-threatening rocks, sucking whirlpools, gushing sky-high water spouts and, finally, a flying, man-eating monster with the face of a woman and six bloodthirsty dog's heads frothing from beneath her breasts. [34]

Despite Tiresias' wise advice about Helios' herds,

and the sworn oaths of all the crew, the cattle and sheep do not survive the knives of Odysseus' hungry men. His hardheaded crewmen make their last mistake, feasting for six days and one final morning on the forbidden herds of Helios.

Then, after Odysseus' ship sails out into open sea, with no land to be seen in any direction, Zeus blasts it with a monstrous thunderstorm. Skies darken, the mast breaks under hurricane winds, sails, rigging, and mast hit the deck, and the ocean bucks beneath them as the black skies roar above. Zeus retaliates on Helios' behalf by blasting them into the sea. Alone in the dark, Odysseus clings to a raft which he fashions from the mast and keel board, lashing them together with a rope once used for a sail. [35]

Ogygia Island is in the middle of this currently roiling ocean. It is the home of Kalypso, daughter of Atlas. It is to this island, and to her care that Odysseus drifts on his keel board. With no ship, no crew, and not even an oar, we finally catch up with Telemakos' father where Menelaus last heard of him. Marooned on her island, as Menelaus was informed, Odysseus lives seven years with Kalypso, sitting on the shore, crying homesick tears.

Finally, Kalypso allows Odysseus to build a raft of trees he cuts down. During his eighth year on Ogygia, Odysseus sails away. If we, in our wildest dreams, imagine Odysseus saves something from the sea and carries it with him on his keel board to Kalypso, we have no record of it.

And if we chase this dream, anyway, and imagine Odysseus carries it on this new raft, we will still arrive at the same sad end. Poseidon transforms smooth sailing and blue skies into mountainous waves and a hurricane. Odysseus clings to his pitiful raft until it disintegrates and then, nearly drowning with every stroke, he finally lands, naked and exhausted, upon the shore of Skheria. [36]

Pleading for help while trying to hide his nakedness,

the shipwrecked sailor finds compassion in Princess Nausicaa when she and her handmaids come to the shore to do their laundry. Offering him some clothing, Nausicaa leads him to her father's palace where Odysseus soon finds the help and hospitality he is so sadly in need of.

Finally, departing Skheria to rejoin his long-suffering wife and son, Odysseus is put on a ship at night while he is sleeping and he is given a quick ride home to Ithaka.

But we will not follow Odysseus home. Our search for the shield of Achilles is as exhausted as Odysseus, presumably submerged by a shipwreck at sea. To search any further we much search the sea, but who imagines we will succeed?

Logic insists that a sea nymph long ago found Achilles' spectacular shield somewhere in the "wine-dark sea" and returned it at once to Thetis.

Perhaps Thetis returned it to Olympos, from whence it first came. Just as I am certain that one day I will return to meet my Maker, the divine shield of Achilles has surely done the same.

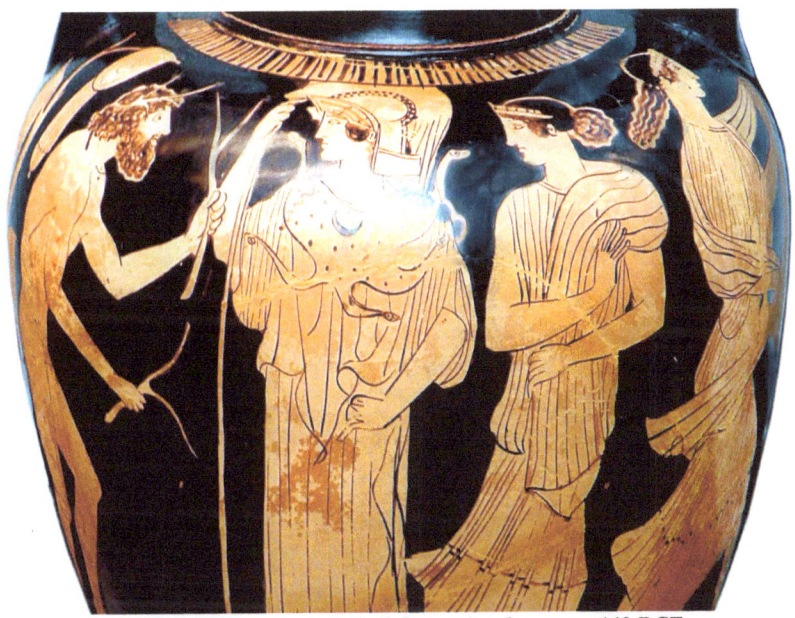

Illustration 41: Attic Red-figure Amphora, ca. 440 BCE,
Odysseus discovered naked by Nausicaa and Athena. Source: CCSA 2.0
Carole Raddato/Vail via Wikimedia Commons

FOOTNOTES:

(22). Homer's *Odyssey*, (online - revised by Timothy Power and Gregory Nagy) with translation by Samuel Butler. London: A.C. Fifield, 1900 (?), Book 5, line 307
(23). *Odyssey*, 24:36-76; **(24)**.11:550-567; **(25)**. 11:530-550; **(26)**. 3:95-200; **(27)**. 4:375-501; **(28)**. 9:30-75; **(29)**. 9:80-96; **(30)**. 9:168-485; **(31)**. 10:1-145; **(32)**. 11:1-3; **(33)**. 11: ; **(34)**.12:271-453; **(35)**. 7:235-299; **(36)**. 7:235-299

VI. The Significance of Achilles' Shield

Testifying to Homer's accuracy,

archaeological artifacts such as swords and daggers of bronze, decoratively inlaid with gold and silver characters, have been found in royal tombs of Mycenae, the ancient Greek realm of King Agamemnon.

Physical evidence of weapons similar to Homer's description of Achilles' shield provides valuable proof of Homer's knowledge. Discovering such glorious treasure not only informs us regarding the physical significance of such weapons, but also of the relationships humans have had with them.

Human history is rendered tangible in the physical form of archaeological artifacts. In our search for archaeological treasures, we find meaning and significance in our collective human life on Earth. With each discovery, we gain extraordinarily perceptive records. From this unique perspective, we gain both a telescopic view into the lost and distant past and a microscopic view of iconic moments in the human experience.

Depicted in the compelling artistry of our ancient ancestors, both the artistic metaphors employed and the moral lessons communicated are as significant as the exciting discovery of the actual archaeological treasure.

However, the ingenious and truly extraordinary significance of the shield of Achilles is that it is an archaeological treasure buried within the pages of Homer's *Iliad*. Not buried under the ancient earth, or as yet undiscovered, Homer's shield of Achilles is accessible to all, offering the same exquisite quality of view, both telescopic and microscopic, as any ancient archaeological artifact.

Employing both perspectives, the following sections focus on the physical, metaphorical, and spiritual significance of the extraordinary shield of Achilles, offering unique views of life in Homer's Ancient Greece.

VI. A. Finding Physical Significance in a Literal Shield

The *Iliad* is not a legend about a war.

In fact, the legendary epic of the war between the Greeks and Trojans doesn't start at the war's beginning, and it ends before the end of the war.

The shield of Achilles and the war for which it is created serve as an exciting backdrop – an epic literary vehicle carrying significant truths. Strip the story of what is not significant to find out what is. It isn't significant who wrote the *Iliad*. It isn't significant who is Homer, when he lived, when he died, if he was blind, or if he ever actually saw a shield such as he describes for the hero, Achilles.

What is the point of the story, why is it being told? What ideas are being shared and what lessons are to be learned? The *Iliad* is a treasure chest of character lessons, of a thousand different characters. All of life's lessons are contained within it, and a variety of responses to many, both positive and negative, are explored. It is a story of the quest for glory, to learn what is glory and how it is attained.

Containing rings within rings,

lessons within lessons, the shield of Achilles contains great morals about peace and war, encapsulated in small symbolic scenes encompassing every aspect of life in broad symbolic categories.

City life is depicted, as well as farm life, social responsibilities, religious duties, hard work, hunger, strife, war, peace, fairness, and sharing. Here are scenes where the lessons to be learned are put to the test. Here are the cycles that are destined to repeat, until the lessons are learned.

Conveniently ascribed to the hands of a god, such a glorious weapon has not yet been found by archaeologists. Is this enough to deny its existence? Of course, if Homer was truly blind, as some scholars believe, our paradox

Mycenae's "Lion Gate" and "Mask of Agamemnon"

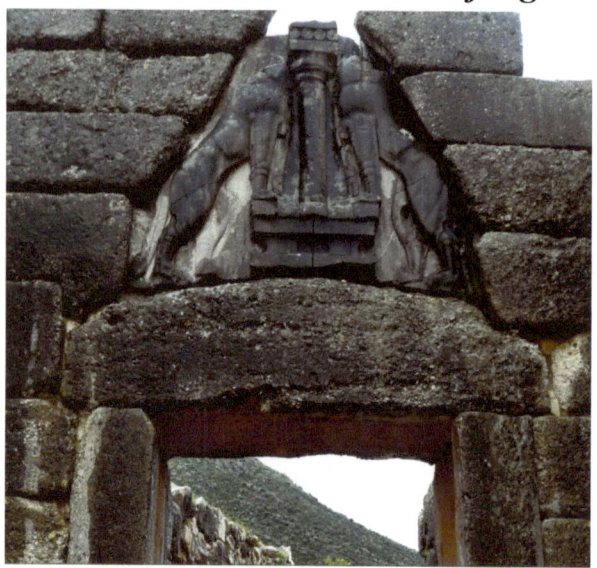

Illustration 42: The "Lion Gate" entrance to Mycenae, ca. 16th century BCE, discovered by Heinrich Schliemann. Source: CCSA 3.0 Rokaszil/Vail via Wikimedia Commons

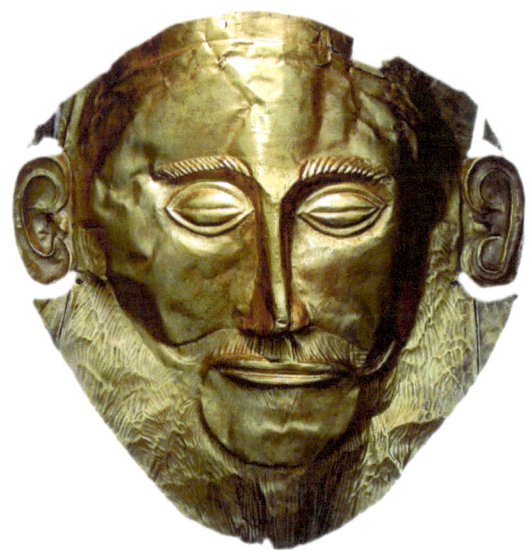

Illustration 43: "Mask of Agamemnon," Gold funerary mask, ca. 16th century BCE, Source: CCSA 3.0 Leo2004/Vail via Wikimedia Commons

grows more paradoxical. We are searching earnestly for a shield, the message of which is perhaps more significant than its physical existence.

Furthermore, we are searching for a shield described in intimate detail by a reportedly blind poet – a shield no one has ever seen, possibly not even the one describing it, and he says it is the handiwork of a god, whom we modern humans comprehend as a sophisticated, imaginary creation of deified, personified allegory. Maybe we are crazy but, if so, we are in good company.

Mycenae, Troy, and the Trojan War

were considered mythical by Classical scholars throughout the ages. Born in 1822, Heinrich Schliemann did not agree, but his amateur opinions were not significant to the scholars of his day. By 1870, fortunately, Schliemann had enough resources and confidence in himself and in Homer to go have a look and do a little digging in the dirt. Today, we can visit the physical sites of Troy and Mycenae, thanks to Heinrich Schliemann, considered by many to be the father of modern archaeology.

So, since Homer was right about Troy and Mycenae, he may also be right about the physical existence of Achilles' shield. Gardner tells us about an archaeological find called the silver siege vase –

> ...*a fragment of a silver vase with repousse' reliefs found at Mycenae. Here there is a battle going on between both light and heavy-armed troops outside the wall of a city; 'and on the wall there stood to guard it their dear wives and infant children, and with these the old men.' The artist who made this cup might well have designed such a work as the shield of Achilles.*[1]

Webster discusses the physical construction of Achilles' shield as described in the *Iliad*, saying:

> *Homer thought of a boss, three zones, and a rim; and this corresponds nearly enough to the five layers of metal which he gives the shield in a later book. [Book 20:270].*[2]

Homer tells us that Hephaistos constructs Achilles' shield with five layers, or plates; two plates are from bronze, two inner plates are composed of tin, and there is an intermediate plate of gold.

In Book 18, starting at line 475, Homer also tells us that Hephaistos prepares molten bronze, gold, and tin for the armor. The shield, when created, is strong, wide, and shining. The rim is three layers thick, or triple-ply, and the shoulder strap is silver.

Mycenaean findings support Homer's words –

currently exhibited in the National Museum of Athens, swords and daggers of bronze, decoratively inlaid with gold and silver characters, have been recovered from the fourth and fifth royal tombs of Mycenae on the Greek Peloponnese Peninsula. [3]

The fifth tomb at Mycenae also contained the famous gold funeral "Mask of Agamemnon." [4] There is no way to know the name of the king for whom this mask was made, but the visage remarkably matches our imagination's image of the High King of Mycenae. The title, "Mask of Agamemnon" has stuck since Schliemann first discovered and named it.

Continuing in Schliemann's footsteps, Carl Blegen uncovered another Mycenaean stronghold, the so-called Palace of Nestor at Pylos. Here, two more daggers of identical construction as the ones at Mycenae have been uncovered. [5] Also found at Pylos is a metal vase with ten images of men's bearded heads[6] inlaid with gold and black niello, a chemical compound containing sulfur. Similarly, a silver cup found at Mycenae was inlaid also with gold and black niello images of men's bearded heads. [7]

Bronze swords were found on the right side of a king buried in the tholos tomb at Dendra in the Argolid, a major center of Mycenaean society. [8] More swords and daggers were laid at his feet, and on the breast of a princess lay another silver cup inlaid with gold and niello. [9] Two more swords inlaid with gold and niello on both sides of the blades were found in Prosymna, another area of the Peloponnese. [10] And, surprisingly far to the north, the largest sword found from the Mycenaean period was unearthed on the island of Skopelos. Its beautiful handle is extremely valuable, covered by gold with repousse' reliefs decorating the entire handle, including a huge, pointed pommel. [11]

The absence of much armor beyond swords and daggers among the many beautiful objects found in the Mycenaean excavations is conspicuous but understandable. Certainly, shields are more useful for the living than for the dead – Homer's *Iliad* even provides a clue that Achaean burial customs may not have included shields.

Following the death of Achilles, his mother holds funeral games in his honor, placing Achilles' glorious armor as the highest prize. It is clearly unthinkable that such armor should be buried. Instead, it becomes an inheritance, a coveted prize for the winner of competitions determining who is *the Best of the Achaeans*.

The earth is the best keeper of secrets,

and so archaeologists hunt more successfully in more conspicuous places. But the ancient Greek model of inheritance did not guarantee a conspicuous final resting place for inherited objects, no matter how famously glorious they may have been. Because Achilles' shield has not been found does not imply it never physically existed. In fact, the physical existence of such similarly inlaid cups, swords, and daggers provides wonderful proof of Homer's knowledge.

We must forgive Homer for ascribing to a god the creation of these artifacts. The days of Homeric heroes were over by the time Homer was born. The artisans working in royal Mycenaean workshops were gone.

Creating character lessons from famous heroes, Homer's timeless epics recreated in words the significant facets of his glorious ancient culture, illuminating times and people that were lost but not forgotten.

The shield of Achilles, similarly lost but not forgotten, communicates to us the truly significant facets of life, enduring throughout the ages of human relationships, so that we might recognize them, too, before they are lost forever.

FOOTNOTES:

(1). Gardner, Ernest A. *Poet and Artist in Greece.* London: Duckworth, 1933 pg. 28.

(2). Webster, T. B. L. *From Mycenae to Homer.* London: Methuen and Company, Ltd., 1977 pg. 214.

(3). Karouzou, Dr. Semni. *National Museum – Illustrated Guide to the Museum.* Athens: Ekdotike Athenon S.A., 1985. Item No.'s 394, 765 and 294, pg. 26, and No.'s 744 and 764, pg. 28.

(4), Karouzou, S. Item No. 624, pg. 28; (5). No.'s 8339 and 8340, pg. 34; (6). No. 7842, pg. 34; (7). No. 2849, pg. 22; (8). No.'s 7325 and 7326, pg. 39; (9). No. 7336, pg. 39; (10). No.'s 8446 and 6416, pg. 40; (11). No. 6444, pg. 41.

Achilles and Briseis

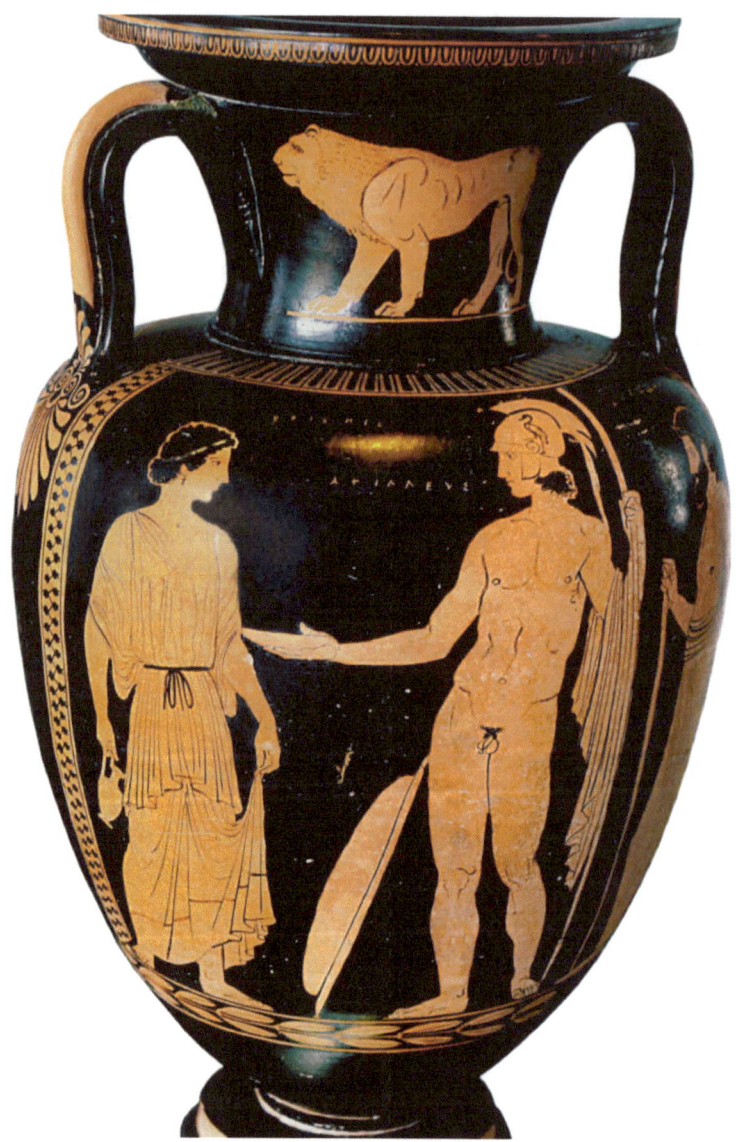

Illustration 44: *Apulian Red-figure Amphora by the Painter of the Berlin Dancing Girl,*
ca. 430-410 BCE, depicting Achilles and Briseis.
Source: *CCSA 3.0 image by AlexanderVanLoon/Vail via Wikimedia Commons*

VI. B. Regarding the Metaphorical Motifs on Achilles' Shield

Achilles, the greatest warrior in history, hates war

with a passion. "Make Love, Not War" could be Achilles' motto. Donning the spectacular new armor presented to him by Thetis and mounting his chariot for battle, Achilles vows he will not stop fighting on this day until all the Trojans hate war. [12]

War is Achilles' worst enemy and, true to his promise, he kills every warrior whom heaven places in his path. [13] By the end of the day, no Trojan still living wants to be outside the walls of Troy.

But this is not how it all starts with Achilles.

When Thetis receives word of war brewing over the kidnapping of Helen, love of peace drives Achilles from his home. Thetis disguises him as a girl, sending him to hide among King Lykomedes' daughters on the island of Skyros.

But wars are not won, nor launched overnight, if we use Helen's words and numbers. At the end of the tenth year of the Trojan War, Helen reports that she has been in Troy for twenty. [14]

So, for a good part of ten years, Achilles enjoys a peaceful life on Skyros, in love with Princess Deidameia. But finally, summoned by Odysseus to join the warriors, Achilles leaves his young son, Neoptolemos, in Deidameia's arms.

Willingly leaving his peaceful life behind, Achilles now leaves for the war. Commanding his army of Myrmidons, he leads them in the service and love of fairness, avenging the abduction of King Menelaos' lawfully wedded wife.

If Achilles can no longer have peace in his life, he will at least have love. For many of the next ten years, Briseis, a young woman awarded to Achilles as a war-prize keeps him company, bringing him comfort and love after long days of warfare.

When Agamemnon offends Achilles by taking Briseis to his tent, Achilles' love for Briseis drives his next action. He restores to himself a kind of personal peace by swearing abstention from battle.

Swinging like the shining scales of a balance,

Achilles lives his life with disciplined passion, wholeheartedly doing a thing, or wholeheartedly refusing to do it. Adding his weight here and removing it there, Achilles ultimately maintains his value of fairness.

With the death of his best friend, Patroklos, the scales swing once again and Achilles springs back into action. With both peace and love now fully vanquished, he is driven instead to chase glory. Glory is another aspect of love, rendering the one glorified beloved.

He is so skilled at the art of chase that only Achilles' reputation can outrun him. And, now, shining in new armor fitting him as lightly as feathers, Achilles flies to the fight as though on wings of blazing passion.

More awesome than charisma, Achilles possesses command; no woman or man can resist him. Every Trojan he approaches sees a war god racing toward him, filled with righteous fury. Every Trojan whom Achilles sees is a destroyer of peace, protecting a guilty thief. Achilles wins no glory for slaughter, but rather for settling the score. He wins for righting the scales of fairness on the battlefield of war.

Achilles is the quintessential warrior, carrying the quintessential shield. In its purest essence, a shield is a defensive device; Achilles' shield is a defensive device so pure that its creation seems a work of pure genius. It is so beautiful that it has the power to stop an enemy in his tracks and, by this mistake, renders him an easy target.

Face to face with Achilles, his enemy pauses to gaze at the extraordinary shield. A wondrous symbol of life, the shield is so eloquently symbolic that the quickest gaze of the hardiest warrior finds something lovingly familiar. It takes his breath away and, instantly, he falls at Achilles' feet.

We can only wonder if it is the shield or the sword that kills him, dying at the hand of Achilles.

This exquisite shield is Achilles' quintessential defense, emblazoned with both winsome emblems of a happy life and deterring emblems of war's horrors. It is an earnest prescription, a brilliant device, shining in defense of peace.

"We can feel the whole life of the Homeric world

stirring and moving and going on its way behind the events of the story," notes Owen, offering his perspective on the shield of Achilles.

Owen continues, "The countryside with its farms, vineyards and pasture lands, scenes of hunting and all the homely crafts, nature in its beauty and calm, and in its storms and terrors – we are thus enabled to see it all without straying from the battlefield."[15]

"But obviously," says Stobart, "an idealising poet in describing such objects permits his imagination to excel anything he has ever seen or heard of. Besides, it was wrought by the lame god Hephaistos, and the gods do not make armour such as you can buy at the shop."[16]

Hogan widens the scope, insisting, "nothing so comprehensive and detailed as this could ever have been seen by Homer or his audience."[17]

And, finally, "Detailed reconstruction of the shield is impossible," states Webster, [18] slamming the door shut in our faces.

For many scholars, the shield of Achilles is purely symbolic. Gardner, in fact, says it is symbolic but represents nothing more than an elaborate work of art. He believes, "though many scenes and figures in varied action are described, there is no attempt to represent or to illustrate a mythical story, or even an actual event. All the scenes are merely typical events of town and country life, in peace and war."[19]

Ferrucci finds Achilles' shield more widely symbolic

"round in shape, encircled by a representation of the Ocean River, which is also the outer boundary of the earth, and with the sun, the moon, and all the constellations depicted in the center, it is a compendium of the cosmos."[20]

Beautifully perceptive, Clarke expands our imaginations further, explaining, "Hephaestus is its maker, just as fire produces all things; he makes the shield at night, just as all matter was created out of the chaos of a primal night; ...he makes it out of gold, silver, bronze, and tin, which are the metal equivalents of the four elements, ether, air, water, and earth. ...The shield itself is round like the world and has five zones, which correspond to the five zones of the earth."[21]

Soaring high on wings of enlightened consciousness, Ferrucci exclaims, "This is the significance of Achilleus' shield. As an image of the hero's consciousness, it reflects the cosmos while representing it, and is thus the first symbolic image of art's capacity to function as a stereoscope."

Ferrucci waxes poetically, "As a similar situation recurs in every great book, the paradox of writing is continually magnified. The first model of reality has been created, the first work contains its own interpretation; art has already the power to formulate art. The cosmos contains the poem, in which resides the shield – the shield that reflects the universe. The poem becomes an image of the cosmos so complete as to discourage any attempt to compete with it."[22]

Taking flight with Ferrucci, we risk flying too close to the sun. Let us turn back at the first scent of burning feathers and return to the shield at hand.

The scenes on Achilles' Shield are metaphorical

representations of life; they are ancient motifs to us, but current with Homer's culture. Like the stained glass windows of many early Christian churches, the scenes depict a story; they hope to teach a lesson.

The first scene, at the epicenter of the shield of Achilles, is undeniably a metaphor for the earth in its heavenly environment. To find the message, to learn the lesson, explore the next three rings:

The inner ring is a metaphor for city life, with associated motifs of social controls. Here are people interested in respecting established limits of behavior in order to maintain social stability. Weddings signify legal relationships; one man accosting another man in the marketplace signifies legal accountability for illegal behavior, and a trial by judges clearly signifies legal justice for all.

These scenes are depicting a society willing to respect what is right and wrong, willing to abide by social and self-control. If I am not accountable for my behavior, nothing will stop me from robbing my neighbor if he has something I want. However, if I will be thrown in jail for robbery, I may be more willing to be a peaceful neighbor, instead of a thief. The seed of government grows or dies according to the communal support for peace.

The middle ring depicts metaphorical war, resulting from man's jealousy, passions, greed, etc., pushing him beyond the limits of social controls. For example, when the son of a king steals another king's wife, retribution follows closely behind. And, as Homer's *Iliad* witnesses, the city of Troy, even with its encircling wall and massive gates can not protect its citizens from the inevitable punishment coming.

The moral begins to clarify, studying the divine shield's scenes of war. Even if Ares and Athena lead the battle, or in other words, no matter how high the technology, or how massive the weapons of destruction, the participants of war will still end up as the victims of Strife, Tumult, and Fate. Everyone suffers and most will die, trampled in the mud and the blood with their brothers.

The outer ring, a metaphorical cycle of peacetime, follows naturally after a cycle of war. Escaping tumult, life retreats to the country. After the war subsides, what is the result? The city is sacked and every good thing is broken, stolen, or burnt. Shops and homes are utterly ruined and there are no more markets. Every salesman-turned-soldier is missing or dead, along with his father and brothers.

After a war, it is time to pack up the donkey with whatever remains and head back to the village, to the ancestral home of Grandma. This is the time to return to tilling the fields, reaping the grain, and gathering the juicy sweet grapes. At least the lions do not carry swords, and there are certainly fewer of them than the warriors who came to steal all the goods and destroy the entire city.

Soon enough, Grandma's home in the country will become crowded again after young sons bring home wives from the harvest dances. Soon enough there will be a surplus of goods, a need for larger markets, and the young people will venture forth to rebuild the ruined cities.

The repetitive waves on the shield's rim

are the generations of humans destined to repeat these cycles of strife, war, and peace. Look again from the beginning and the full message of Achilles' shield becomes profoundly clear.

The earth, moon, sun, and stars in the center are unable to change their natural cycles. But the man-made cycles of strife, war, and peace, while predictably repetitive, are not really involuntary. These are timeless lessons about valuing social order and controls, about maintaining standards of fairness, and about appreciating peace.

Utilizing the oral tradition, the best medium available to him, Homer eternally memorialized the positive effects of order and negative impacts of strife. Achilles' shield, the "Shield of Memory," as Atchity terms it, is a quintessential weapon of defense, ingeniously defending peace.

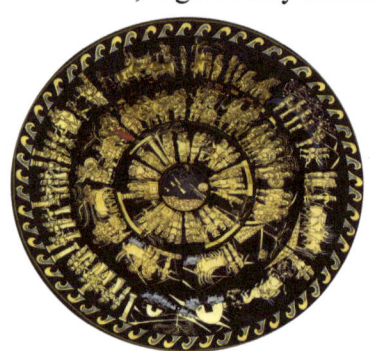

FOOTNOTES:

(12). Homer's *Iliad, Book 19, line 423*, (online) translation by A.T. Murray, Ph.D. Cambridge, MA, Harvard University Press; London, William Heinemann, 1924.

(13). *Iliad*, 21:104; **(14).** 24:765.

(15). Owen, S.T., *The Story of the Iliad*. Ann Arbor: University of Michigan Press, 1966, pg. 189.

(16). Stobart, J.C., *The Glory that was Greece*. New York: Frederick A. Praeger, 1969, pg. 47.

(17). Hogan, J.C., *A Guide to the Iliad*. New York: Anchor Books, 1979, pp. 239-240.

(18). Webster, T. B. L., *From Mycenae to Homer*. London: Methuen and Company, Ltd., 1977, pg. 214.

(19). Gardner, E. A., *Poet and Artist in Greece*. London: Duckworth, 1933, pp. 27-28.

(20). Ferrucci, F., *The Poetics of Disguise*. Ithaca: Cornell University Press, 1980, pg. 29.

(21). Clarke, H., *Homer's Readers*. Newark: University of Delaware Press, 1981, pg. 80.

(22). Ferrucci, F., *The Poetics of Disguise*. Ithaca: Cornell University Press, 1980, pp..30-31.

VI. C. Appreciating the Spiritual Allegories on Achilles' Shield

Peace is a prize shared with the living and the dead -

a body not properly laid to rest is a soul unable to find peace, unable to pass on to the hereafter. A deceased body prevented from being buried is still today considered an inhumane atrocity.

Patroklos, not yet buried, complains to Achilles all night long in Achilles' dreams. He must have his burial, he must find peace, and Patroklos cries to Achilles to take care of it quickly.

And, in the case of Hektor's funeral, peace is likewise granted to the living. Achilles guarantees a temporary suspension of the war, promising King Priam eleven days of peace for the funeral rites of the Trojan hero.

A funeral provides opportunities unmatched in any other assembly, whether it is today or in the earliest of ancient Greek days. It is an opportunity to pay respect and honor to the deceased, allowing the soul to pass on in peace. It is a time of religious worship, marked by rituals of sacrifice recognizing the Immortal Power(s) controlling life and death. It is a time of fellowship with one another, a momentous social gathering.

People who have shared in the life of the one now passing on congregate and share with the others what part they played, and what they remember best. All that remains when we die are our deeds, witnesses of our fleeting lives. And, based on our faith in our beliefs, an attainment or withholding of *kleos*, the ancient Greek concept of Immortal Glory.

A funeral is also an opportunity for personal gain. We see an informal system of gift-giving, something akin to the concept of inheritance in the ancient Greek funeral games, in the sharing of wealth and personal effects as prizes to the winners of games held in the deceased's honor.

Ancient Funerals & Funeral Game Prizes

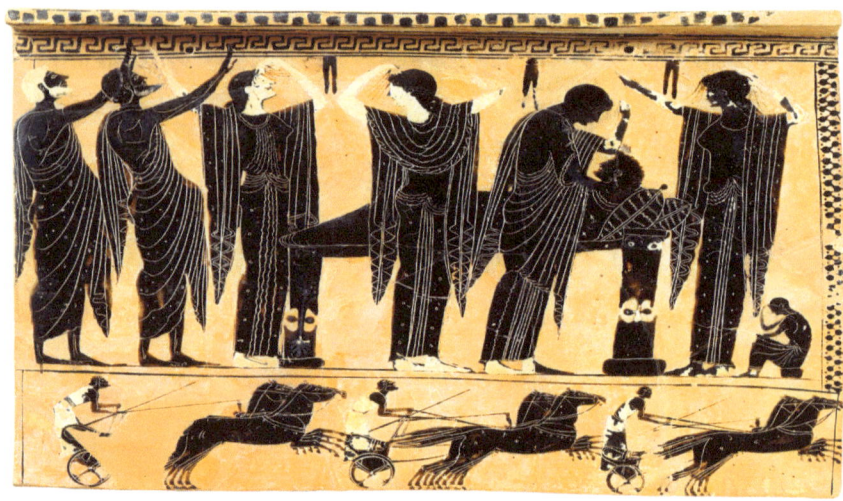

Illustration 45: Attic Black-figure Terracotta Funerary Plaque, ca. 520-510 BCE, funeral of a man, possibly Patroklos or Achilles, and chariot races at the funeral games held in his honor. Source: CC0 Metropolitan Museum of Art/Vail via Wikimedia Commons

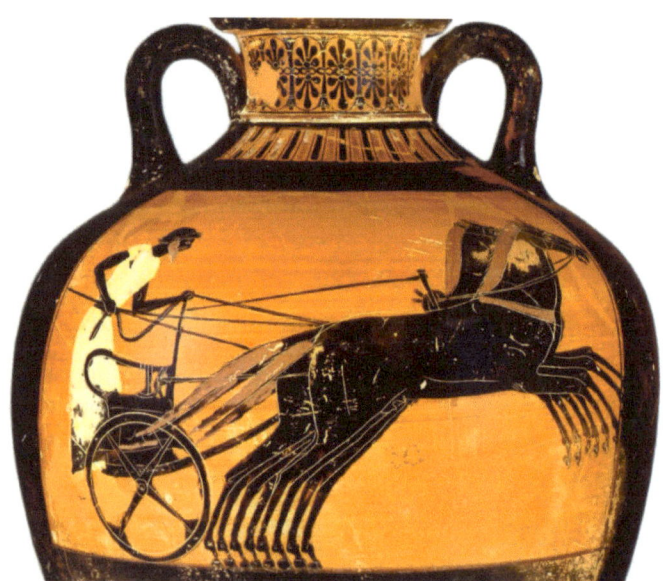

Illustration 46: Attic Black-figure Amphora, ca. 490-480 BCE. These amphorae, often filled with olive oil, were specially designed as prizes for winners of the Panathenaic Games. Source: CC0 Getty Open Content/Vail via Wikimedia Commons

Zinon Papakonstantinou, in *Prizes in Early Archaic Greek Sport*, analyzes this ancient practice of gift-exchange:

> *An initial examination of the prizes and their distribution during the funeral games of Patroclus suggests that the circulation of these valuable objects was an integral part of aristocratic gift-exchange and that therefore such prizes reaffirmed social hierarchies and consolidated networks of power relationships of Homeric elites.* [23]

When Achilles dies, Thetis shares some of her son's wealth with the soldiers who win competitions in his honor. For the highest prize, she promises her son's glorious armor to *the Best of the Achaeans*, the top contender of the funeral games for Achilles.

> ***...But thy mother asked of the gods beautiful prizes***
> ***and set them in the midst of the list for the chiefs of the Achaeans.***
> ***Ere now hadst thou been present at the funeral games***
> ***of many men that were warriors,***
> ***when at the death of a king the young men gird themselves***
> ***and make ready the contests,***
> ***but hadst thou seen that sight***
> ***thou wouldst most have marvelled at heart,***
> ***such beautiful prizes did the goddess, silver-footed Thetis,***
> ***set there in thy honor; for very dear wast thou to the gods.*** [24]

Funeral games lead to fair sharing,

providing a logical resolution of the deceased's property, especially if he has great wealth or has an extensive social network. And athletic prowess as a competitor is not the only means of winning a prize.

The competition of poetry recital finds a voluntarily captive audience and many competitors glad to recite their best stories, perhaps even including the life story of the newly deceased. And if, by their sharing, the contenders are judged worthy of a prize from the deceased's belongings, so much the better for everyone.

Funeral games contribute greatly in nationalizing the ancient Greeks. The competitions carry such honor, such potential for earning *kleos*, that to win is of ultimate personal value. Characteristics such as discipline, strength, sharing, and fairness are epitomized by the contenders, naturally affecting them in all fields of life. By encouraging competition that is self-governed by fairness, the games nurture the seed of national governance.

Expanding beyond the boundaries of social networks, growing side by side with Government, the Games encourage and protect the value of fairness, ultimately uniting entire cities, regions, and nations.

Ancient funeral games give birth to the Olympics.

With roots in early funeral games, [25] and growing as regional worship events, the Panathenaic Games in Athens, Pythian Games in Delphi, Nemeian Games in Nemea, the Isthmian Games of Corinth and, of course, the Olympic Games at Elis all blossom and become mammoth competitions, inviting huge numbers of participants and viewers.

In the 8th century BCE, an Olympics legend records, the city-states of Elis and Pisa leave off fighting after the oracle of Delphi advises King Iphitos of Elis to prevent losing by organizing games in honor of the gods. [26]

A truce is declared and all attend the games which, hereafter, are called the "Olympics" in honor of the Olympian gods. Forming boards of city-state members, the organizers of the Games request each city-state to leave off fighting and send representatives instead to settle matters between them in friendly competitions. [27] In this case, the winners bring home prizes instead of war booty, and the city-states are rewarded by seeing their citizens honored, rather than killed or enslaved.

The cost of games, prizes, and publicly celebrated honor is an excellent price to pay for Peace. It is a simple, civilized solution to war, brilliantly executed. The value of fairness is maintained, and Peace is the ultimate prize shared by these fair contenders, uniting them all as a nation.

Homer's *Iliad* is the ultimate prize-winning poem in the poetry recital competitions, loved and repeated perennially after its first composition. [28]

The *Iliad* resurfaces and bobs on each successive ring of new generations, floating like a shining beacon of light on a beautiful river called Peace.

Look at the blossoming of Literature, Drama, History, Philosophy, Art, and Science following the rise of the Panhellenic Games, especially the Quadrennial Panathenaic Games following the ascendancy of Athens as the imperial power in the region.

Mining Homer for spiritual gems,

Homer's *Iliad* becomes every student's primer with the spread of education in Classical Greece. Like many scriptural texts today, such as the *Torah*, *Bible*, or *Qur'an*, the *Iliad* became an indispensable resource, with students of innumerable generations religiously mining it for invaluable treasures.

And, as each new generation is inspired, they begin reaching deeper and higher, producing finer and finer works. Each fresh young student examines the ideas of the others before him and builds upon them with new ideas. By this process of development, all the arts and sciences have been born and are today still growing.

The ancient Greek ideals are still present today, most tangibly evident in our recurring celebration of the international Olympic Games. Sadly, it seems that many today consider the Olympics almost as superfluous as a long, drawn-out description of a shield in the midst of an explosive battle.

Nevertheless, the beautifully simple ideals expressed in both Olympic Games and Achilles' shield still remain - the lessons to be learned are simple and are aiming at identical targets:

- *Appreciate the Value of Fairness*
- *Come Together*
- *Put an End to Down-Spiraling Cycles of War*
- *Win the Prize of Peace*

Unfortunately, the intangible value of Fairness is often buried under Jealousy's boots, for the sake of Personal Gain. Greed and Jealousy are selfish, knowing only how to lie, telling us what we want is worth more in our hands than in the hands of others. When this happens, there will always be War; it is the Immortal Equalizer.

Only when enough casualties are dragged to Death by War will the fear of Death and respect for Life grow in value. Only then will the miserliness of

Greed be exposed and behaviors begin to change. Soon, the scales will tip in favor of Peace, and War will subside for a while.

The language of Allegory is easily understood,

and the ancient Greeks were masters of this medium. Today we prefer to restrain our ideals from growing lives of their own. Associating partners with our God is unacceptable in many of our religions, so our allegories are capitalized to indicate the names of abstract concepts.

But in the early Greek conceptualization, abstract concepts grow arms, legs, and faces. As abstract identities uncontrollable by humans, they become recognized as Powerful Immortals. And, once Immortal, they become objects of worship, wrapped in the mantle of Religion.

Achilles is himself a kind of allegory of Justice. He is an Equalizer, a restorer of Fairness. It is not surprising that his shield is a gift created by an Immortal Being. It is an exceptional gift that his mother, Silver-Footed Thetis, bestows upon the heroic forefathers of Western Civilization.

Achilles' divine shield is an allegory of Peace, not easily attained, bestowed only by Immortal Power. And, even if we do not believe in a world ruled by Immortal Power, Peace is still the ultimate Prize – the gloriously authentic Golden Apple awarded *"To The Most Fair."*

FOOTNOTES:

(23). Papakonstantinou, Z. *Prizes in Early Archaic Greek Sport.* Oregon, Nikephoros 15, 2002, pp. 51-67.

(24). Homer's *Odyssey* translated by A.T. Murray, Ph.D. (online) Book 24:85-95

(25). Renfrew, C., *The Minoan-Mycenaean Origins of the Panhellenic Games* in Raschke, W.J. (Ed.), *The Archaeology of the Olympics: The Olympics and Other Festivals in Antiquity,* Wisconsin: University of Wisconsin Press, 1988.

(26). NOSTOS. *Brief History of the Olympic Games.* Online text by NOSTOS Hellenic Information Society. See also Valavanis, P. *The Olympics: From Ancient Greece to the World* (online) 2016.

(27) *AGON The spirit of Competition in Ancient Greece* – brochure supported by the Stavros Niarchos Foundation accompanying the *AGON* exhibition at the Capital Museum, Beijing; July 31-Oct 14, 2008.

(28). Nagy, G. *Homer the Preclassic.* Berkeley and Los Angeles, University of California Press, 2010, Chapter 2, pg 31.

VII. Historical Motifs and Notes to Scenes on Achilles' Shield

Cross-referencing historical similarities

with Achilles' shield is a delightful challenge that any reader might undertake upon reading Homer's extraordinary description in Book 18 of the *Iliad*. Recognizing that historical similarities might be identified on ancient Greek artifacts, especially among terracotta vases, I undertook a challenge to reconstruct a literal shield of Achilles based only on Homer's words and accomplished with only historically relevant designs.

Reducing the scenes to artistic motifs greatly facilitated my research. Thus, ancient Greek motifs of horses, warriors, women, etc, as found on early black-figure pottery and other historical artifacts could then be incorporated into my reconstruction.

The ancient Greeks clearly loved illustrating Homeric life and times. They left us a veritable gold mine, as open as our books, computers, desires, and minds. What our mining expeditions uncover depends on our efforts–so thrilling in the process, and so satisfying in the acquisition!

Sharing these discoveries, our golden nuggets of Homeric insight, adds invaluable wealth to the treasury available to future lovers of Ancient Greece, delightfully influencing future imaginations and profoundly enriching future search expeditions.

Compiled below are my golden nuggets–ancient Greek sources of similar artistic motifs that influenced my reconstruction. Several interesting notes are also offered, insights into Homeric life and times that are relevant to individual scenes depicted upon the timeless shield of Achilles.

Historical Motifs - Epicenter: Creation

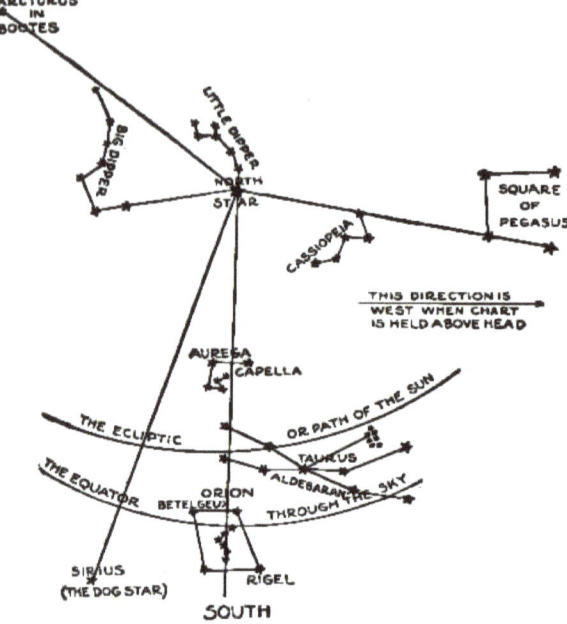

1920 Star Map Showing the Big Dipper, Little Dipper, Taurus (including Hyades and Pleiades), and Orion.

From A. Frederick Collins, The Book of Stars, Fig. 27.

Source: CC0 Archive.org/Vail via Wikimedia Commons

FIG. 27.—STAR MAP SHOWING SIX CHIEF CONSTELLATIONS.

Illustration 47: Star Map

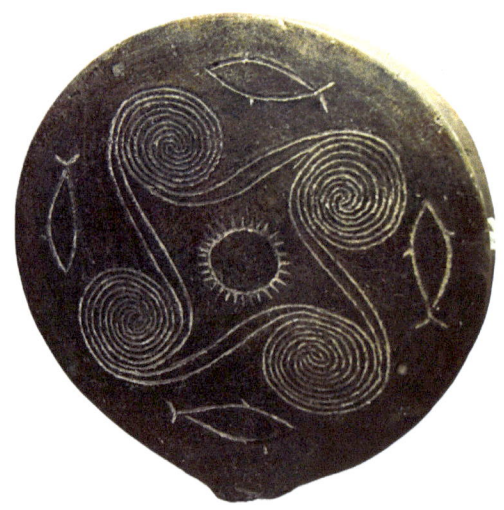

Sun, ocean waves, and fish.

Early Cycladic Terracotta "frying pan" (use is undetermined) from Naxos, ca. 2700-2500 BCE.

Source: CCSA 3.0 Zde/Vail via Wikimedia Commons

Illustration 48: Early Cycladic "Frying Pan"

VII. A. Reference Notes - Epicenter: CREATION

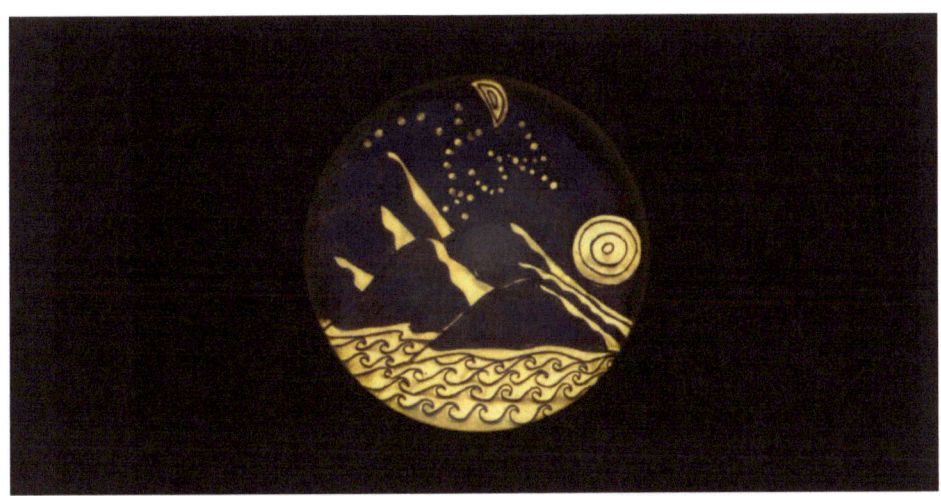

Illustration 49: Epicenter: Creation. From the Shield of Achilles
by Kathleen Vail © All Rights Reserved

"Earth, heaven and sea he made with an unwearied sun, and moon..."

Earth's primal elements are indelibly etched onto everyday wares and dwellings by creative humans from the earliest ages. Still today, at the core of our frail beings, we are both drawn to and overawed by the powerful sun, moon, stars, and sea.

Star maps depict constellations such as those identified by Homer at the center of Achilles' shield. Shown here are simplifications of Hyades and Pleiades, both of the Taurus constellation. Positioned relative to Taurus is Orion, the Hunter, with belt and club (some say sword) depicted. Ursa Major, or the Great Bear, is shown simplified to the Big Dipper, also known as the Wain, or chariot, identified by its cart and stem with which it is hooked to a team of horses.

Hogan notes in *A Guide to the Iliad*, regarding Homer's usage of the constellations Pleiades, Hyades, Orion, and the Great Bear, "The constellations mentioned here are perhaps chosen for their usefulness to

Historical Motifs - Epicenter: Creation, Cont'd

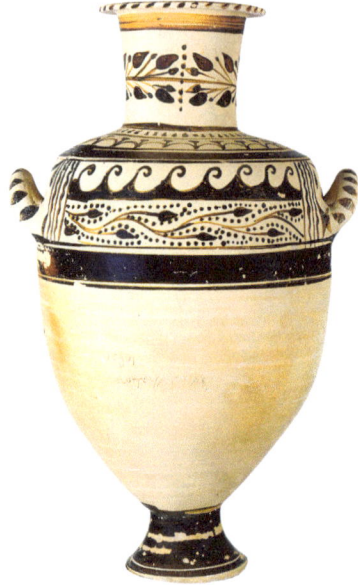

A beautiful line of waves decorates this water vessel.

Greek Black-figure Hydria, or Hadra Vase from Alexandria, Egypt, ca. 213 BCE.

Source: CC0 Metropolitan Museum of Art/Vail via Wikimedia Commons

Illustration 50: Black-figure Hydria

Sappho reading one of her poems to three student-friends.

Red-figure Hydria or Kalpis by the Group of Polygnotos, ca. 440–430 BCE.

Source: CCSA 2.5 Marsyas/Vail via Wikimedia Commons

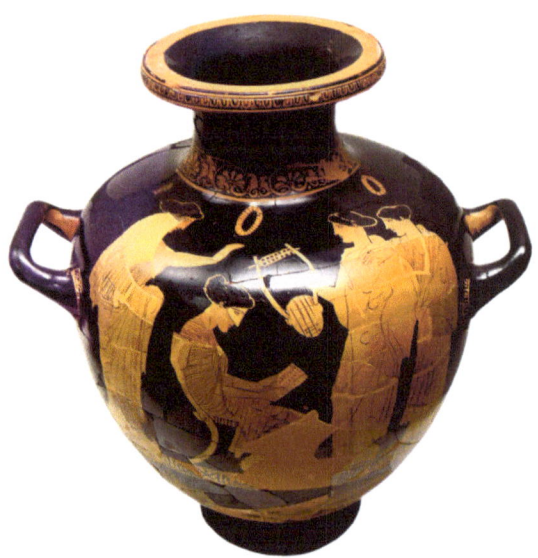

Illustration 51: Red-figure Hydria

the farmer and sailor." [1] Hesiod, likewise, bears witness to this seasonal usefulness in the following verses:

But when the Pleiades and the Hyades and strong Orion begin to set,
then it is that you should be mindful to plow in season. [2]

The agricultural significance of Homer's choice of these constellations is further analyzed by Robert Hannah in his excellent article entitled, *The Constellations on Achilles Shield.*[3]

The legendary female lyric poet, Sappho of Lesbos, Greece (ca. 630-570 BCE), was likewise familiar with the constellations in her night sky, as she wistfully records in the following fragment of lovely poetry:

The moon is set.
And the Pleiades.
It's the middle of the night.
Time passes.
But I sleep alone. [4]

Documented sources for the motifs in this image include:

Ocean Waves:

– Early Cycladic Terracotta "Frying Pan," from Naxos, ca. 2700-2500 BCE. At the National Archaeological Museum of Athens, Inv. No. 6140A. CCSA 3.0 image by Zde/Vail via Wikimedia Commons.

– Greek Black-figure Hydria, or Hadra Vase from Alexandria, Egypt, ca. 213 BCE. At the Metropolitan Museum of Art. Casagrande-Kim, R., *When the Greeks Ruled Egypt: From Alexander to Cleopatra,* cat. 123, p. 104.

FOOTNOTES:

(1). Hogan, J.C. *A Guide to the Iliad.* New York: Anchor Books, 1979.

(2). Nagy, G. *Translation: Hesiod's Works and Days* (Center for Hellenic Studies online) lines 614-617.

(3). Hannah, Robert *The Constellations on Achilles' Shield (Iliad 18. 485-489).* Volume 2, Number 4 Electronic Antiquity: Communicating the Classics. Dec. 1994.

(4). Dubnoff, J. *Translation: Poetry of Sappho,* Center for Hellenic Studies-online, fr. 8.

Historical Motifs - Inner Ring: Wedding Procession

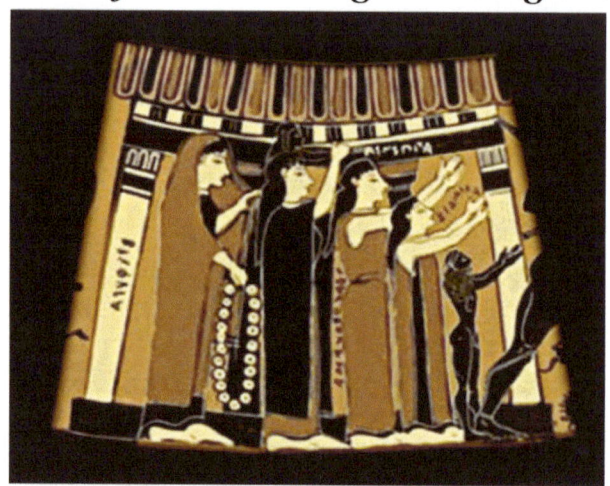

Illustration 52: The "Amphiaraos Krater" (detail)

Women under a columned porch. Detail from the Amphiaraos Krater,
a Late Corinthian Red-ground Column Krater, ca. 560 BCE.
Source: CC0 Vail/ Universitats Bibliothek via Wikimedia Commons

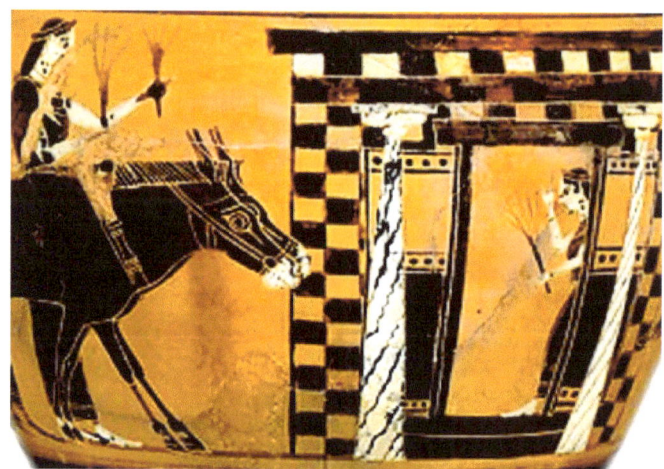

Illustration 53: Attic Black-figure Lekythos

A wedding procession by torchlight approaches the bride's home
in this earliest known depiction of an Attic wedding.
Attic Black-figure Lekythos, ca. 550-530 BCE.
Source: CC0 Metropolitan Museum of Art/Vail via Wikimedia Commons

VII. B. Reference Notes - Inner Ring: CIVIL LIFE

VII. B. 1. Wedding Procession

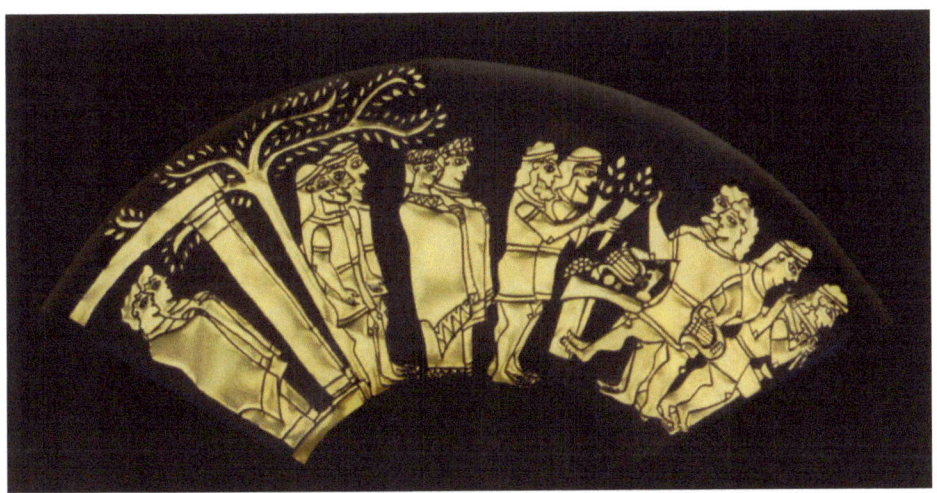

Illustration 54: Inner Ring: Wedding Procession. From the Shield of Achilles by Kathleen Vail © All Rights Reserved

"Two cities he pictured, of eloquent men..."

Documented sources for the motifs in this image include:

Feasts:

– Celebe, ca. 6th Century BCE, "Eurytios Krater" now at the Louvre, Paris; Fowler, *A Handbook of Greek Archaeology*, fig. 367.

Men in Short Garments:

– Attic Amphora, "Heracles Killing Nessos," ca. 610-600 BCE, at the National Museum of Athens; Richter, *A Handbook of Greek Art*, fig. 407.

– Celebe, ca. 6th Century BCE, "Eurytios Krater" now at the Louvre, Paris; Fowler, *A Handbook of Greek Archaeology*, fig. 367.

– Attic Black-figure Volute Krater, "The Francois Vase," ca. 570 BCE, Mingazzini, *Greek Pottery Painting*, plate 7.

Historical Motifs - Wedding Procession, Cont'd.

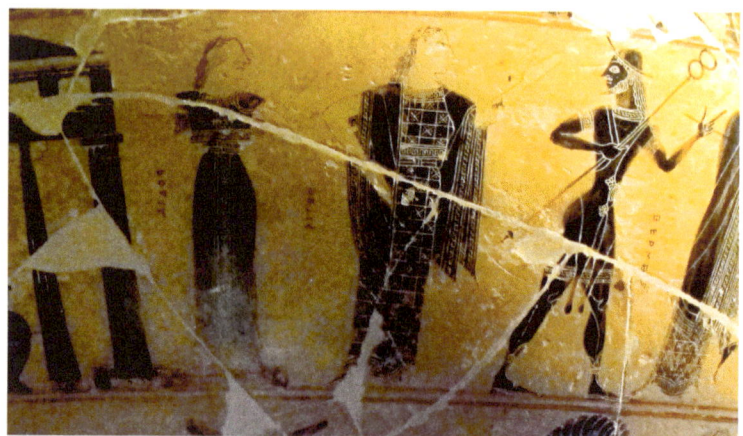

Illustration 55: The Francois Vase (detail)

Guests arriving for the wedding of Peleus and Thetis. Detail from the "Francois Vase," an Attic Black-figure Volute Krater signed by the potter Ergotimos and the painter Kleitias, ca. 570-565 BCE. Source: CCSA 3.0 image by Sailko/Vail via Wikimedia Commons

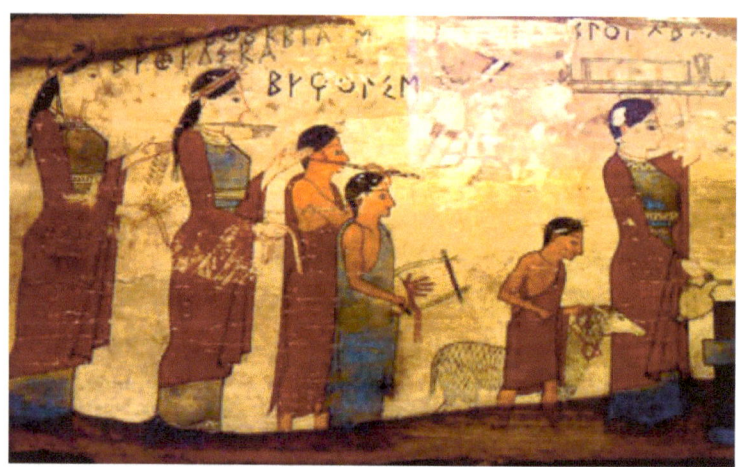

Illustration 56: Corinthian Miniature Painting

Women with wreaths in hair and long robes covering the shoulders. Corinthian miniature painting of sacrificial lamb, ca. 540 BCE. Source: CCSA 2.5 image by Marsyas/Vail via Wikimedia Commons

Pipes and Lyres:

– Pipes: Protocorinthian Olpe, "The Chigi Vase," by the MacMillan Painter, ca. 650-640 BCE, in the Villa Giulia, Beazley, *Greek Sculpture and Painting*, fig. 19. Also Mingazzini, *Greek Pottery Painting*, plate 6.

– Lyres: Corinthian Miniature Painting of a lamb being taken for sacrifice on an altar, ca. 540 BCE, Karouzou, *National Museum – Illustrated Guide to the Museum*, item 16464.

Trees:

– Attic Red-figure Amphora by Andokides, ca. 530-520 BCE. Paris, Musée Du Louvre

– Cup by the Corinthianizing Painter, ca. 660 BCE, in the Berkeley Museum, and Beazley, *The Development of Attic Black-figure*, plate 83, no. 2.

– Lekythos by the Cactus Painter, "Herakles at the Tree of the Hesperides," Boardman, *Athenian Black Figure Vases*, fig. 233.

– Corinthian Bottle by Timonidas, ca. 580 BCE, Cook, *Greek Art – Its Development, Character and Influence*, plate D, page 277.

Women Under Columned Porch:

– Corinthian Krater, "The Departure of Amphiaraos," ca. 560 BCE, in the Berlin St. Museum, Pfuhl, *Masterpieces of Greek Drawing and Painting*, fig. 14.

Women With Wreaths in Hair and/or Covered Shoulders:

– Corinthian Celebe, ca. 550 BCE, in the Vatican, Fowler, *A Handbook of Greek Archaeology*, fig. 366.

– Corinthian Miniature Painting of a lamb being taken for sacrifice on an altar, ca. 540 BCE, Karouzou, *National Museum – Illustrated Guide to the Museum*, item no. 16464.

– The Francois Vase, ca. 570 BCE, Mingazzini, *Greek Pottery Painting*, color plate 7.

– Eretrian Amphora, ca. 675 BCE, in the National Museum of Athens, Richter, *A Handbook of Greek Art*, fig. 413.

Historical Motifs - Inner Ring: Conflict in the Market

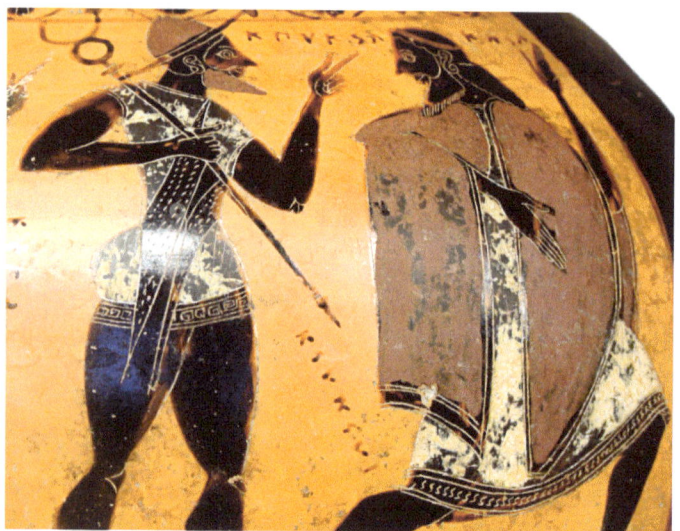

Hermes confronting Paris about the Judgement of "The Most Fair."

Detail from an Attic Black-figure Amphora, ca. 560-550 BCE.

Source: CC0 Bibi Saint-Pol/Vail via Wikimedia Commons

Illustration 57: Attic Black-figure Amphora (detail)

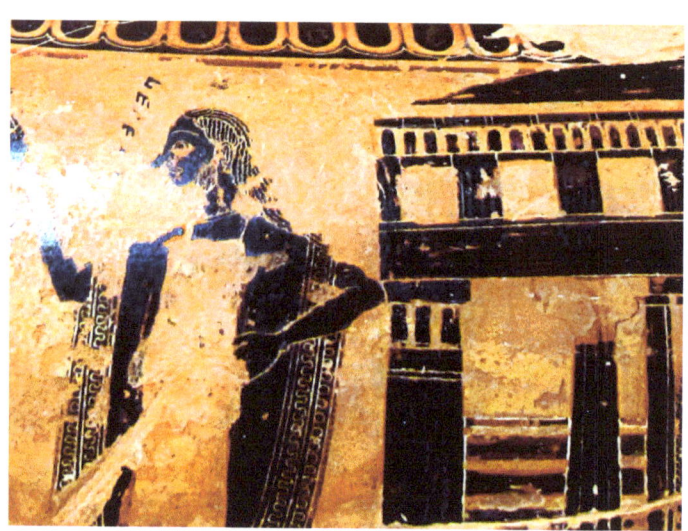

Illustration 58: Francois Vase (detail)

Peleus receiving wedding guests in front of a columned portico. Detail from the "Francois Vase," an Attic Black-figure Volute Krater, ca. 570-565 BCE. Source: CCSA 3.0 Sailko/Vail via Wikimedia Commons

VII. B. 2. Conflict in the Market

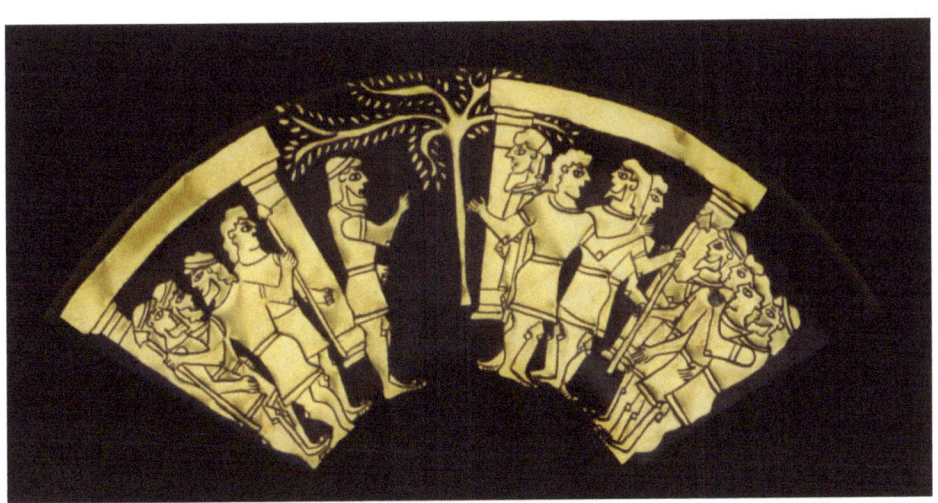

Illustration 59: Inner Ring: Conflict in the Market. From the Shield of Achilles
by Kathleen Vail © All Rights Reserved

"*Then in the market, surrounded by men, two argued the blood-price...*"

Broadening our appreciation of this scene and the following scene of the Judgement of the Elders, Dr. Gregory Nagy notes that the litigation scenes on Achilles' shield reflect a seminal moment in the evolutionary development of the self-governing *polis*.

The following passages from Nagy's essay, *The Shield of Achilles: Ends of the Iliad and Beginnings of the Polis*, offer an interesting perspective:

> *This evolutionary model is the lens through which I see the picture on the shield of Achilles, with its concentric circles of limits expanding further and further outward. [48]*

> *I repeat what I said earlier, this time going one step further. The logic of the litigation scene spills over into the logic of a surrounding circle of supposedly impartial elder adjudicators who are supposed to define the rights and wrongs of the case.*

Historical Motifs - Conflict in the Market, Cont'd

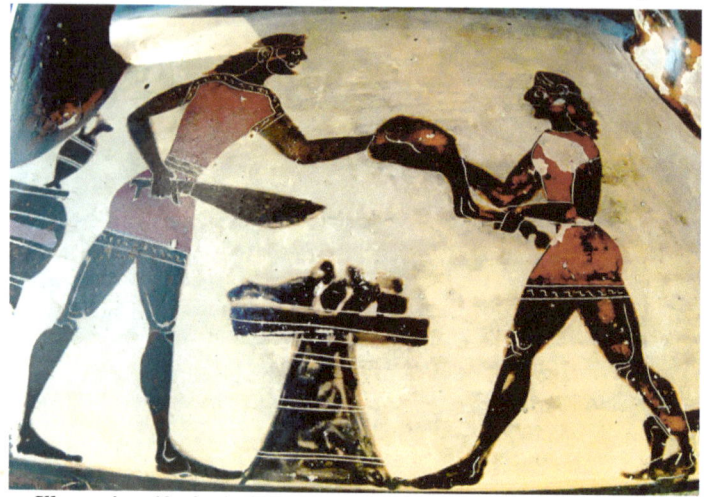

Illustration 60: Corinthian Black-figure "Eurytios Krater" (detail)

Men in everyday short garments preparing a leg of lamb for a feast. Detail from "Eurytios Krater," a Corinthian Black-figure Column Krater, ca. 600 BCE. Source: CCA 2.5 Marie-Lan Nguyen/Vail via Wikimedia Commons

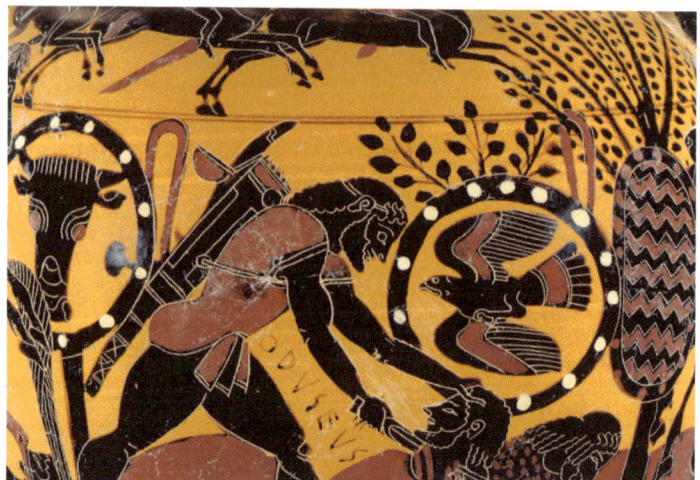

Illustration 61: Chalkidian Black-figure Neck Amphora (detail)

Odysseus slaying a Thracian warrior - note trees far right. Detail from a Chalkidian Black-figure Neck Amphora, ca 540 BCE Source: CC0 Getty Open Content/Vail via Wikimedia Commons

Next, the logic of this inner circle {86|87} of elders spills over into the logic of an outer circle of people who surround the elders, the people who will define who defines most justly. Next, it spills over into the logic of the outermost circle, people who are about to hear the Iliad. These people who hear Homeric poetry, as I said, are to become the people of the polis. Going one step further, these people are even ourselves. [1]

Documented sources for the motifs in this image include:

Columns:

– Attic Black-figure Lekythos, ca. 550-530 BCE, vonBothmer, *The Amasis Painter and His World: Vase-Painting in Sixth-Century B.C. Athens,* pl. 4.

– Attic Red-figure Amphora by Andokides, ca. 530-520 BCE. Paris, Musée Du Louvre.

– Carpenter, *Dionysian Imagery in Archaic Greek Art*, plate 2.

– The Francois Vase, ca. 570-565 BCE, Mingazzini, *Greek Pottery Painting*, color plt 7.

– The "Sophilos Dinos," ca. 570 BCE, The British Museum Collection online.

Men in Short Garments: (please see additional references, above)

– Attic black-figure Amphora , ca. 560-550 BCE; Beazley, *Attic Black-Figure Vase Painters.*

– Corinthian Black-figure Celebe, ca. 6th Century BCE, "Eurytios Krater" now at the Louvre, Paris; Fowler, *A Handbook of Greek Archaeology,* fig. 367.

Trees: (please see additional references, above)

– Chalkidian Black-figure Neck Amphora, ca. 540 BCE; Boardman, *The History of Greek Vases*, fig. 103.

FOOTNOTES:

(1). Nagy, G. *The Shield of Achilles: Ends of the Iliad and Beginnings of the Polis.* (online; Harvard Center for Hellenic Studies) Chapter 4, *Homeric Responses*, 2003.

Historical Motifs - Judgement of the Elders

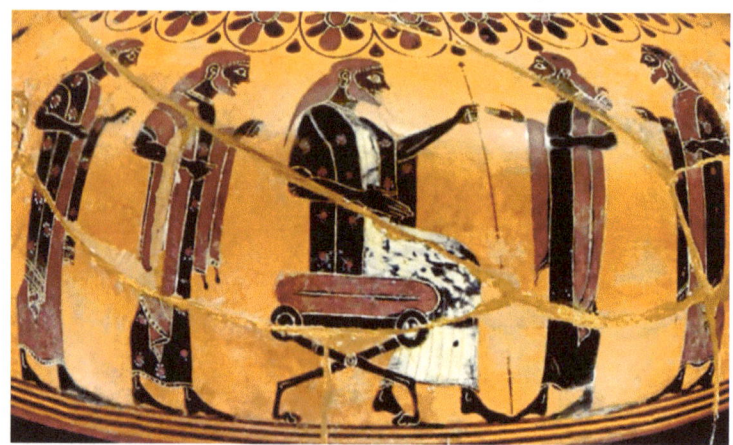

Illustration 62: Nikosthenic Amphora (detail)

A king on his throne, surrounded by elder statesmen all wearing long garments.
Detail from a Black-figure Nikosthenic Amphora, ca. 530 BCE.
Source: CC0 Marie-Lan Nguyen/Vail via Wikimedia Commons

King Arkesilas wearing long garments, watching over the bundling of wool.

Detail from a Laconian Black-figure Cup by the Arkesilas Painter, ca. 565-560 BCE.

Source: CCSA 2.5 Marie-Lan Nguyen/Vail via Wikimedia Commons

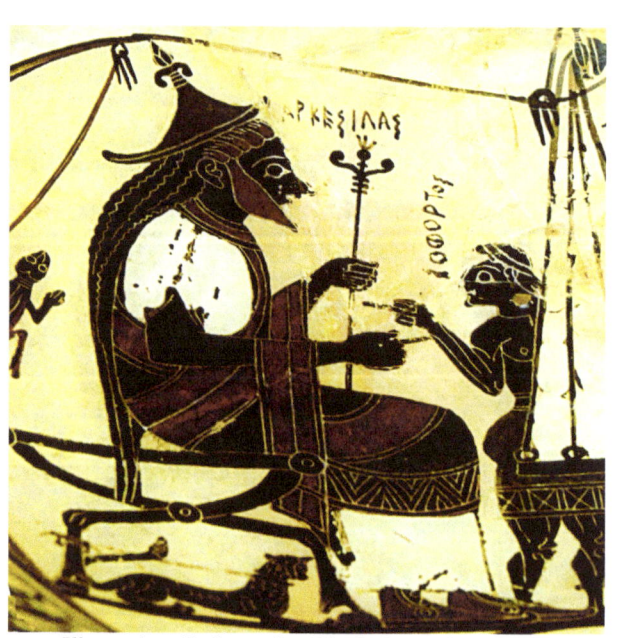

Illustration 63: Laconian Black-figure Cup (detail)

VII. B. 3. Judgement of the Elders

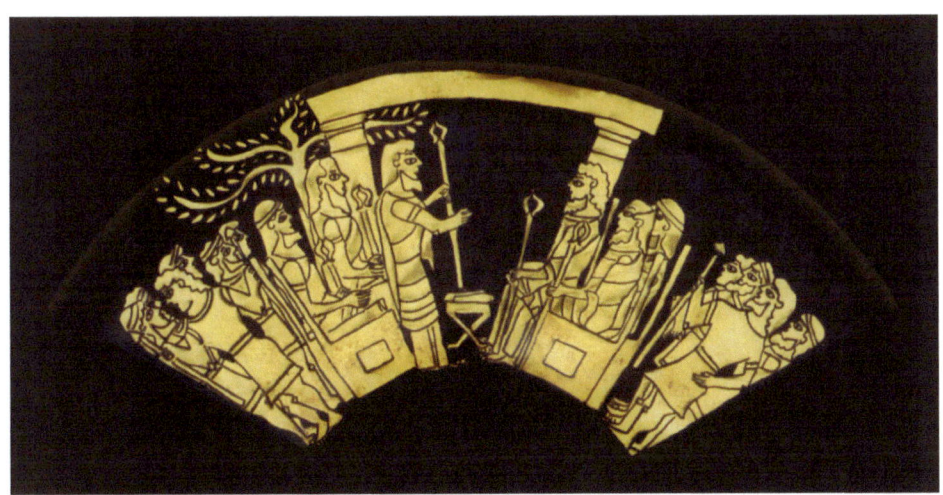

"The Elders each sat in the sacred circle on seats of smooth-polished..."

Referring to this scene of the Judgement of the Elders, Gernet points out:

> *If we accept that the poet knew what he was talking about, then we can agree that our task is not to settle the question of the fact, but to propose criteria for decisive proof.*

> *...The judgement itself – or at least that which takes its place – is not to be discussed. An arrangement was agreed whereby the exercise of vengeance was unconditionally suspended: if the ransom were not paid, the avenger would again be free to act and would kill his adversary.*

> *...From this comes the kind of pressure that finally calls for the appeal to justice. Theoretically, however, the initiative comes not from the one we might call the 'plaintiff,' from the one who has the 'right to vengeance': the initiative comes from the one who has submitted to vengeance and who 'tells the people his case.'*

Historical Motifs - Judgement of the Elders, Cont'd

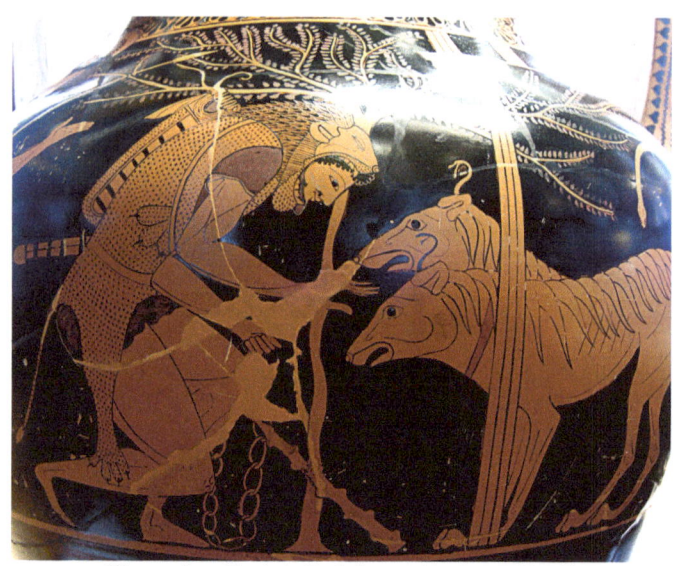

Illustration 65: Attic Red-figure Amphora (detail)

Heracles approaches Cerberus at a columned portico representing the entrance to Hades. Also, note a tree of the Hesperides beside Heracles.
Attic Red-figure Amphora by the Andokides Painter, ca. 530–520 BCE
Source: CC0 Bibi Saint-Pol/Vail via Wikimedia Commons

Elderly man seated between two men and two women.

Attic Black-figure Neck Amphora ca. 550–540 BCE.

Source: CC0 Metropolitan Museum of Art/Vail via Wikimedia Commons

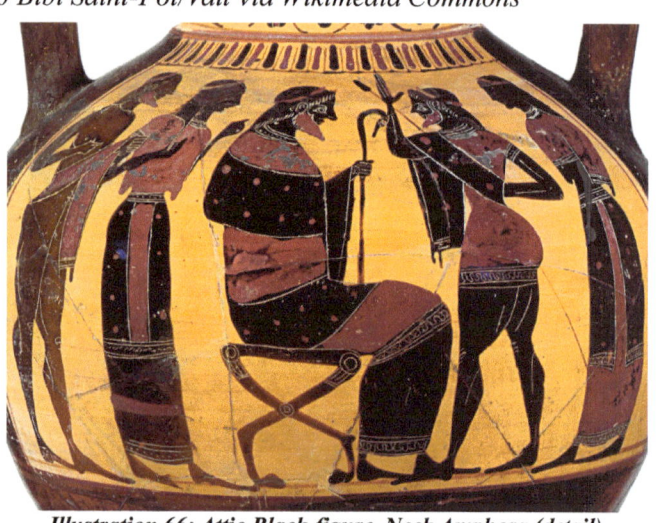

Illustration 66: Attic Black-figure Neck Amphora (detail)

...We have here the image, at once schematic and poetic, of a primitive procedure whose mark is preserved in later law. [1]

Crawford and Whitehead note that this judgement by the elders is a *"typical feature of the early 'Polis'."* They recognize this scene as *"the orderly resolution of disputes by pronouncement of the aristocratic elders of the community."* [2]

Offering a comparison between Homer and Hesiod, Crawford and Whitehead state:

The Boiotion poet and pessimist Hesiod will have been familiar with the Homeric description of the shield of Achilles; his own view of the dispensation of justice, however, is a strikingly different one. In the scene on the shield the implication is clear that the ordinary man can hope to get a fair deal from his aristocratic judges, even if one party will necessarily be the loser. [3]

I would also like to add that this judgement scene not only depicts the origin of Western legal procedures; likewise, the two bars of gold show us just as clearly the origin of high legal fees!

Documented sources for the motifs in this image include:

Columns: (please see references, above)

Men in Short Garments: (please see references, above)

Men in Long Garments:

– Corinthian Celebe, ca. 550 BCE, in the Vatican; Fowler, *A Handbook of Greek Archaeology*, fig. 366.

– Laconian Black-figure cup by the Arkesilas Painter, ca. 565-560 BCE.

– Oinochoe by the Amasis Painter, ca. 560 BCE, at the New York Metropolitan Museum of Art; VonBothmer, *The Amasis Painter and His World*, fig. 33.

Old Men:

Historical Motifs - Judgement of the Elders, Cont'd

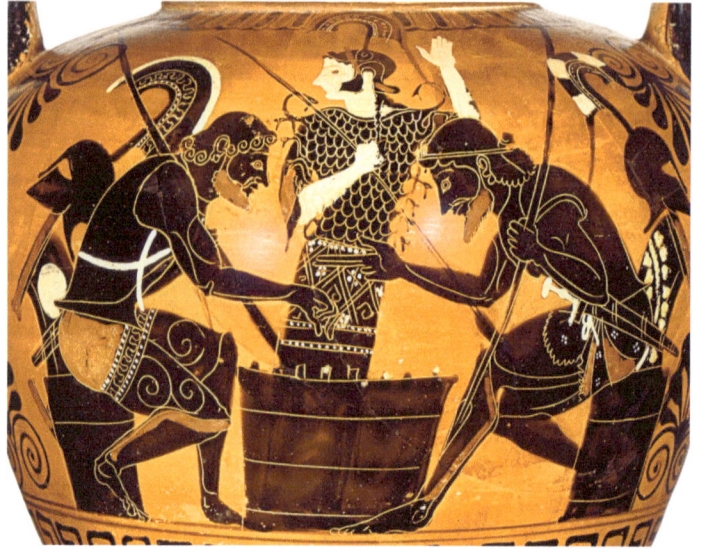

Achilles and Ajax Playing a Board Game Overseen by Athena.

Detail from an Attic Black-figure Neck Amphora ca. 510 BCE.

Source: CC0 Getty Open Content/Vail via Wikimedia Commons

Illustration 67: Attic Black-figure Neck Amphora (detail)

Herakles Entering Olympos

Detail from an Attic Black-figure Olpe, ca. 540 BCE.

Source: CC0 Bibi Saint-Pol/Vail via Wikimedia Commons

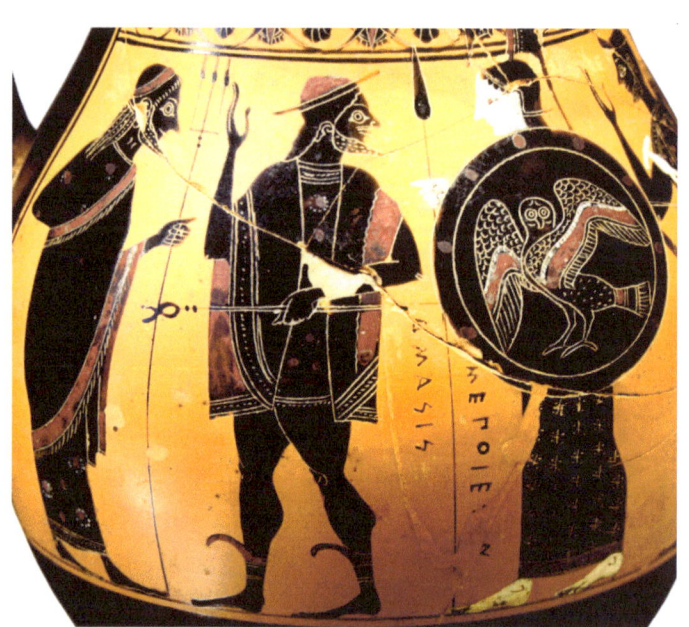

Illustration 68: Attic Black-figure Olpe (detail)

– Attic Black-figure Neck Amphora of Panathenaic Shape attributed to the Princeton Painter, ca. 550-540 BCE, Metropolitan Museum of Art; Beazley, *Attic Black-figure Vase-painters*, pg. 298.

– Attic Black-figure Amphora, "Warriors and Old Men," ca. 520-500 BCE, at the New Orleans Museum of Art; New Orleans Museum of Art, *Greek Vases from Southern Collections*, pg. 63.

– Corinthian Bottle by Timonidas, ca. 580 BCE; Cook, *Greek Art – Its Development, Character and Influence*, plate D, page 277.

Stone and Fold-up Seats:

– Attic Bilingual Amphora of Panathenaic Shape by the Andokides Painter, ca. 530 BCE, Red-figure Side B depicting Achilles and Telamonian Aias (Ajax) playing a board game.

– Attic Black-figure Neck Amphora by the Medea Group, ca. 510 BCE, J. Paul Getty Museum; Wescoat, B. *Poets and Heroes*, Exh. Cat., pp. 48-49, no. 12, ill.

– Attic Black-figure Amphora, "Warriors and Old Men," ca. 520-500 BCE, at the New Orleans Museum of Art; New Orleans Museum of Art, *Greek Vases from Southern Collections*, pg. 63.

– Attic Black-figure Olpe by the Amasis Painter, ca. 540 BCE, at the Louvre Museum, Dept. of Greek, Etruscan, and Roman Antiquities. Atlas database: entry 6882.

– Skyphos by the Theseus Painter, ca. 550 BCE, at the British Museum; Boardman, *Athenian Black Figure Vases*, fig. 246.

Trees: (please see references, above)

FOOTNOTES:

(1).   Gernet, L. *The Anthropology of Ancient Greece*. Baltimore: The Johns Hopkins University Press, 1981, pp. 174-175.

(2).   Crawford, M. and Whitehead, D. *Archaic and Classical Greece*. Cambridge: University Press, 1983, pg. 43.

(3).   Crawford, M. and Whitehead, D., pg. 44.

Historical Motifs - Middle Ring: City Under Siege

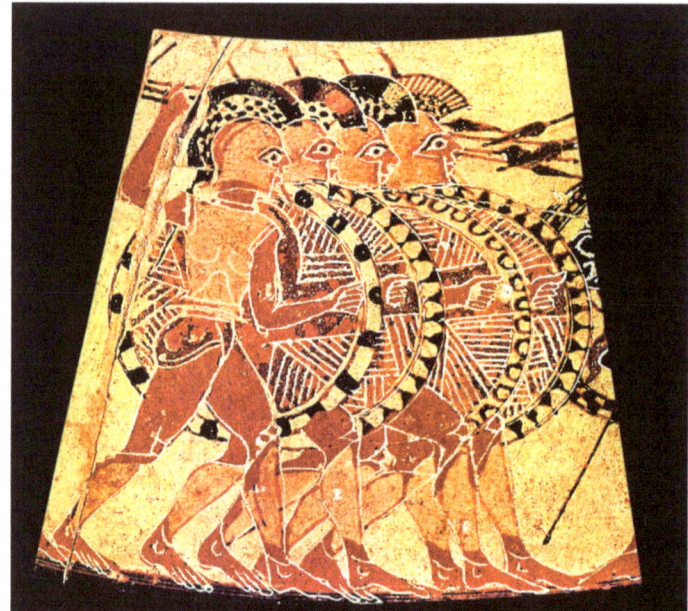

Armed hoplite warriors in tight formation for battle.

Detail from the "Chigi Vase," a Protocorinthian Olpe, ca. 650-640 BCE.

Source: CC0 Szilas/Vail via Wikimedia Commons

Illustration 69: Chigi Vase (detail)

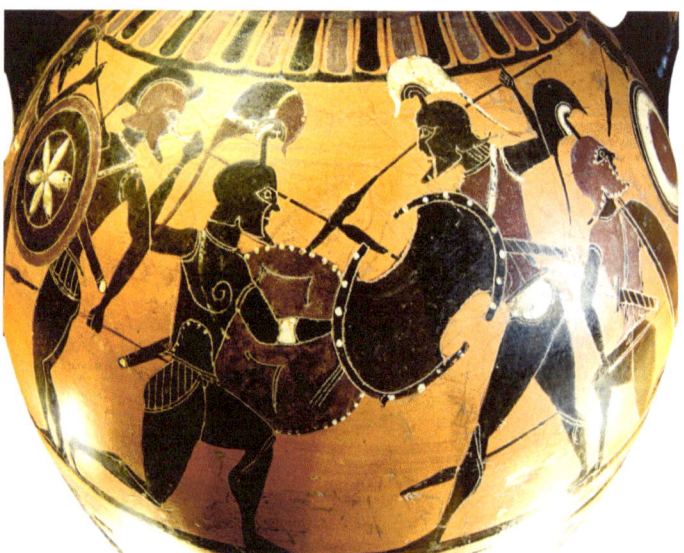

Battling warriors in full armor.

Detail from an Attic Black-figure Amphora, ca. 570-565 BCE.

Source: CC0 Bibi Saint-Pol/Vail via Wikimedia Commons

Illustration 70: Attic Black-figure Amphora (detail)

VII. C. Reference Notes - Middle Ring: WARTIME

VII. C. 1. City Under Siege

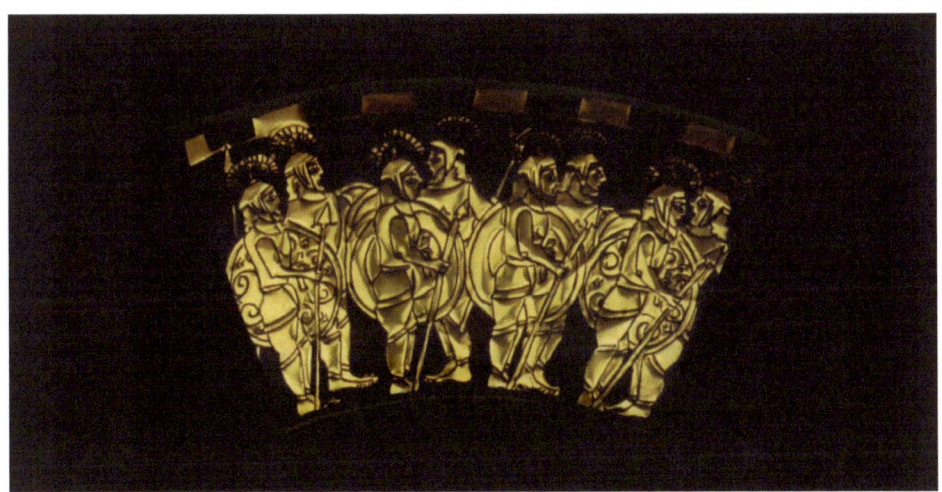

Illustration 71: Middle Ring: City Under Siege. From the Shield of Achilles by Kathleen Vail © All Rights Reserved

"Wartime, next, in the other city, displayed in preparations..."

Documented sources for the motifs in this image include:

<u>**Armor:**</u>

– Shields, breastplates, and helmets: Protocorinthian Olpe, "The Chigi Vase," by the MacMillan Painter, ca. 650-640 BCE, in the Villa Giulia; Beazley, *Greek Sculpture and Painting*, fig. 19. Also in Mingazzini, *Greek Pottery Painting*, plate 6.

– Oinochoe, by the Amasis Painter, ca. 560 BCE, at the New York Metropolitan Museum of Art; VonBothmer, *The Amasis Painter and His World*, fig. 33.

– Chalcidian Psykter-Amphora, with battle of Greeks and Trojans, ca. 540 BCE, in Melbourne, at the National Gallery of Victoria; Richter, *A Handbook of Greek Art*, fig. 414, a and b.

– Deianira Lekythos in the manner of the Gorgon Painter; Boardman, *Athenian Black Figure Vases*, fig. 16.1.

Historical Motifs - City Under Siege, Cont'd

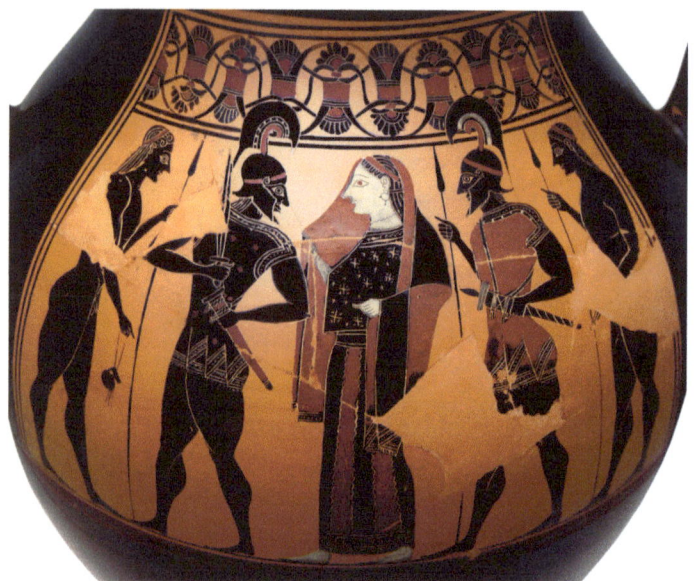

Recovery of Helen by Menelaus.

Detail from an Attic Black-figure Amphora by the Amasis Painter, ca. 550 BCE.

Source: CC0 Bibi Saint-Pol/Vail via Wikimedia Commons

Illustration 72: Attic Black-figure Amphora (detail)

Row of Hoplite Warriors.

Detail from a Corinthian Black-figure Alabastron, ca 590-570 BCE

Source: CC0 Metropolitan Museum of Art/Vail via Wikimedia Commons

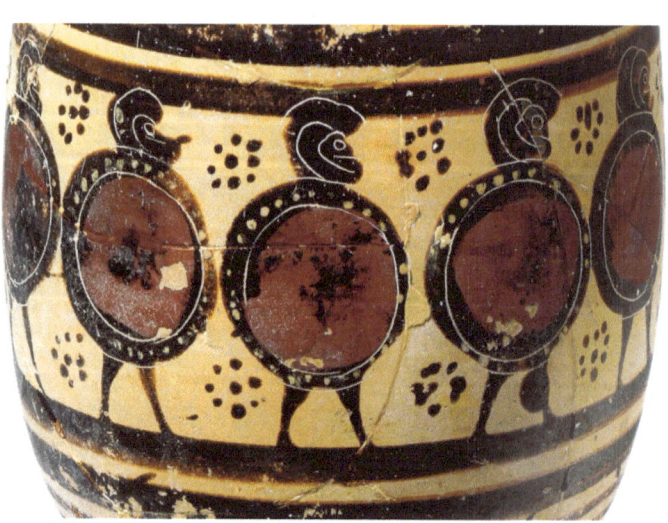

Illustration 73: Corinthian Black-figure Alabastron (detail)

– Armour and Helmet from a Geometric period grave, ca. 8th century BCE, at Argos Archaeological Museum; Homan-Wedeking, *The Art of Archaic Greece*, fig. 8.

– Bronze Helmet, ca. 560-550 BCE, and bronze breastplate, ca. 540 BCE, from the Sanctuary of Zeus at Olympia; Homan-Wedeking, *The Art of Archaic Greece*, figs. 6, 7, 9.

– Bronze Breastplate and Helmet, ca. 7th century BCE, at the New York Metropolitan Museum of Art, exhibition 1979-1980;The Metropolitan Museum of Art, *Greek Art of the Aegean Islands*, pp. 140, 141, 144 and 145.

Warriors:

– Celebe, ca. 6th Century BCE, now at the Louvre, Paris; Fowler, *A Handbook of Greek Archaeology*, fig. 367.

– Protocorinthian Olpe, "The Chigi Vase," by the MacMillan Painter, ca. 650-640 BCE, in the Villa Giulia; Mingazzini, *Greek Pottery Painting*, plate 6, pg. 21.

– Chalcidian Psykter Amphora, with battle of Greeks and Trojans, ca. 540 BCA, in Melbourne, at the National Gallery of Victoria; Richter, *A Handbook of Greek Art*, fig. 414, a and b.

– Oinochoe, by the Amasis Painter, ca. 560 BCE, at the New York Metropolitan Museum of Art; VonBothmer, *The Amasis Painter and His World*, fig. 33.

– Cycladic Polychrome Terracotta Krater, at the New York Metropolitan Museum of Art; The Metropolitan Museum of Art, *Greek Art of the Aegean Islands*, pp. 122-123.

– Corinthian Black-Figure Alabastron, ca 590–570 BCE, at the New York Metropolitan Museum of Art; Hôtel Drouot, *Antiquités Grecques et Romaines, Collection de M.E. Vente Drouot 2-4 Juin 1904*. no. 110, p. 16, pl. III.

Historical Motifs - Middle Ring: Arming for a Raid

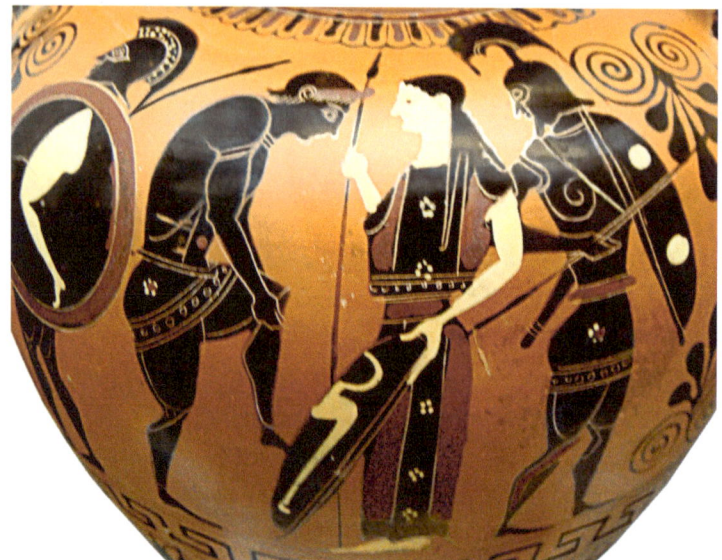

Warrior arming for battle, assisted by a woman.

Detail from an Attic Black-figure Amphora, ca 530-510 BCE.

Source: CC0 Bibi Saint-Pol/Vail via Wikimedia Commons

Illustration 74: Attic Black-figure Amphora (detail)

Warrior arming for battle, assisted and advised by a woman and two men.

Detail from an Attic Black-figure Amphora, ca 560-540 BCE.

Source: CC0 Bibi Saint-Pol/Vail via Wikimedia Commons

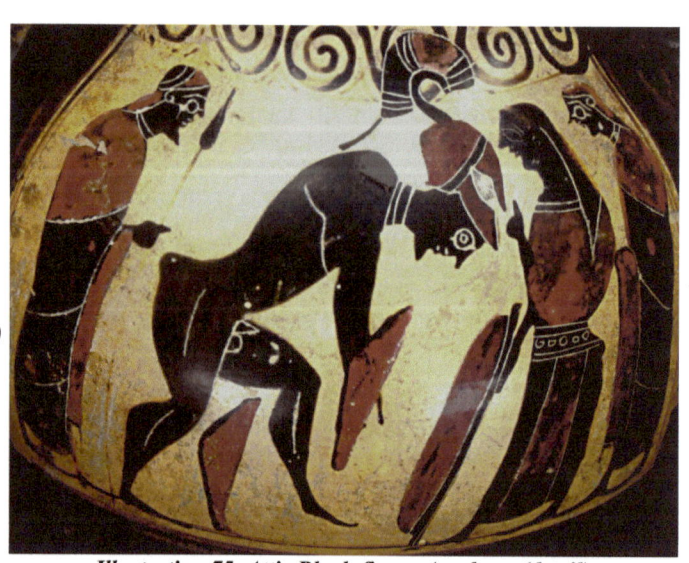

Illustration 75: Attic Black-figure Amphora (detail)

VII. C. 2. Arming for a Raid

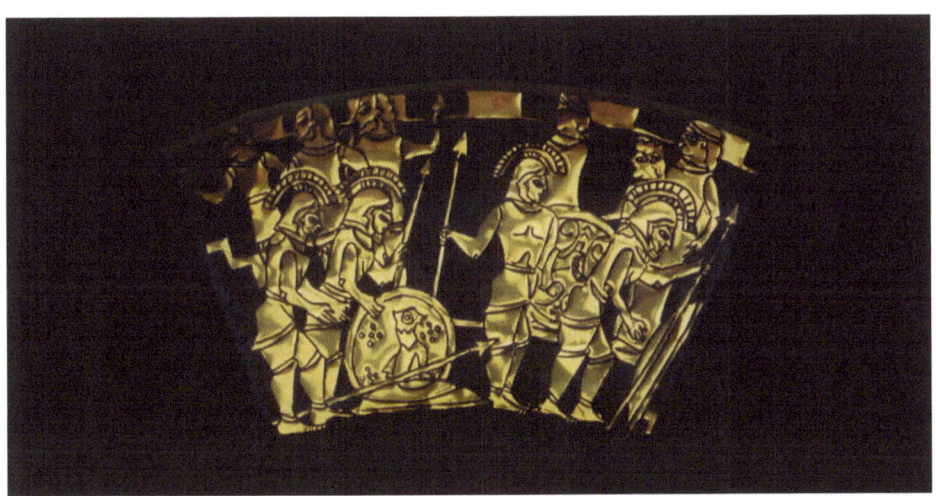

"The townsmen were hungry, but bowing to neither, they quickly..."

Documented sources for the motifs in this image include:

<u>**Armor:**</u> (please see references, above)

<u>**Old Men:**</u> (please see references, above)

<u>**Warriors:**</u> (please see references, above)

<u>**Women and Children:**</u> (please see references, above)

Historical Motifs - Ares and Athena Lead the Raid

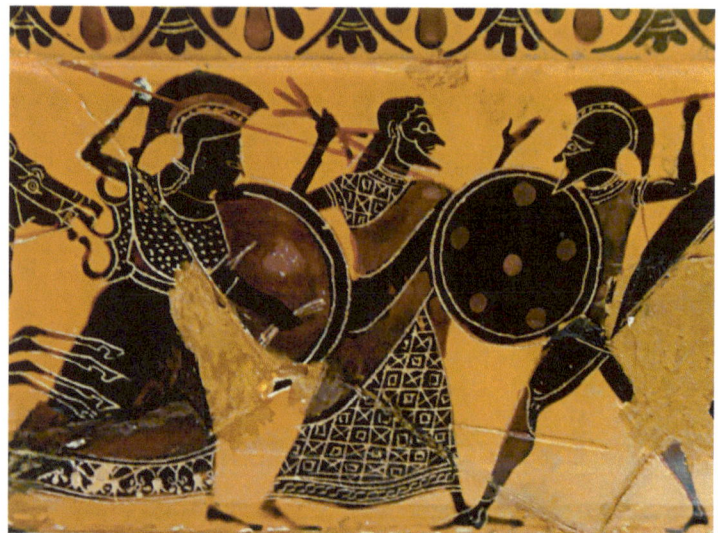

Zeus intervening between Athena & Ares

Detail from an Attic Black-figure Volute Krater, ca. 540–510 BCE.

Source: CC0 Marie-Lan Nguyen/Vail via Wikimedia Commons

Illustration 77: Attic Black-figure Volute Krater (detail)

Athena wearing the war aegis.

Detail from "The Burgon Vase," an Attic Black-figure Panathenaic Amphora, ca 570-560 BCE.

Source: CC0 Marie-Lan Nguyen/Vail via Wikimedia Commons

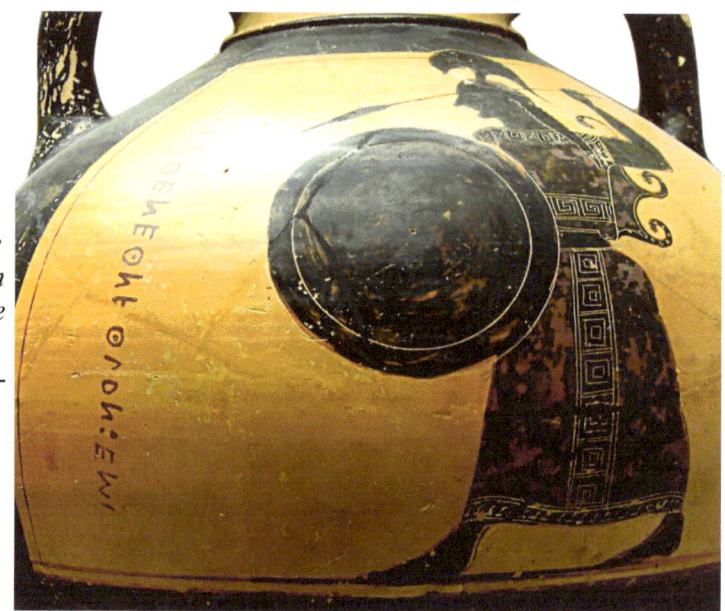

Illustration 78: "The Burgon Vase," Attic Black-figure Amphora (detail)

VII. C. 3. Ares and Athena Lead the Raid

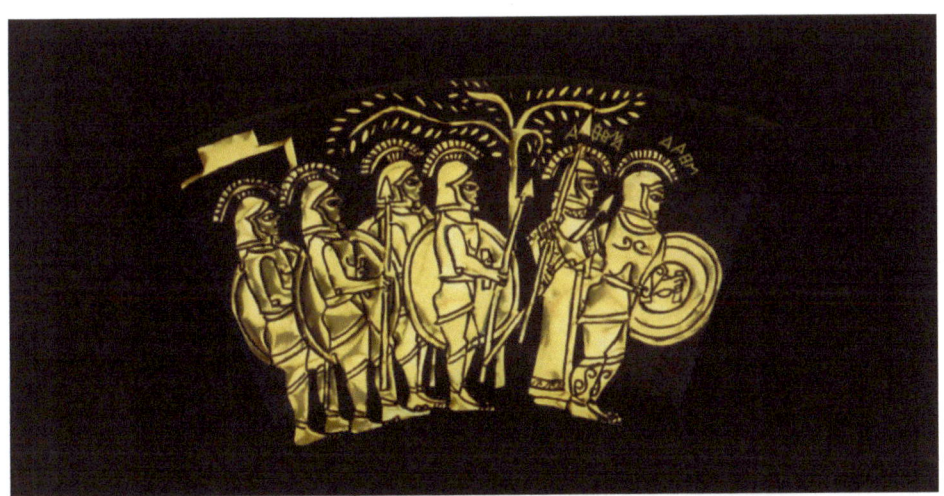

Illustration 79: Middle Ring: Ares & Athena Lead the Raid. From the Shield of Achilles by Kathleen Vail © All Rights Reserved

"The men filed out through a secret gate led by Ares and Athena..."

Documented sources for the motifs in this image include:

Armor: (please see references, above)

Athena:

– Panathenaic Amphora, "The Burgon Vase," ca. 570-560 BCE; Folsom, *Attic Black-Figured Pottery*, plate 14d.

– Attic Black-figure Volute Krater, ca. 540-510 BCE. CC0 Marie-Lan Nguyen/Vail via Wikimedia Commons.

Trees: (please see references, above)

Warriors: (please see references, above)

Historical Motifs - Middle Ring: Warriors Hiding

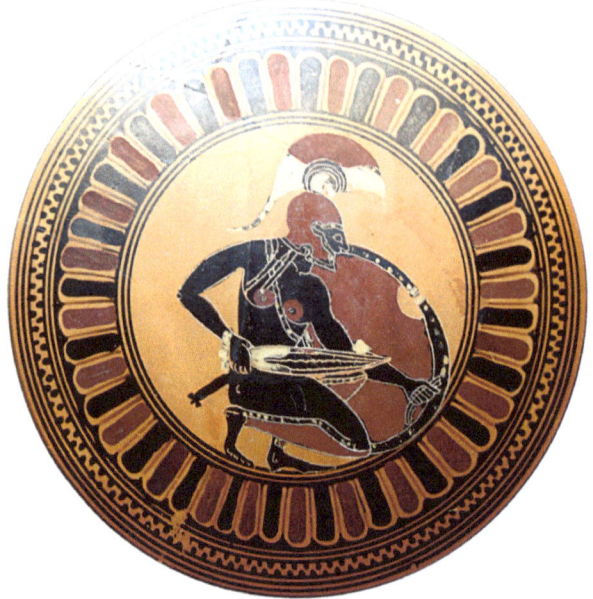

Kneeling warrior, perhaps Achilles, with an unsheathed sword and planning an ambush.

Tondo of an Attic Black-figure Kylix by the C Painter, ca. 560 BCE.

Source: CC0 Bibi Saint-Pol/Vail via Wikimedia Commons

Illustration 80: Attic Black-figure Kylix Tondo

Achilles crouched behind a tree, hiding prior to an ambush.

Detail from an Attic Black-figure Lekythos by the Athena Painter, ca. 480 BCE.

Source: CC0 Bibi Saint-Pol/Vail via Wikimedia Commons

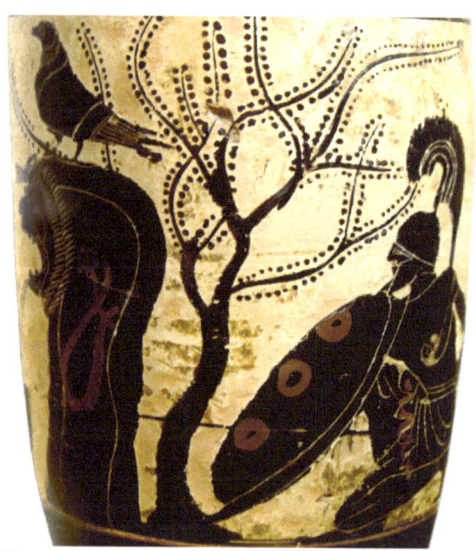

Illustration 81: Attic Black-figure Lekythos (detail)

VII. C. 4. Warriors Hiding

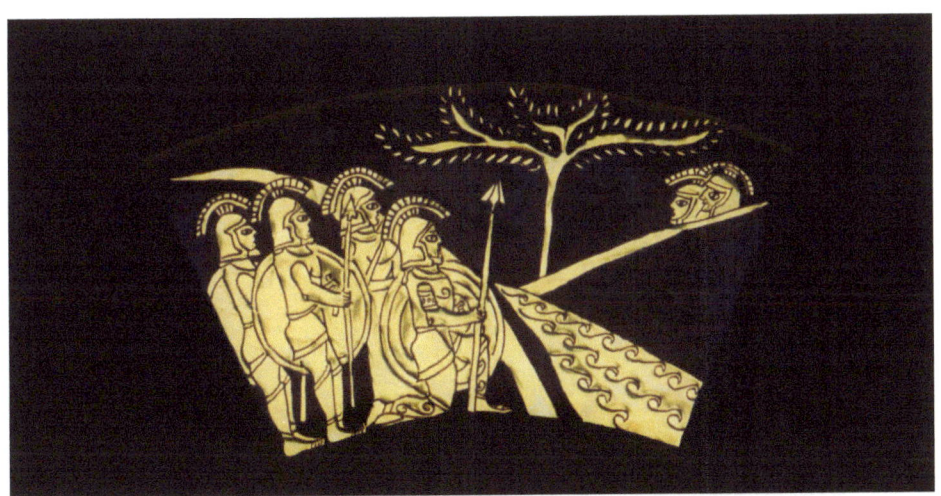

Illustration 82: Middle Ring: Warriors Hiding. From the Shield of Achilles
by Kathleen Vail © All Rights Reserved

"When the warriors came to their ambush point..."

Documented sources for the motifs in this image include:

Armor: (please see references, above)

Athena and Ares: (please see references, above)

Trees: (please see references, above)

Warriors: (please see references, above)

Historical Motifs - Middle Ring: Peaceful Herdsmen

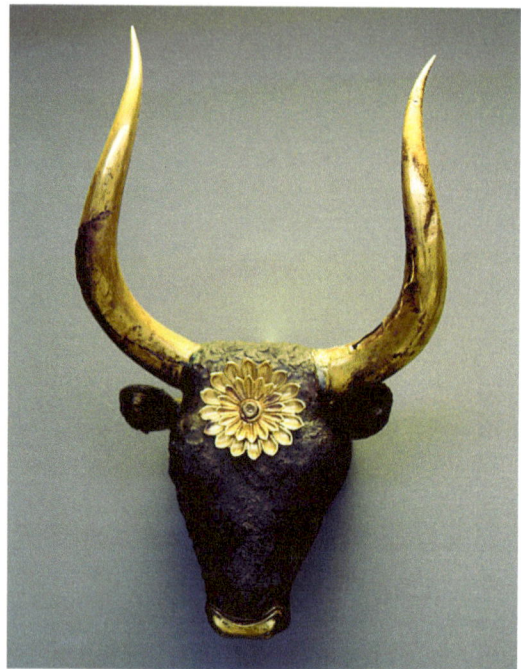

Bull's head libation vessel.

Mycenaean Rhyton, or libation vessel, in the shape of a bull's head, made of bronze, semi-precious stones, and gilded, ca. 16th century BCE.

Source: CCSA 3.0 Zde/Vail via Wikimedia Commons

Illustration 83: Mycenaean Bull's Head Rhyton

Lamb's head libation vessel depicting youth playing the lyre and the aulos, or double pipe.

Attic Red-figure Rhyton in the shape of a lamb's head, ca. 460 BCE.

Source: CCA 2.5 Marie-Lan Nguyen/Vail via Wikimedia Commons

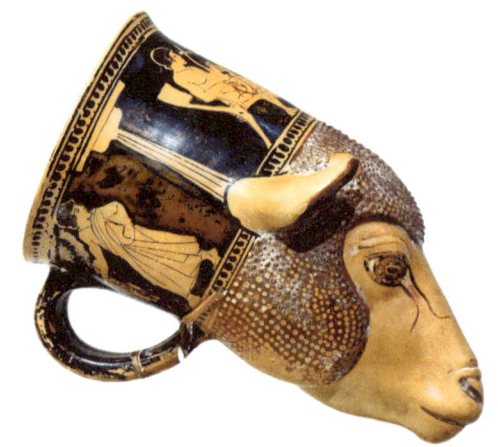

Illustration 84: Attic Red-figure Lamb's Head Rhyton

VII. C. 5. Peaceful Herdsmen

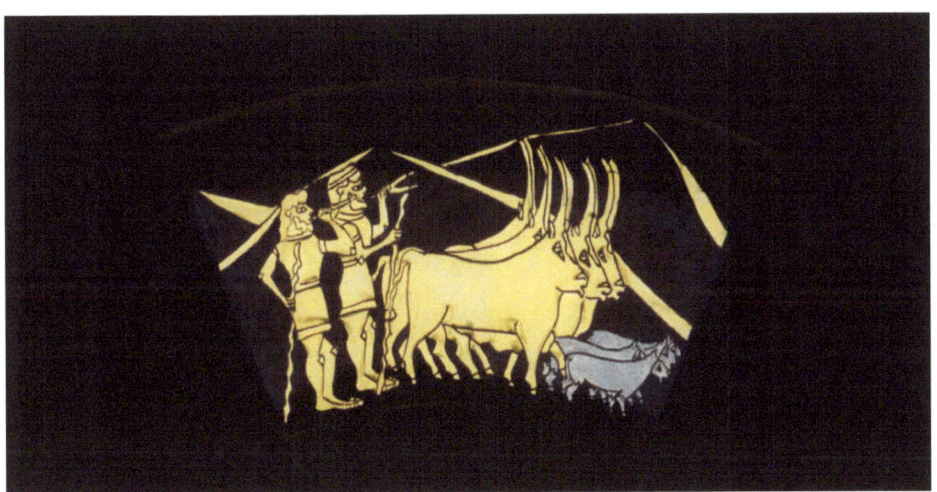

Illustration 85: Middle Ring: Peaceful Herdsmen. From the Shield of Achilles by Kathleen Vail © All Rights Reserved

"Then the flocks and herds both came in view..."

The references to oxen depicted in many scenes on the shield of Achilles are significant, for as Robinson tells us, "Far more than on agriculture, however, the Achaeans depended for their livelihood on the pasturage of flocks and herds. They kept goats, sheep and swine; but their most prized possession was the ox, an animal doubly useful for ploughing as well as for food." [1]

Documented sources for the motifs in this image include:

Bulls:

– Protocorinthian Oinochoe, ca. 625 BCE, at the Metropolitan Museum of Art; Picon, *Art of the Classical World in the Met Museum of Art*, 2007; no. 61, pp 64, 418.

– Italo-Ionian Amphora, "The Judgement of Paris," in Munich's Antiker Kleinkunst; Pfuhl, *Masterpieces of Greek Drawing and Painting*, fig. 14.

Historical Motifs - Peaceful Herdsmen, Cont'd

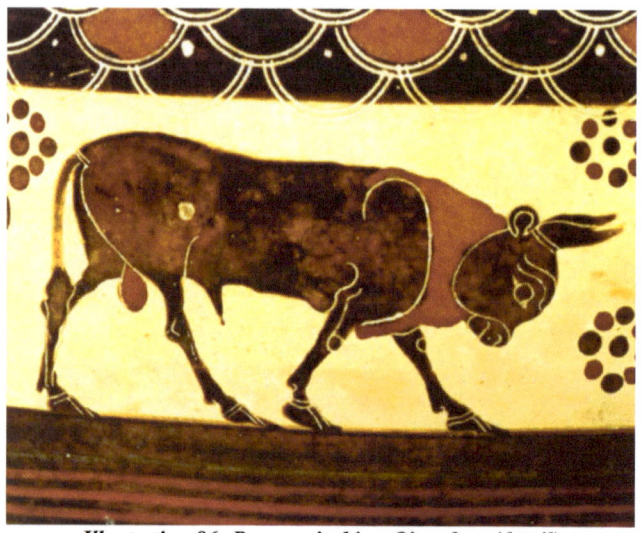

Bull in a charging stance.

Detail from a Protocorinthian Black-figure Oinochoe, ca. 625 BCE.

Source: CC0 Metropolitan Museum of Art/Vail via Wikimedia Commons

Illustration 86: Protocorinthian Oinochoe (detail)

Shepherd riding a ram while piping.

Detail from an Attic Red-figure Pelike, ca. 570 BCE.

Source: CCA 2.5 Marie-Lan Nguyen/Vail via Wikimedia Commons

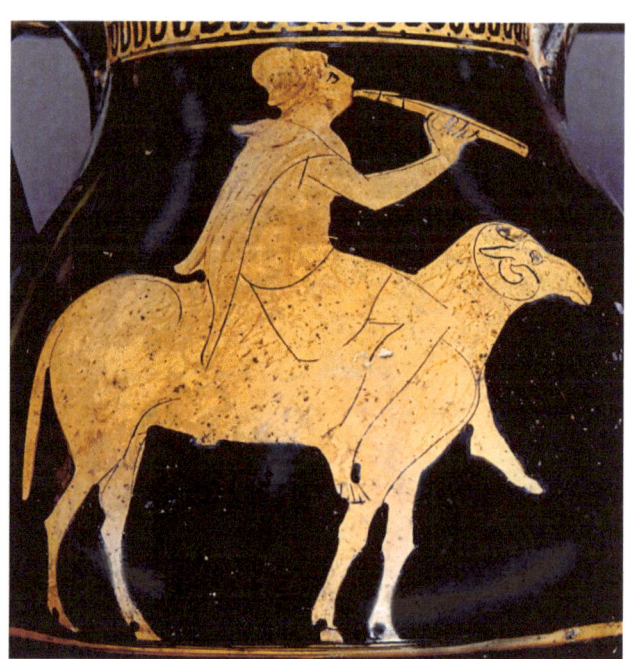

Illustration 87: Attic Red-figure Pelike (detail)

– Ionic Black-figure Amphora, "Hermes Steals the Cow Io From the Giant Argos," ca. 6th century BCE; Buschor, *Greek Vase Painting*, plate XL, fig. 77.

– Late Minoan Rhyton, or Libation Vessel, made from terracotta in the form of a bull's head, ca. 1450-1400 BCE. Metropolitan Museum of Art; Picon, *Art of the Classical World in the Met Museum of Art*, 2007; no, 14, pp 38, 411.

– Mycenaean Rhyton, or Libation Vessel in the shape of a bull's head, made from bronze, inlaid semi-precious stones and gilded, ca. 16th century BCE. National Archaeological Museum of Athens; Karouzou, *National Museum – Illustrated Guide to the Museum*, 1985; no. 384.

Men in Short Garments: (please see references, above)

Pipes: (please see additional references, above)

– Attic Red-figure Pelike, ca. 470 BCE, depicting a shepherd riding a ram while playing an aulos, or double pipe.

Sheep:

– Corinthian Miniature Painting of a lamb being taken for sacrifice on an altar, ca. 540 BCE, now in the National Museum of Athens, illustrated in Karouzou's, *National Museum – Illustrated Guide to the Museum*, item no. 16464.

– Attic Red-figure Rhyton in the shape of a lamb's head, attributed to the Painter of London E 100, ca. 460 BCE, depicting youths playing the aulos and lyre. Metropolitan Museum of Art; Picon, *Art of the Classical World in the Met Museum of Art*, 2007; no. 137, pp. 124, 432

– Attic Red-figure Pelike, ca. 470 BCE, depicting a shepherd riding a ram while playing an aulos, or double pipe.

FOOTNOTES:

(1). Robinson, C. E., *Everyday Life in Ancient Greece*, Oxford: The Clarendon Press, 1933. pg. 18.

Historical Motifs - The Raiding Party Attacks

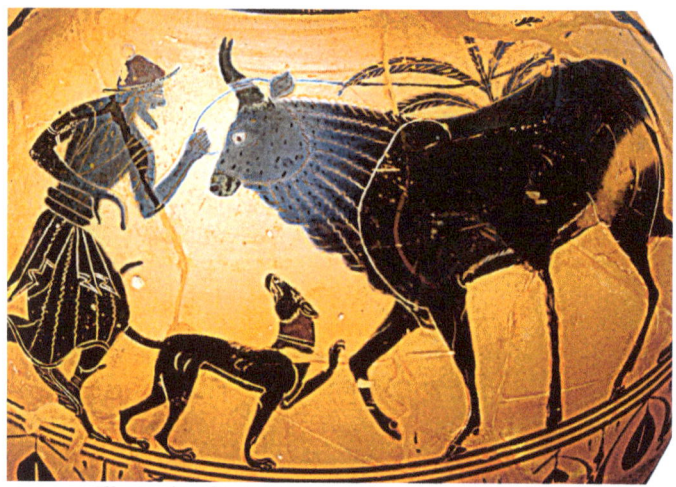

Hermes stealing the cow, Io.

Detail from an Ionic Black-figure Amphora, ca. 6th century BCE.

Source: CC0 Bibi Saint-Pol/Vail via Wikimedia Commons

Illustration 88: Ionic Black-figure Amphora (detail)

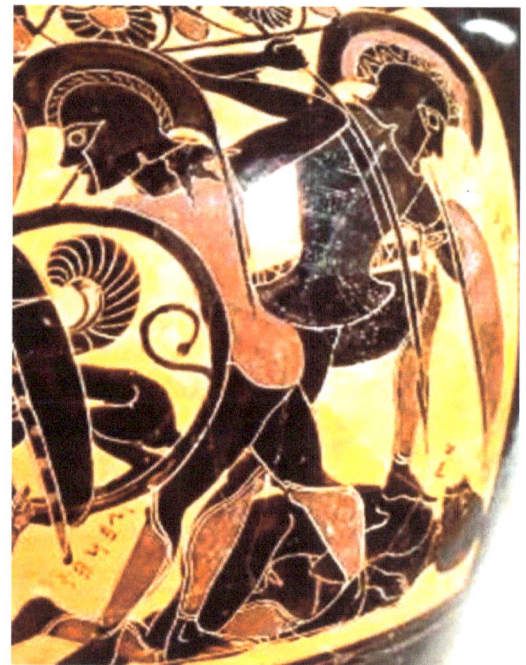

Warriors attacking their enemies.

Detail from a Chalkidian Black-figure Psykter Amphora attributed to the Inscriptions Painter, ca. 540 BCE.

Source: CC0 Autralia National Gallery of Victoria/Vail via Wikimedia Commons

Illustration 89: Chalkidian Psykter Amphora (detail)

VII. C. 6. The Raiding Party Attacks

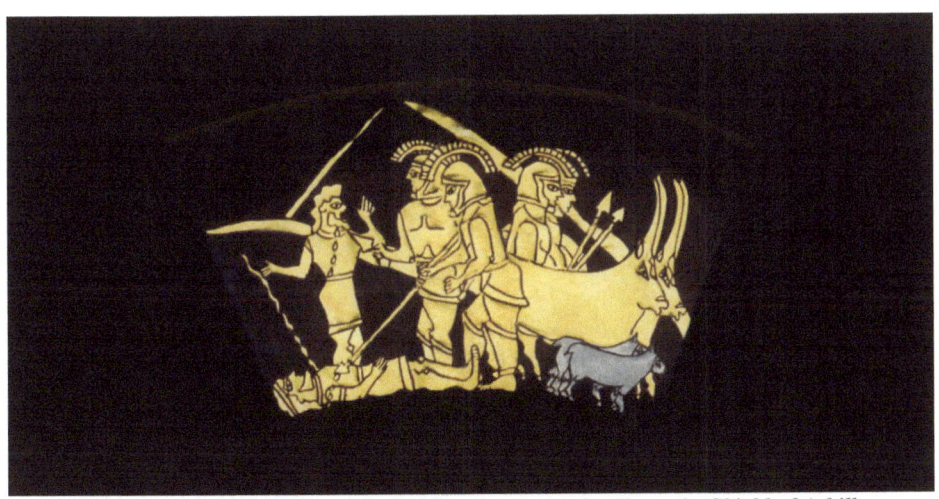

"In a sudden rush the signal blared and the raiding troop..."

Documented sources for the motifs in this image include:

Bulls: (please see references, above)

Men in Short Garments: (please see references, above)

Sheep: (please see references, above)

Warriors: (please see references, above)

Historical Motifs - The Troops Are Alerted

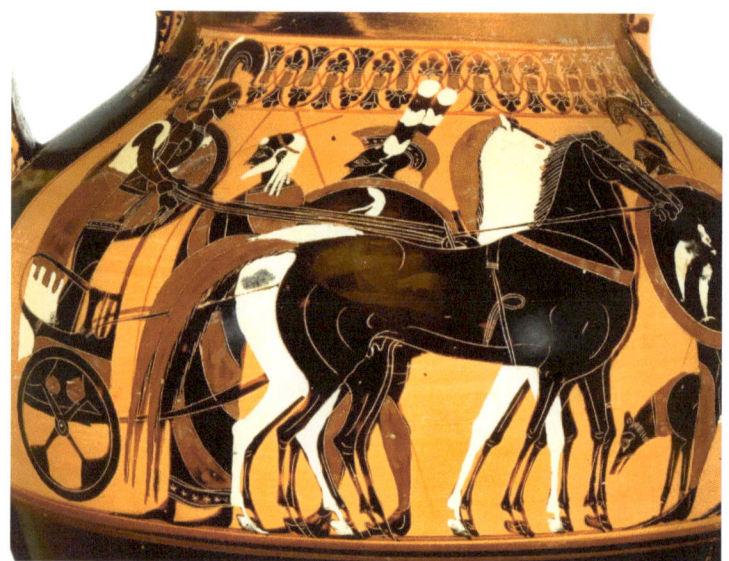

Warrior and his charioteer.

Detail from an Attic Black-figure Amphora, ca. 540-530 BCE.

Source: CC0 Metropolitan Museum of Art/Vail via Wikimedia Commons

Illustration 91: Attic Black-figure Amphora (detail)

Achilles and his chariot driver.

Detail from a Corinthian Black-figure Hydria, ca. 570-550 BCE.

Source: CCSA 3.0 Walters Art Museum/Vail via Wikimedia Commons

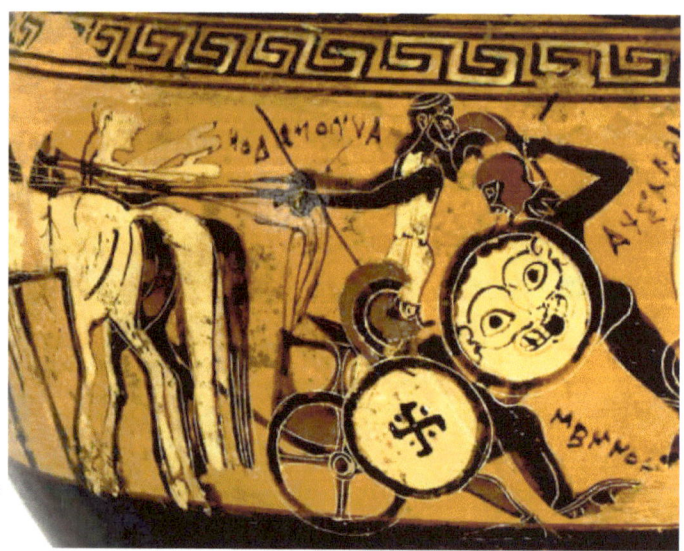

Illustration 92: Corinthian Black-figure Hydria (detail)

VII. C. 7. The Troops Are Alerted

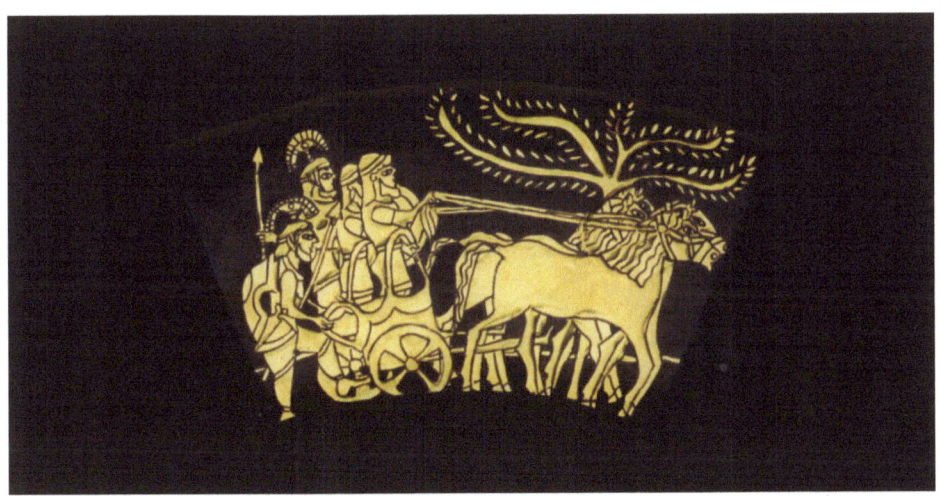

Illustration 93: Middle Ring: The Troops Are Alerted. From the Shield of Achilles by Kathleen Vail © All Rights Reserved

"The troops at the city walls heard the sounds of lowing..."

Documented sources for the motifs in this image include:

<u>Armor:</u> (please see references, above)

<u>**Chariots and Horses:**</u>

– Attic Black-figure Amphora, ca. 540-530 BCE, in the Metropolitan Museum of Art; Beazley, *Attic Black-figure Vase Painters,* pp. 307, 693, no. 55.

– Attic Black-figure Amphora, ca. 530-520 BCE, in the Walters Art Museum, and on exhibition at Alexander S. Onassis Public Benefit Foundation (USA), New York. 2009-2011.

– Attic Black-figure Amphora, ca. 500-490 BCE, at the Metropolitan Museum of Art; Beazley, *Paralipomena: Additions to Attic Black-Figure Vase-Painters and to Attic Red-Figure Vase-Painters [2nd edition]*, Oxford, 1971, pg. 129.

Historical Motifs - The Troops Are Alerted, Cont'd

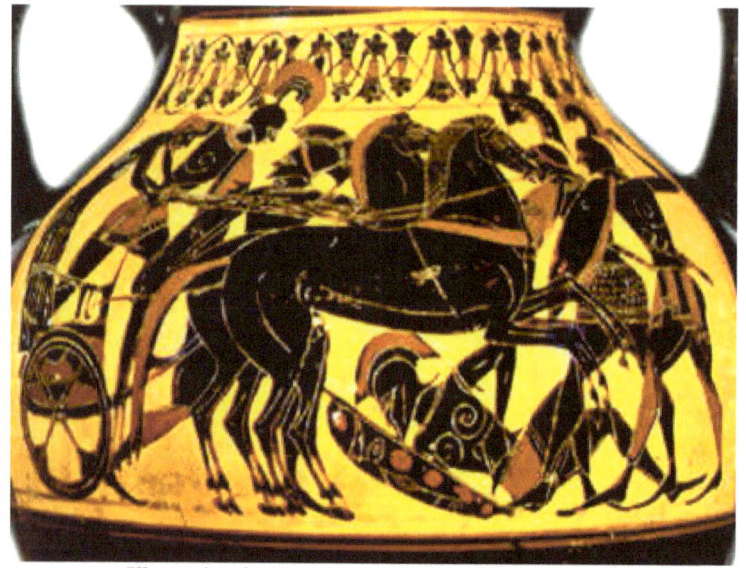

Warrior and his charioteer in battle.

Detail from an Attic Black-figure Amphora, ca. 500-490 BCE.

Source: CC0 Metropolitan Museum of Art/Vail via Wikimedia Commons

Illustration 94: Attic Black-figure Amphora (detail)

Warrior mounting his chariot and taking leave of his father.

Detail from an Attic Black-figure Amphora, ca. 530-520 BCE.

Source: CCSA 3.0 Walters Art Museum/Vail via Wikimedia Commons

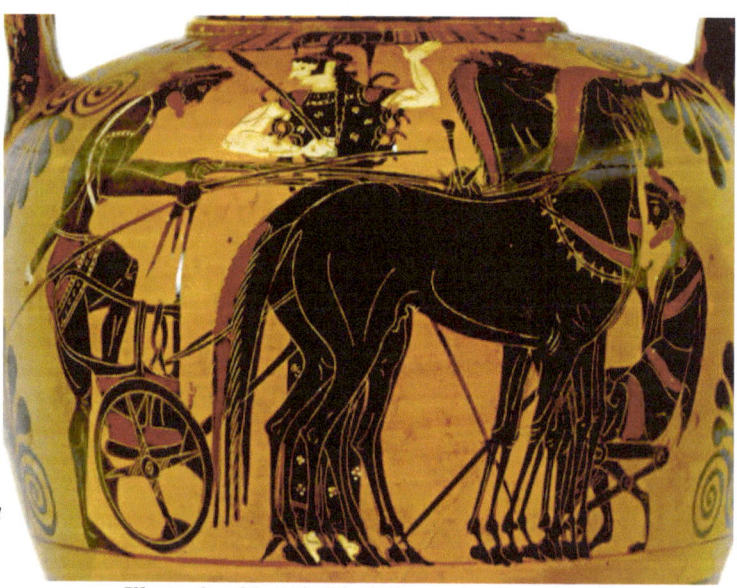

Illustration 95: Attic Black-figure Amphora (detail)

– Attic Amphora, ca. 620 BCE, in the National Museum of Athens; Richter, *A Handbook of Greek Art*, fig. 406.

– Corinthian Black-figure Amphora, ca. 570-550 BCE, in the Walters Art Museum, and on exhibition at Alexander S. Onassis Public Benefit Foundation (USA), New York. 2009-2011

– Chalcidian Psykter-Amphora, with battle of Greeks and Trojans, ca. 540 BCE, in Melbourne, at the National Gallery of Victoria; Richter, *A Handbook of Greek Art*, fig. 414, a and b.

– Corinthian Celebe, ca. 550 BCE, in the Vatican; Fowler, *A Handbook of Greek Archaeology*, fig. 366.

– Greek Black-figure Volute Krater, ca. 525-500 BCE, in the Walters Art Museum, and on exhibition at Alexander S. Onassis Public Benefit Foundation (USA), New York. 2009-2011

– Protocorinthian Olpe, "The Chigi Vase," by the MacMillan Painter, ca. 650-640 BCE, in the Villa Giulia; Brilliant, *Art of the Ancient Greeks*, figs. 2-19.

Men in Short Garments: (please see references, above)

Trees: (please see references, above)

Warriors: (please see references, above)

Historical Motifs - Battle!

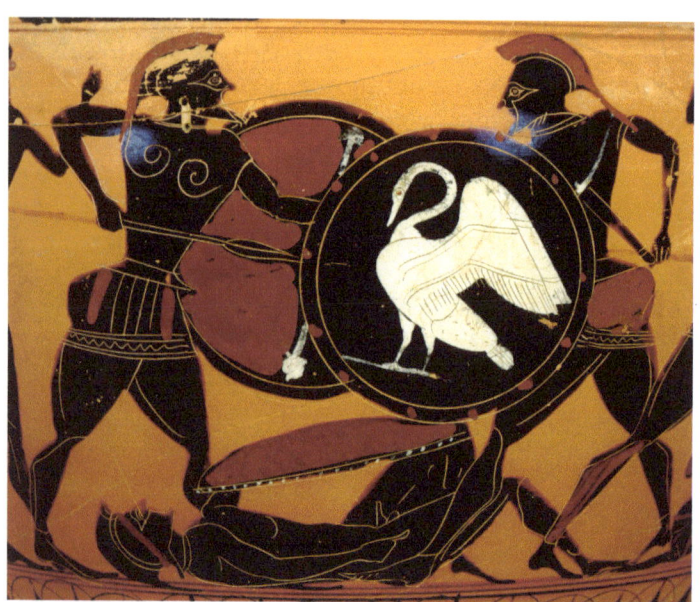

Warriors battling over the body of Patroklos.

Detail from an Attic Black-figure Neck Amphora by the workshop of Exekias, ca. 540 BCE.

Source: CC0 Getty Open Content/Vail via Wikimedia Commons

Illustration 96: Attic Black-figure Neck Amphora (detail)

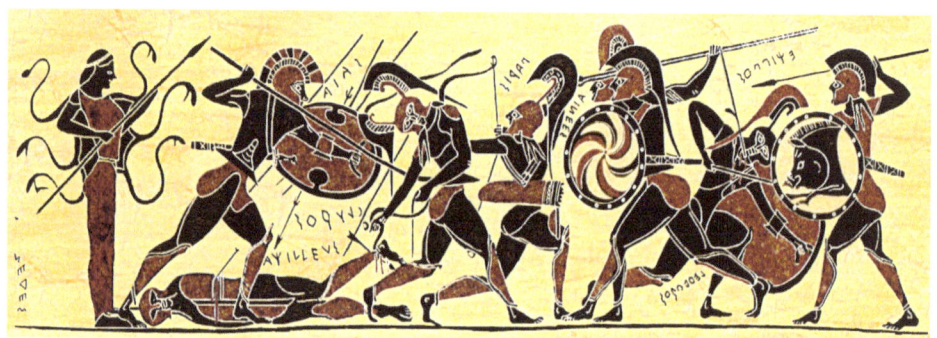

Illustration 97: Chalkidian Black-figure Amphora (drawing)

The Death of Achilles in the Trojan War:
1927 B&W Drawing by A. Rumpf of a lost Chalkidian Black-figure Amphora by the Inscriptions Painter, ca. 540-530 BCE (colorized by Vail).
Source: CC0 image by Rumpf/Vail via Wikimedia Commons

VII. C. 8. **Battle!**

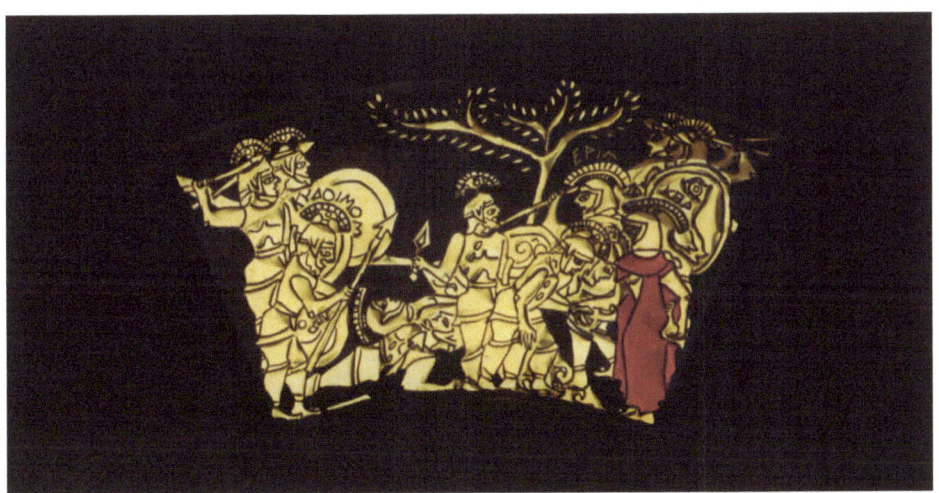

Illustration 98: Middle Ring: Battle! From the Shield of Achilles
by Kathleen Vail © All Rights Reserved

"Upon the riverbanks fighting began as foes threw spears..."

Documented sources for the motifs in this image include:

<u>**Armor:**</u> (please see references, above)

<u>**Trees:**</u> (please see references, above)

<u>**Warriors:**</u> (please see references, above)

Historical Motifs - Plowing the Field

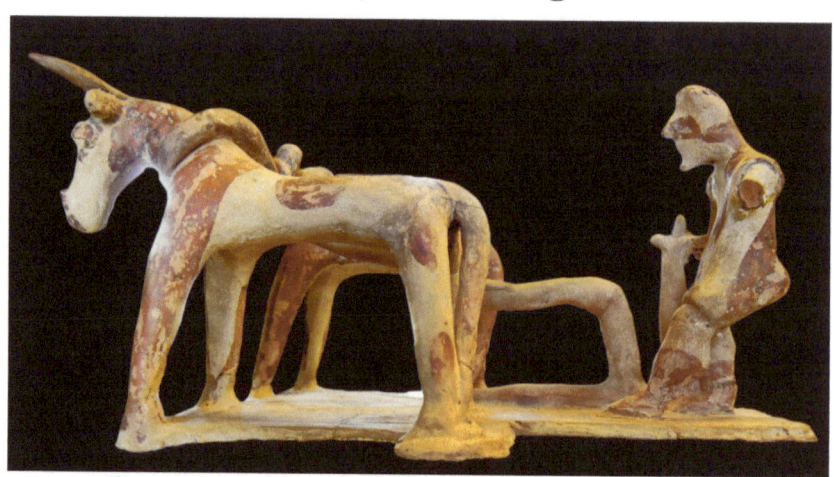

Illustration 99: Ancient Greek Terracotta Figurine of a Plowman

*Farmer plowing his field with his pair of oxen. Terracotta Figurine
from Thebes, Boeotia, ca. 600-575 BCE.
Source: CCA 2.5 Marie-Lan Nguyen/Vail via Wikimedia Commons*

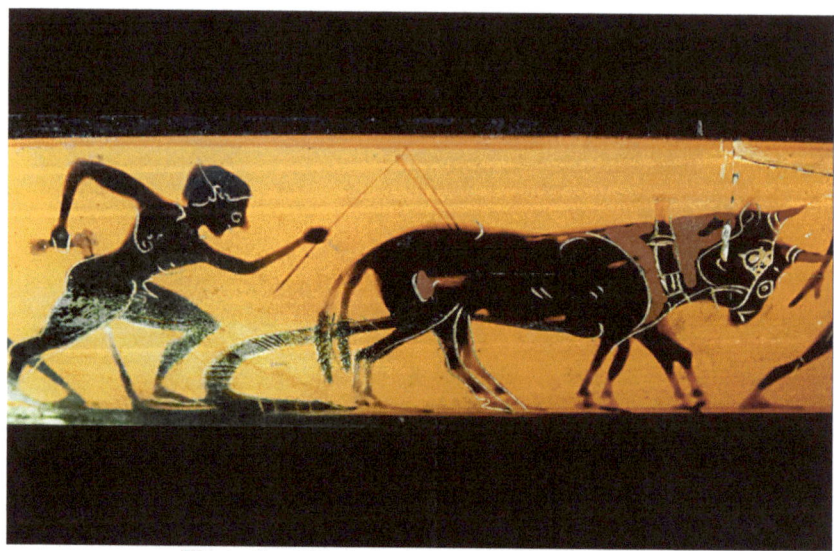

Illustration 100: A plowman and his team of oxen

*A plowman and his team of oxen. Attic Black-figure Band Cup, ca. 525 BCE.
Source: CCA 2.5 Marie-Lan Nguyen/Vail via Wikimedia Commons*

VII. D. Reference Notes - Outer Ring: PEACETIME

VII. D. 1. Plowing the Field

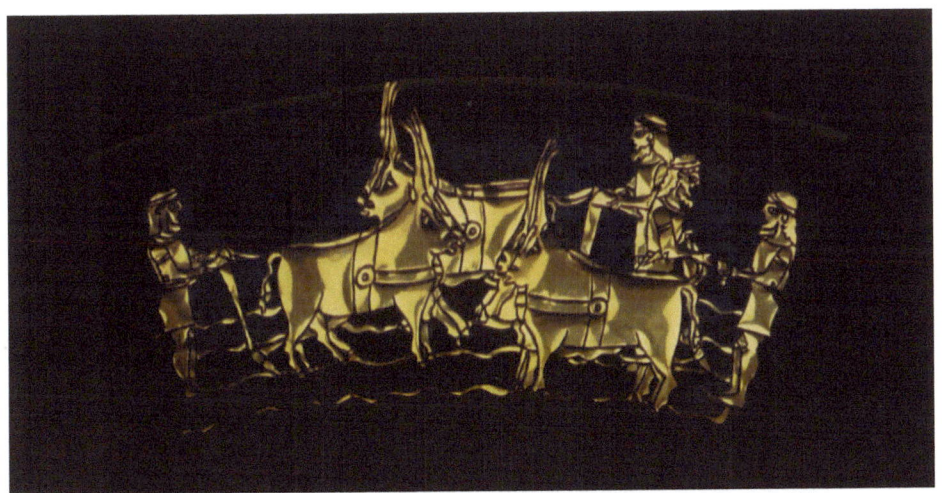

Illustration 101: Outer Ring: Plowing the Field. From the Shield of Achilles
by Kathleen Vail © All Rights Reserved

"Hephaistos put next a freshly plowed field with many plowmen..."

Agricultural activities described on the shield of Achilles' outer ring of peacetime scenes seem at first glance rather common or even quite generic. However, Homer offers some poignant cross references in Book 18 of the *Odyssey*, clearly resonating with the narration of a field being plowed in this scene and the grain being harvested in the next.

Dressed in the guise of a poor beggar, Odysseus must suffer the taunts of Eurymakhos, the leader of Penelope's unwelcome suitors, before Odysseus can execute his plan for revenge. Turning to Odysseus, Eurymakhos snidely demands:

> *"Stranger, will you work as a servant, if I send you to the outer limits of the field and see that you are well paid? Can you build a stone fence, or plant trees? I will have you fed all the year round, and will find you in shoes and clothing. Will you go, then? Not*

Historical Motifs - Plowing the Field, Cont'd

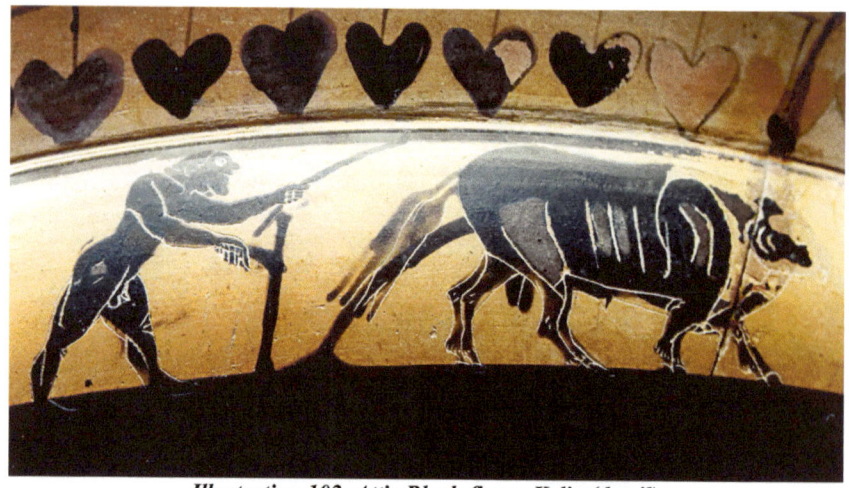

Illustration 102: Attic Black-figure Kylix (detail)

Farmer plowing his field with his pair of oxen.
Detail from an Attic Black-figure Kylix, or Band Cup, ca. 560-550 BCE
Source: CCA 2.5 Marie-Lan Nguyen/Vail via Wikimedia Commons

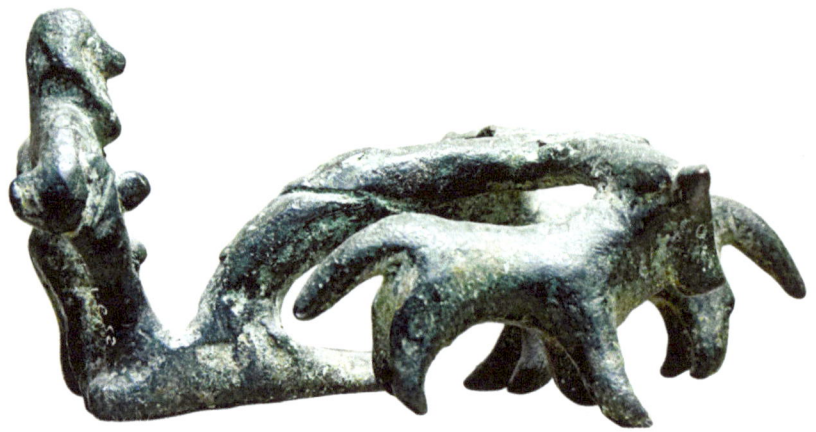

Illustration 103: Ancient Greek Bronze Figurine of a Plowman

Plowman driving a team of two oxen.
Greek Bronze figurine, ca. 6th Century BCE.
Source: CCA 2.5 Marie-Lan Nguyen/Vail via Wikimedia Commons

you; for you have got into bad ways, and do not want to work; you had rather fill your belly by going round the dêmos begging."

"Eurymakhos," answered Odysseus, "if you and I were to work one against the other in early summer [hôra] when the days are at their longest – give me a good scythe, and take another yourself, and let us see which will fast the longer or mow the stronger, from dawn till dark when the mowing grass is about. Or if you will plough against me, let us each take a yoke of tawny oxen, well-mated and of great strength and endurance: turn me into a four acre field, and see whether you or I can drive the straighter furrow." (1)

Documented sources for the motifs in this image include:

Bulls Plowing: (please see additional bull references, above)

– Greek Terracotta Figurine from Thebes, Boeotia, ca. 600-575 BCE. In the collections of the Louvre, Department of Greek, Etruscan, and Roman Antiquities.

– Greek figurine crafted of bronze, probably made in Asia Minor, ca. 6th century BCE. In the British Museum, Upper floor, Room 69.

– Attic Black-figure Kylix, or Band Cup, by the Painter of the Burgon Sianas, ca. 560-550 BCE. In the British Museum, Upper floor, room 69: Greek and Roman life.

– Greek Black-figure Kylix, or Band Cup, ca. 525 BCE. Musée du Louvre, Dép. des Antiquités Grecques et Romaines.

Men in Short Garments: (please see references, above)

FOOTNOTES:

(1). Butler, S., Homer's *Odyssey* Book 18, Lines 356-374

Historical Motifs - Harvesting the Grain

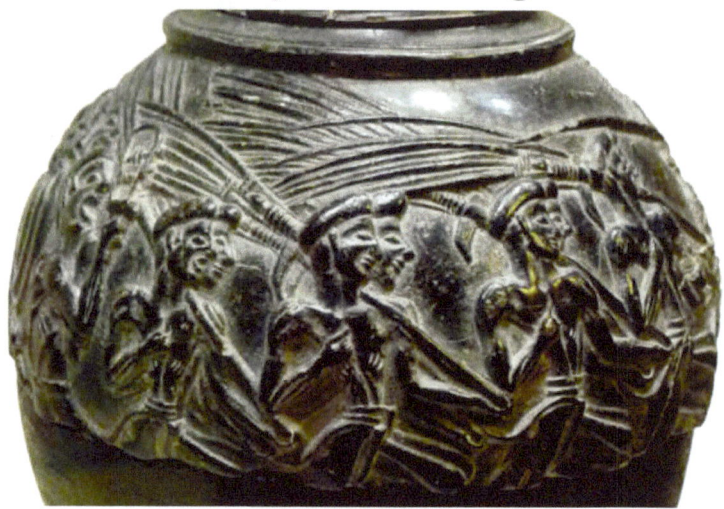

Illustration 104: The "Harvester Vase"

Men participating in a Reaping/Harvesting Festival. Detail from the "Harvester Vase," a Minoan ceremonial vessel carved from serpentine, ca. 1500-1450 BCE. Source: CCSA 3.0 Aeleftherios/Vail via Wikimedia Commons

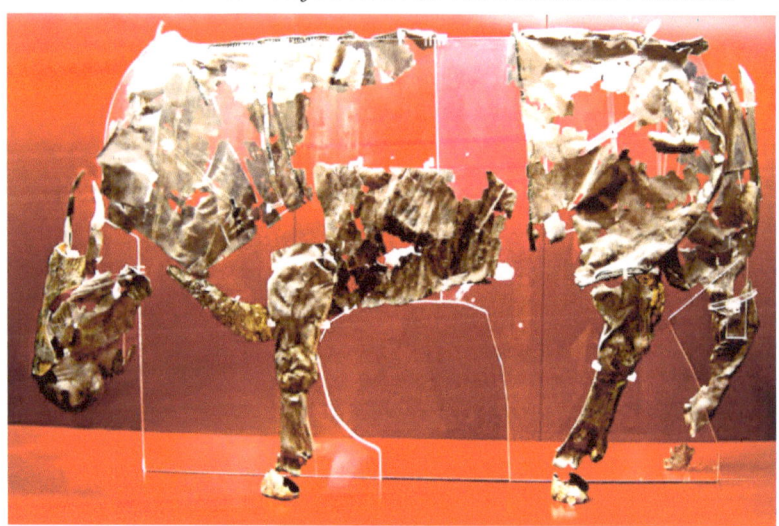

Illustration 105: Silver Repoussé Bull from Delphi

Ancient Greek Silver Repoussé Bull from Delphi, ca. 6th Century BCE. Source: CCSA 3.0 Ricardo André Frantz/Vail via Wikimedia Commons

VII. D. 2. **Harvesting the Grain**

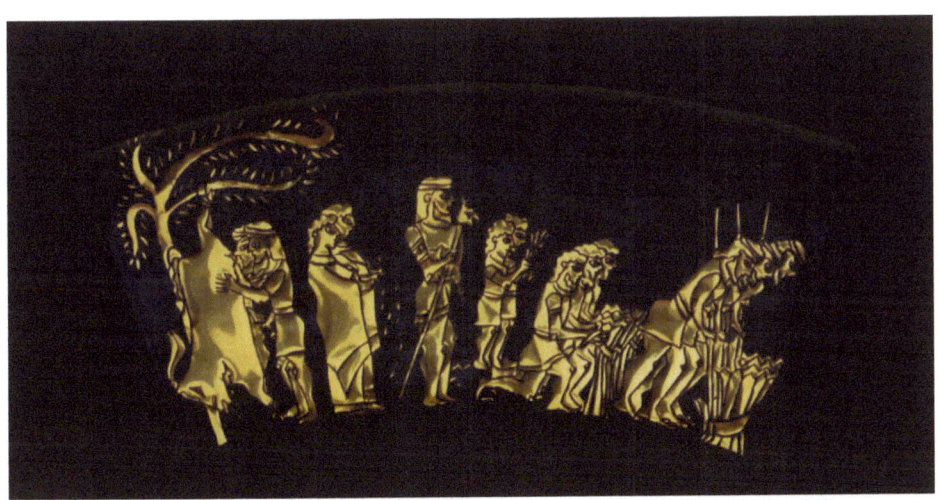

Illustration 106: Outer Ring: Harvesting the Grain. From the Shield of Achilles
by Kathleen Vail © All Rights Reserved

"He also placed there a wealthy king's field where men..."

Chadwick reports many Linear B tablets from Pylos appear to record large quantities of wheat; however, he believes most of these tablets are in fact lists of persons holding land, which is measured in grain. "At neither site," says Chadwick of the Pylos and Knossos tablets, "is the king mentioned by name; we have only the title 'the king' (*wa-na-ka*). He had an important officer who may have been his second-in-command, perhaps the chief of the army. His court was composed of officers called 'Followers' (*e-qe-ta*), or as we might say, 'Companions.'"[1]

Finley tells us more about the tablets, defining the word *temenos* as a "'royal land' or privately owned estate, belonging to a king." Citing the "only certain appearance on the tablets," of the word *temenos*, Finley says, "One Pylos tablet has on its first line the words '*wanakatero temeno tosoja pema*,' followed by the Grain ideogram and the numeral 30..." He continues, "*Temenos* is therefore a land term, connected with the '*wanax*' (as at times in Homer) and the '*lawagetas*'(unknown in Homer)."[2]

Historical Motifs - Harvesting the Grain, Cont'd

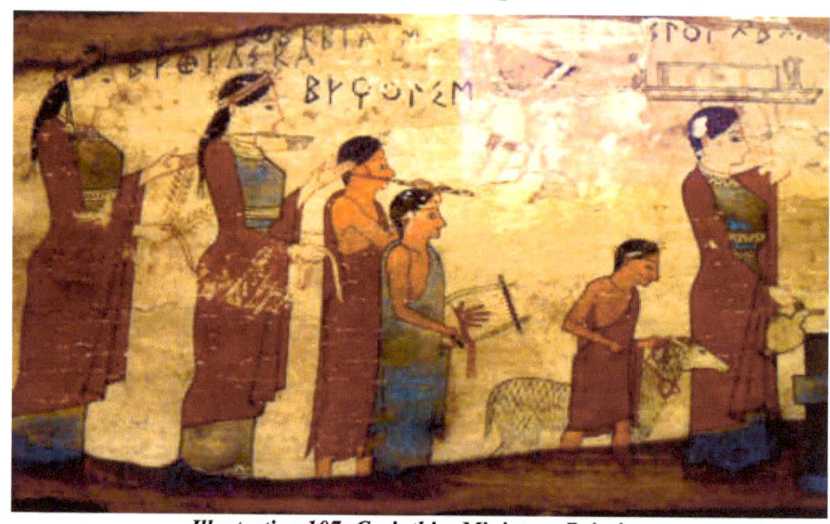

Illustration 107: CorinthianMiniature Painting

A woman (far left) carrying sacred barley in a sacrificial procession. Corinthian miniature painting of a sacrificial lamb, ca. 540 BCE. Source: CCSA 2.5 Marsyas/Vail via Wikimedia Commons

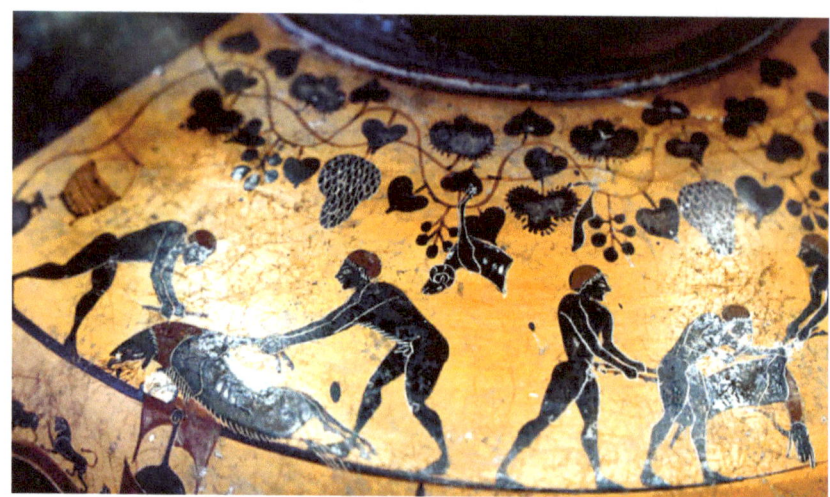

Illustration 108: The "Ricci Hydria"

Men engaged in butchering activities. Black-figure "Ricci" Hydria, ca. 530 BCE. Source: CCSA 4.0 Sailko/Vail via Wikimedia Commons

Another remarkable glimpse into Mycenaean culture is evident in this scene, regarding the religious ritual of sacrifice. Homer tells us the women are winnowing barley to prepare the laborer's supper, while the king's men are butchering a great ox they have sacrificed.

In many instances in both the *Iliad* and the *Odyssey*, when an animal is sacrificed, barley grains are scattered as an integral part of the ritual. At Aulis, prior to deploying to Troy, Agamemnon offers a sacrifice to Zeus, petitioning him for fair winds and victory:

> *They stood in a circle about the ox and took up the scattering barley; and among them powerful Agamemnon spoke in prayer: ... Now when all had made prayer and flung down the scattering barley, first they drew back the victim's head, cut his throat and skinned him...* [3]

The ritual of scattering barley during a sacrifice also occurs when Agamemnon returns Chryseis to her father. Barley is so integral to the ritual, in fact, that it can not be neglected. In the *Odyssey*, Homer tells us of Odysseus' men slaughtering Helios' cattle:

> *They plucked the leaves that shone on a tall oak – having no barley meal – to strew the victims, performed the prayers and ritual, knifed the kine and flayed each carcass...* [4]

Documented sources for the motifs in this image include:

Bulls : (please see references, above)

Men in Short Garments: (please see references, above)

Trees: (please see references, above)

Women and Children: (please see references, above)

FOOTNOTES:

(1). Chadwick, J., *Linear B and Related Scripts,* pg. 37.
(2). Finley,M. I., *Economy and Society in Ancient Greece.* pp. 225, 230-231.
(3). Lattimore, R., *The Iliad of Homer.* Book 2:410-411, and 421-422, pg. 87.
(4). Fitzgerald, R., *Translation of the Odyssey by Homer.* Book 12:355-360, pg. 221.

Historical Motifs - Gathering the Grapes

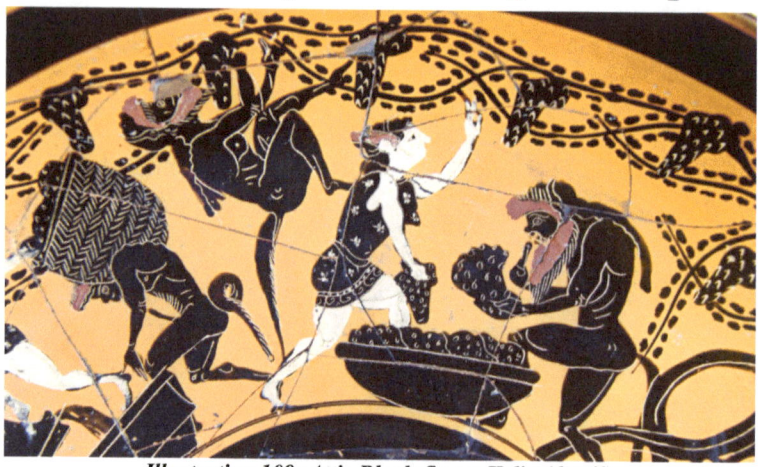

Illustration 109: Attic Black-figure Kylix (detail)

Satyrs and Maenads harvesting grapes into baskets.
Detail from an Attic Black-figure Kylix, ca. end of 6th century BCE.
Source: CC0 Bibi Saint-Pol/Vail via Wikimedia Commons

A young man and his music teacher, holding a lyre, perhaps Herakles and Linos.

Detail from an Attic Red-figure Amphora, ca.440–430 BCE

Source: CCA 2.5 Marie-Lan Nguyen/Vail via Wikimedia Commons

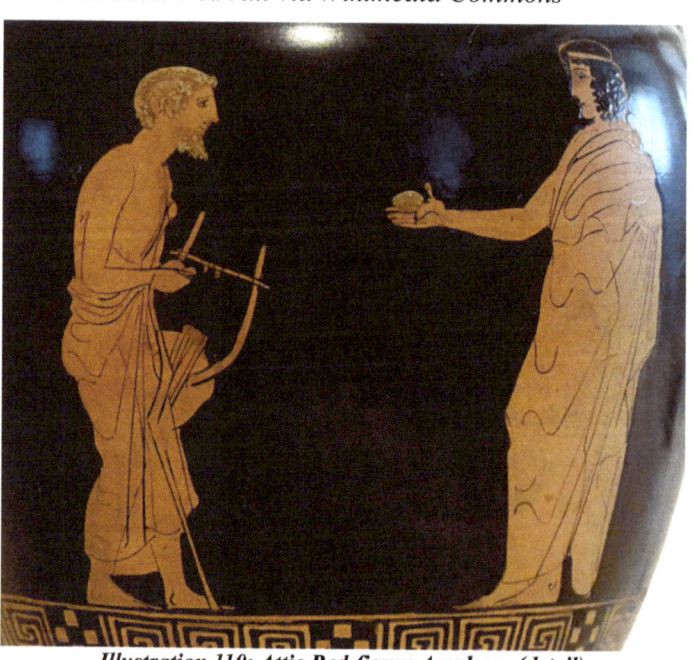

Illustration 110: Attic Red-figure Amphora (detail)

VII. D. 3. Gathering the Grapes

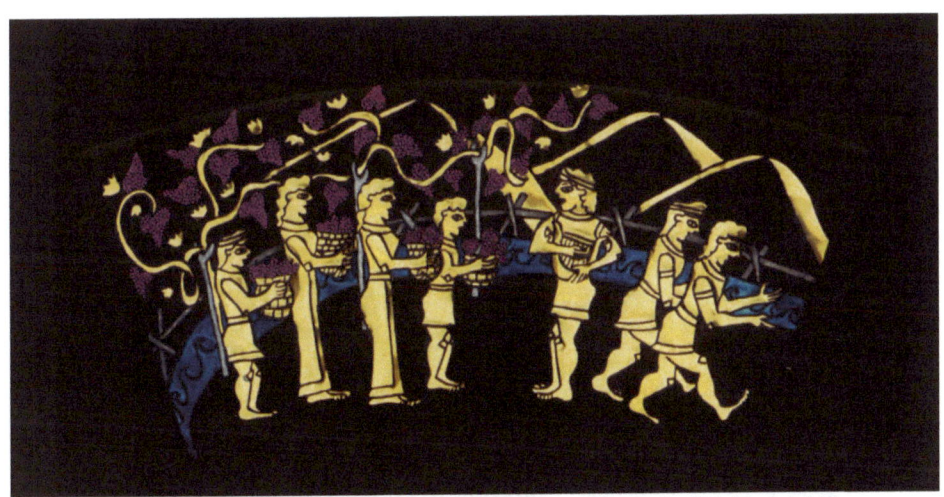

Illustration 111: Outer Ring: Gathering the Grapes. From the Shield of Achilles by Kathleen Vail © All Rights Reserved

"A vineyard in gold he next created, with vines hung heavy..."

According to Pache, various ancient Greek legends agree that the "delicate song of Linos" which Homer refers to in this scene is a harvest song sung in memory of Linos. The identity of Linos, however, is not so well agreed upon. He may have been a son of Apollo and a Muse; a son of Apollo and a mortal; or even a rival god of music with similarities to an early Egyptian myth. [1]

As the son of Apollo and a Muse in one popular legend, Linos is the inventor of rhythm and melody, teaching his musical skills to his brother Orpheus. Unfortunately, Linos also teaches music to Herakles, who kills Linos with his own lyre after being reprimanded for making mistakes. In another legend, Linos is a highly-skilled musical rival ultimately killed by Apollo.

According to yet another legend, Pausanias reports that Apollo curses the people of Argos with a plague of infant deaths because of his anger over two murders. One is the death of Psamathi, a mortal consort of Apollo, and

Historical Motifs - Gathering the Grapes, Cont'd

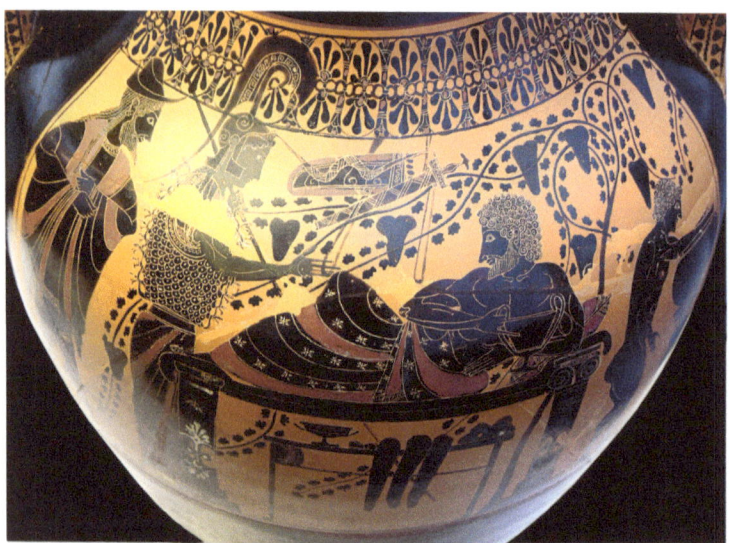

Herakles and Athena in a vineyard.

Detail from an Attic Black-figure Amphora, ca. 6th century BCE.

Source: CC0 Bibi Saint-Pol/Vail via Wikimedia Commons

Illustration 112: Attic Black-figure Amphora (detail)

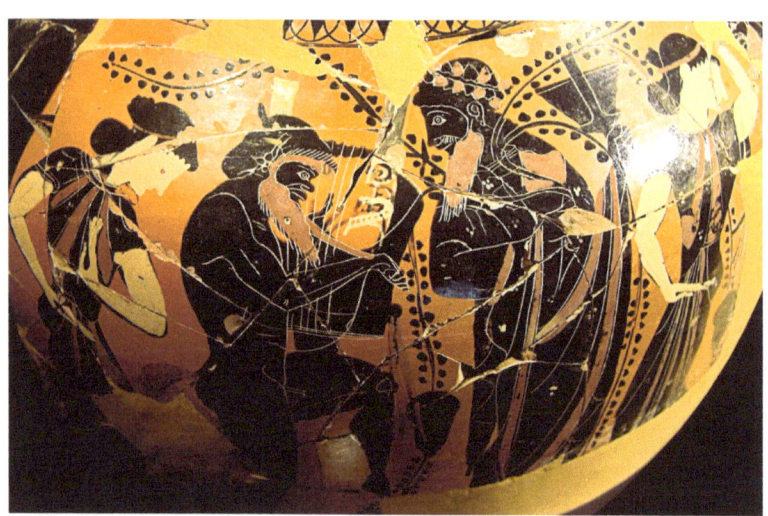

Illustration 113: Greek Black-figure Vase (detail)

A satyr plays a lyre in a vineyard for two dancing maenads and Dionysos. Detail from a Greek Black-figure vase, ca. 520 BCE. Source: CCSA 4.0 Zde/Vail via Wikimedia Commons

the other is the death of Linos, Psamathi's baby. Psamathi's father, the king of Argos, kills his daughter after learning of her immodesty. Clearly anticipating this mortal danger, it is exactly due to fear of her father's wrath that she left her newborn son, Linos, although fathered by Apollo, abandoned on a hillside to die. [2]

Agreeing with Pausanias, Conon relates in his *Narrations* that Apollo's plague leaves the people of Argos only after the Oracle at Delphi banishes Psamathi's father. The oracle also prescribes prayers and songs of penitence to be composed for Linos and performed annually in Argos. [3]

Regarding this same scene of remorseful singing on the shield of Achilles, Ferrucci notes, "We are not far from a time foreseen by Helen in her encounter with Hektor: 'us two, on whom Zeus set a vile destiny, so that hereafter we shall be made into things of song for the men of the future.'" [4]

Documented sources for the motifs in this image include:

Baskets and/or Grapevines:

– Attic Black-figure Amphora by the Lysippides Painter, ca. 6th century BCE, now at Munich. Beazley, *The Development of Attic Black-Figure*, plate 79, no. 2.

– Attic Black-figure Kylix by the Chiusi Painter, ca. end of 6th century BCE, now at the Cabinet des Medailles, BNF, Paris.

– Carpenter, *Dionysian Imagery in Archaic Greek Art*, plate 21.

Lyres: (please see references, above)

Men in Short Garments: (please see references, above)

Trees: (please see references, above)

Women: (please see references, above)

FOOTNOTES:

(1). Pache, C., *Baby and Child Heroes in Ancient Greece, pg. 67.*
(2). Perseus Digital Library at Tufts, *Pausanias' Description of Greece, 1.43.7-8.*
(3). Kiesling, B., *Conon, Fifty Narrations – From the Bibliotheca of Photius. no. 19.*
(4). Ferrucci, F., *The Poetics of Disguise,* pg. 29.

Historical Motifs - Herding the Cattle to Pasture

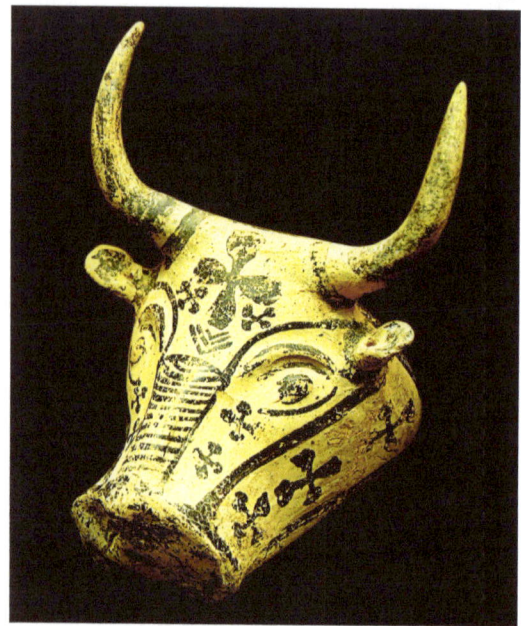

Bull's head with straight horns

Terracotta Mycenaean Rhyton, or libation vessel, ca. 1300-1200 BCE.

Source: CC0 Marie-Lan Nguyen/Vail via Wikimedia Commons

Illustration 114: Mycenaean Bull's Head Rhyton

A man and his dog.

Detail from an Attic Black-figure Lekythos, ca. 480 BCE

Source: CC0 Metropolitan Museum of Art/Vail via Wikimedia Commons

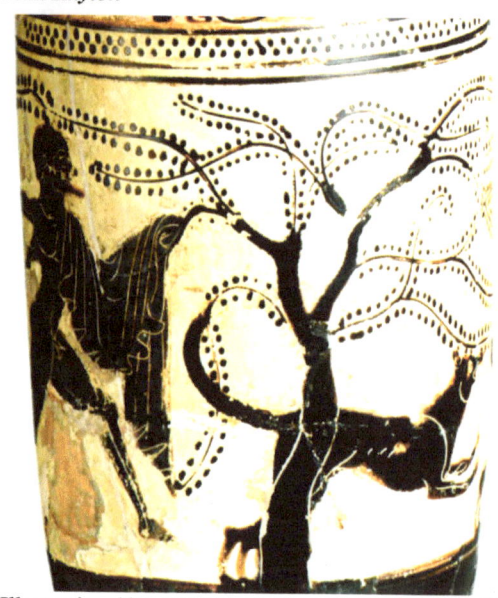

Illustration 115: Attic Black-figure Lekythos (detail)

VII. D. 4. **Herding the Cattle to Pasture**

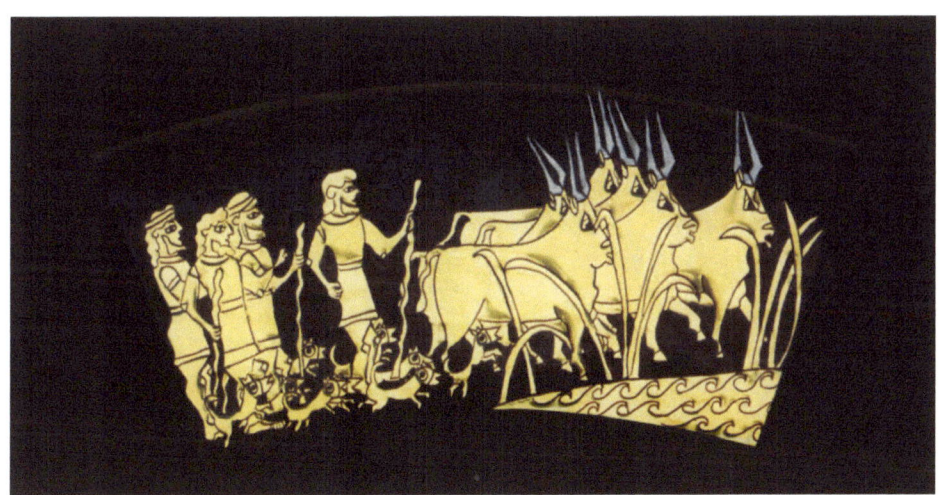

Illustration 116: Outer Ring: Herding Cattle to Pasture. From the Shield of Achilles by Kathleen Vail © All Rights Reserved

"A herd of oxen he next placed there, with gold bodies..."

This scene is a wonderful illustration of the land and herd owners in ancient Greece. The theme is familiar throughout the *Iliad*, but perhaps most clearly recalled by Homer among his description of the gifts offered by Agamemnon to Achilles, hoping to solicit Achilles' return to battle:

> *He will grant you seven citadels, strongly settled...near the sea, at the bottom of sandy Pylos, and men live among them rich in cattle and rich in sheepflocks, who will honour you as if you were a god with gifts given and fulfil your prospering decrees underneath your sceptre.* [1]

In a very clear example of Homer's ancient knowledge being proven by the findings of modern archaeologists, Chadwick tells us about inscriptions written on the clay tablets found at Pylos which reflect Agamemnon's promise of men bound to service under Achilles.

"The holders of land," notes Chadwick, "clearly had obligations to fulfill

Historical Motifs - Herding Cattle to Pasture, Cont'd

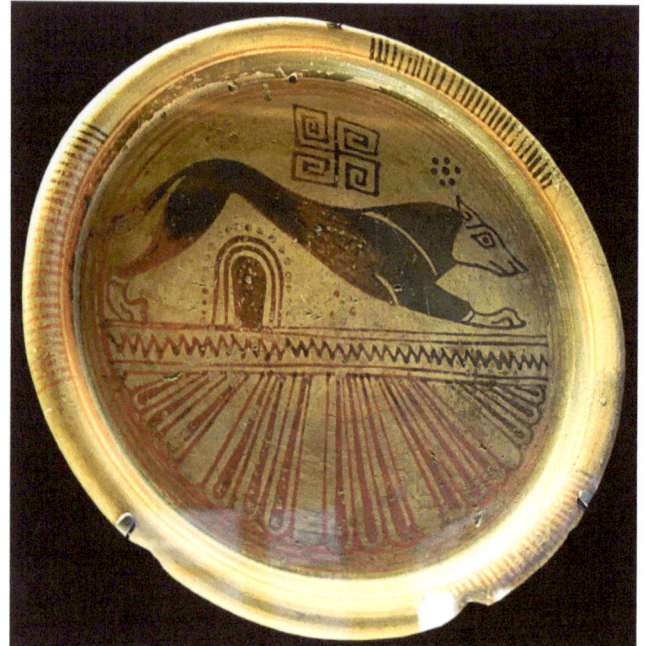

Running dog.

Ancient Greek Orientalizing Plate, ca. 600-575 BCE.

Source: CCSA 3.0 Loïc Evanno /Vail via Wikimedia Commons

Illustration 117: Ancient Greek Orientalizing Plate

Actaeon being devoured by his dogs. Detail from an Attic Black-figure Lekythos, ca. 480–470 BCE

Source: CCSA 2.5 Marsyas/Vail via Wikimedia Commons

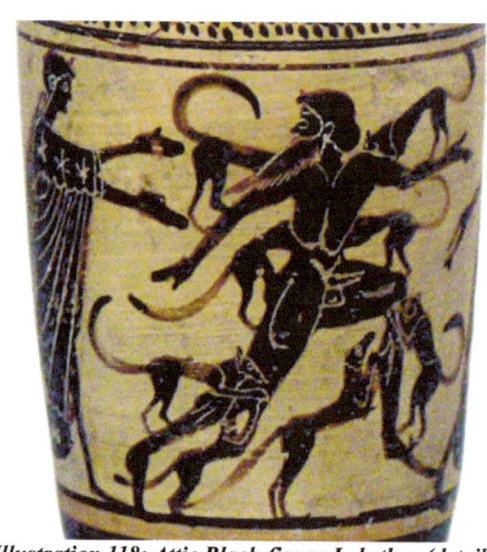

Illustration 118: Attic Black-figure Lekythos (detail)

in return for their holding, for we have notes that some of them had not met their obligations; these [obligations] probably included military service in time of war." [2]

Documented sources for the motifs in this image include:

Bulls : (please see references, above)

Dogs:

    – Attic Black-figure Lekythos, ca. 480 BCE, in the Metropolitan Museum of Art; Beazley, *Attic Black-figure Vase-painters*, pp. 522, 704, no. 7.

    – Attic Black-figure Lekythos, ca. 480–470 BCE, in the National Archaeological Museum of Athens.

    – Carpenter, *Dionysian Imagery in Archaic Greek Art*, plate 21.

    – Celebe, ca. 6th Century BCE, now at the Louvre, Paris; Fowler, *A Handbook of Greek Archaeology*, fig. 36.

    – Italo-Ionian Amphora, "The Judgement of Paris," in Munich's Antiker Kleinkunst; Pfuhl, *Masterpieces of Greek Drawing and Painting*, fig. 12.

    – Lip Cup, signed by Tleson, ca. 550 BCE. Boardman, *Athenian Black Figure Vases*, fig. 110.

Men in Short Garments: (please see references, above)

River:

    – Dagger from Mycenae. Bronze, inlaid with silver and gold. Mycenaean Late Bronze Age, 16th century BCE. National Archaeological Museum of Athens, N 765.

FOOTNOTES:

(1). Lattimore, R. *The Iliad of Homer*, Book 9:291-298, pg. 206.
(2). Chadwick, J. *Linear B and Related Scripts*, pg. 37.

Historical Motifs - Outer Ring: Lion Attack

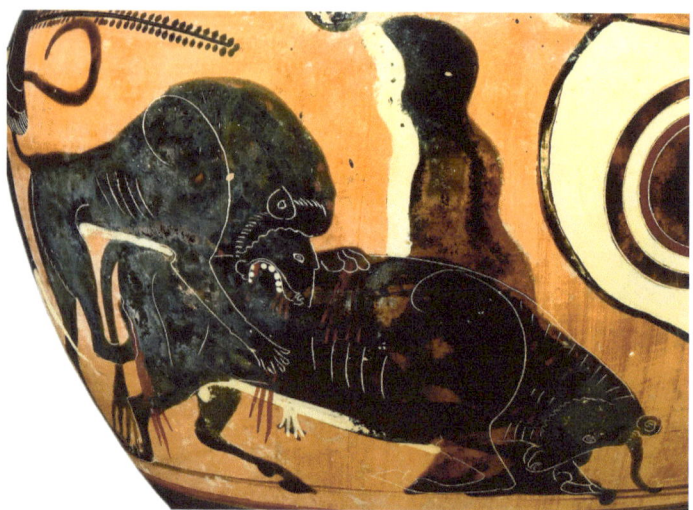

Lion attacking a bull.

Detail from an Attic Black-figure Column Krater, ca. 2nd half of 6th century BCE.

Source: CC0 Getty Open Content/Vail via Wikimedia Commons

Illustration 119: Attic Black-figure Column Krater (detail)

Large lion sculpture.

Cretan Terracotta Lion Sculpture, ca. 6th century BCE.

Source: CC0 Cmessier/Vail via Wikimedia Commons

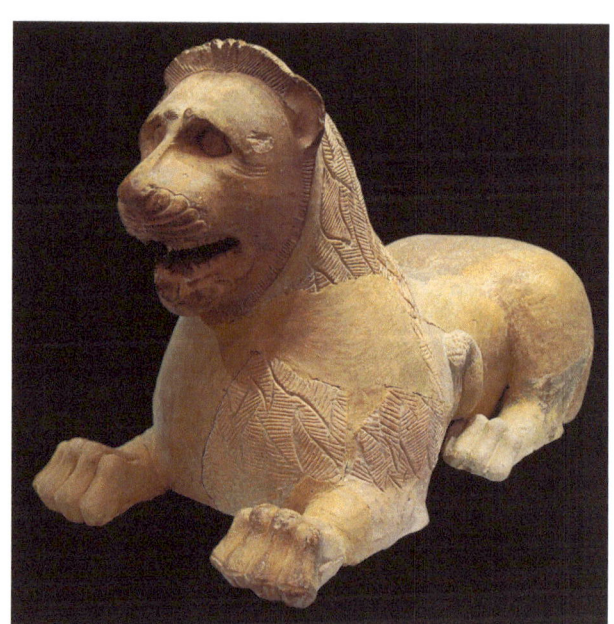

Illustration 120: Cretan Terracotta Lion Sculpture

VII. D. 5. **Lion Attack**

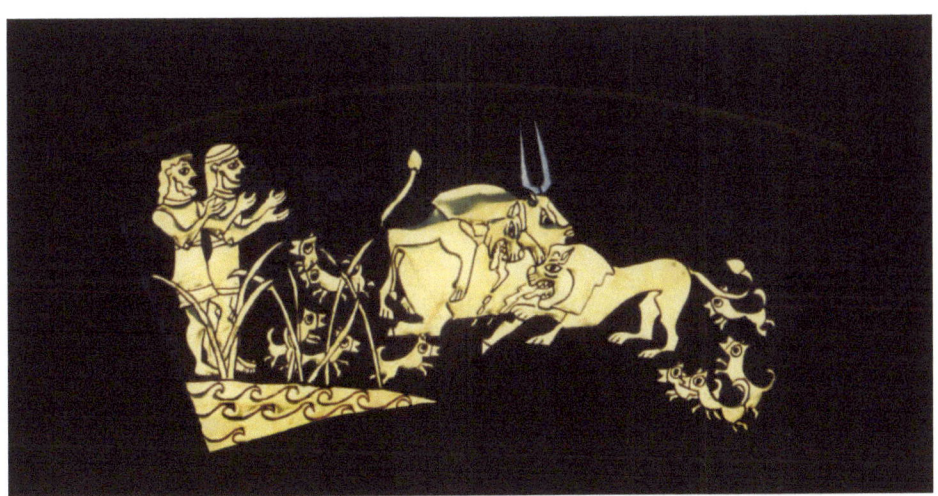

*Illustration 121: Outer Ring: Lion Attack. From the Shield of Achilles
by Kathleen Vail © All Rights Reserved*

"Then a pair of lions charged a bull: In two huge bounds assaulted..."

Documented sources for the motifs in this image include:

Bulls : (please see references, above)

Dogs : (please see references, above)

Lions:

– Attic Black-figure Column Krater, ca. Second half of 6th century BCE. J. Paul Getty Museum; Spivey, N. and Squire, M., *Panorama of the Classical World*, p. 125, fig. 208.

– Attic Black-figure Tondo of a Kylix, or Lip Cup, ca. 540 BCE. J. Paul Getty Museum; Clark, *Corpus Vasorum Antiquorum. The J. Paul Getty Museum 2 (USA 25)*, pp. 52-53; fig. 30; pls. 100, 103.

Historical Motifs - Lion Attack, Cont'd

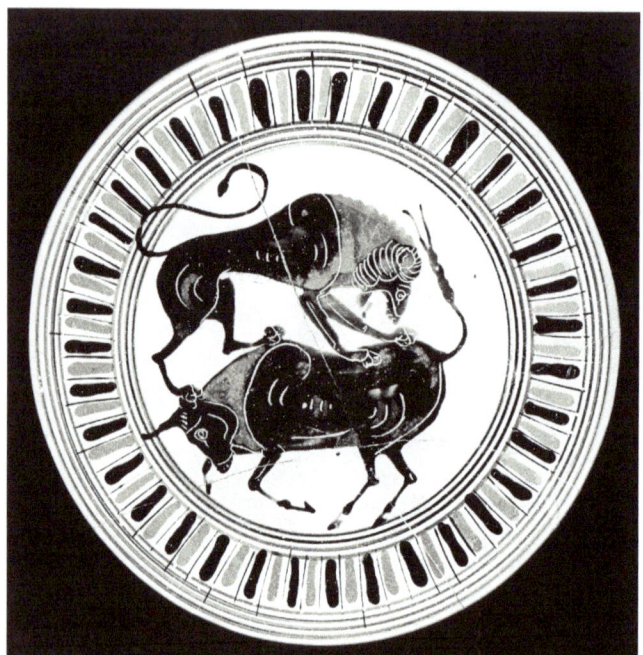

*Lion attacking
a bull.*

*Attic Black-figure
Tondo of a Kylix,
ca. 540 BCE.*

*Source: CC0 Getty
Open Content/Vail
via Wikimedia
Commons*

Illustration 122: Attic Black-figure Kylix Tondo

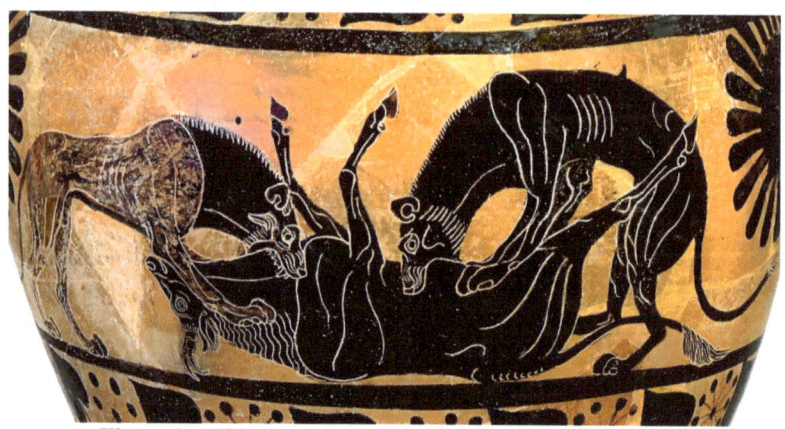

Illustration 123: Greek Caeretan Black-figure Hydria (detail)

*Two lions attacking a bull. Detail from a Greek Caeretan Black-figure Hydria,
ca. 520-510 BCE. Source: CC0 image by the Metropolitan Museum
of Art/Vail via Wikimedia Commons*

– Corinthian Bottle by Timonidas, ca. 580 BCE; Cook, *Greek Art – Its Development, Character and Influence*, plate D, page 277.

– Corinthian Jug, ca. 625 BCE, from Rhodes, at Oxford; Beazley, *Greek Sculpture and Painting*, fig. 17.

– Cretan Large Terracotta Lion Sculpture, ca. 6th century BCE, in the Archaeological Museum of Heraklion, Crete.

– Greek Caeretan Black-figure Hydria attributed to the Eagle Painter, ca. 520-510 BCE. Metropolitan Museum of Art; Picon, *Art of the Classical World in the Met Museum of Art*, 2007; no. 64, pp. 67, 419.

– Neck Amphora, "Heracles Fights the Lion," by the Antimenes Painter; Boardman, *Athenian Black Figure Vases*, fig. 189.

– Neck Hydria, "Harnessing of Athena's Chariot," by the Antimenes Painter, ca. 520-500 BCE; Folsom, *Attic Black-Figured Pottery*, plate 10d.

– Protocorinthian Olpe, "The Chigi Vase," by the MacMillan Painter, ca. 650-640 BCE, in the Villa Giulia; Mingazzini *Greek Pottery Painting*, plate 6, pg. 21.

Men in Short Garments: (please see references, above)

Historical Motifs - Valley of Sheep

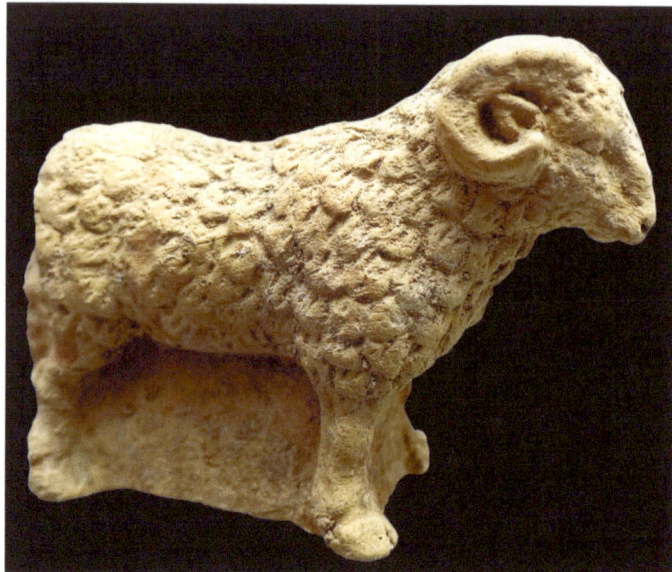

Ram statuette.

Terracotta statuette of a ram from Boeotia, Greece, ca. 4th century BCE.

Source: CC0 Daderot/Vail via Wikimedia Commons

Illustration 124: Greek Terracotta Statuette of a Ram

Ram and panther.

Corinthian Black-figure Pyxis by the Stobart Painter, ca. 580-570 BCE.

Source: CCSA 3.0 Marcus Cyron/Vail via Wikimedia Commons

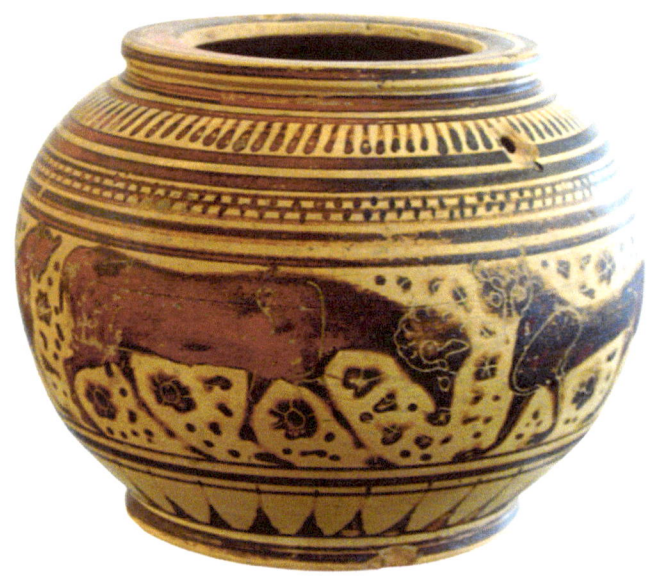

Illustration 125: Corinthian Black-figure Pyxis

VII. D. 6. Valley of Sheep

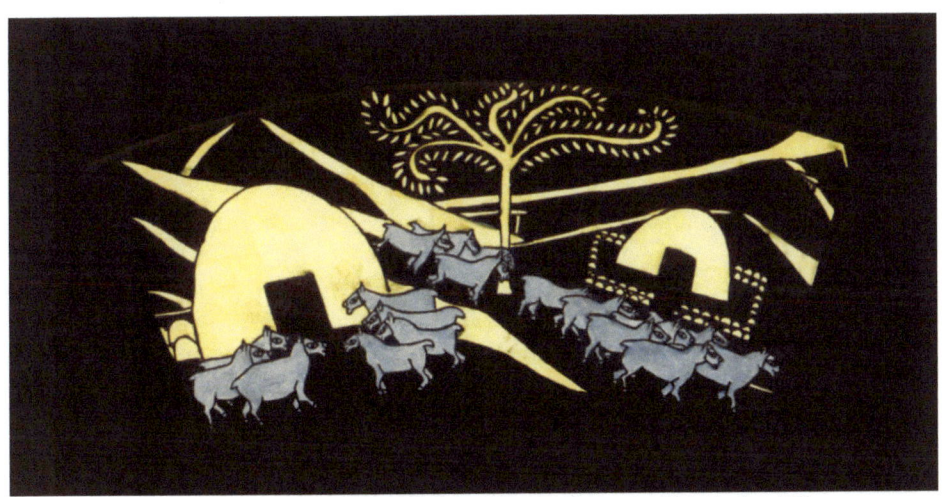

*Illustration 126: Outer Ring: Valley of Sheep. From the Shield of Achilles
by Kathleen Vail © All Rights Reserved*

"The Bandy-legged god put next on the shield a wide valley..."

Documented sources for the motifs in this image include:

<u>Sheep</u> : (please see additional references, above)

— Corinthian Black-figure Pyxis by the Stobart Painter, ca. 580-570 BCE. In the Ancient Collection Museum of the University of Leipzig, Inv, No. T 2335.

— Greek Terracotta Ram Statuette, from Boeotia, ca. 4th century BCE. Exhibited at Martin von Wagner Museum, Wurzburg, Germany.

<u>Trees</u> : (please see references, above)

Historical Motifs - Circle-Dancing

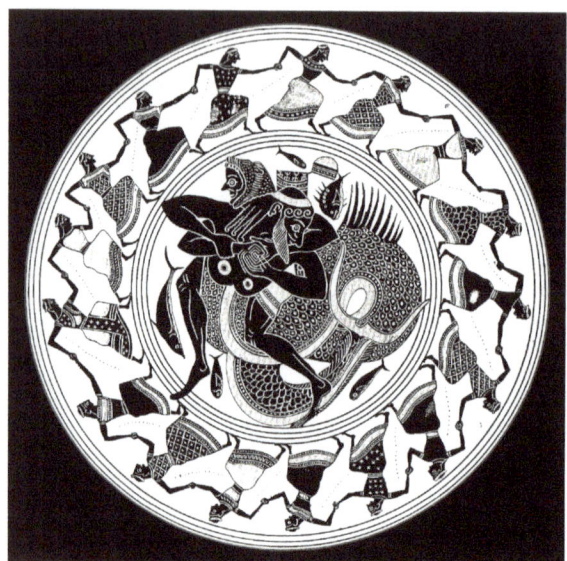

Women holding hands and dancing in a circle.

Detail from a drawing of an Attic Black-figure Kylix Tondo, ca. 550 BCE.

Source: CCSA 3.0 Universitatsbibliothek Heidelberg/Vail via Wikimedia Commons

Illustration 127: Attic Black-figure Kylix Tondo

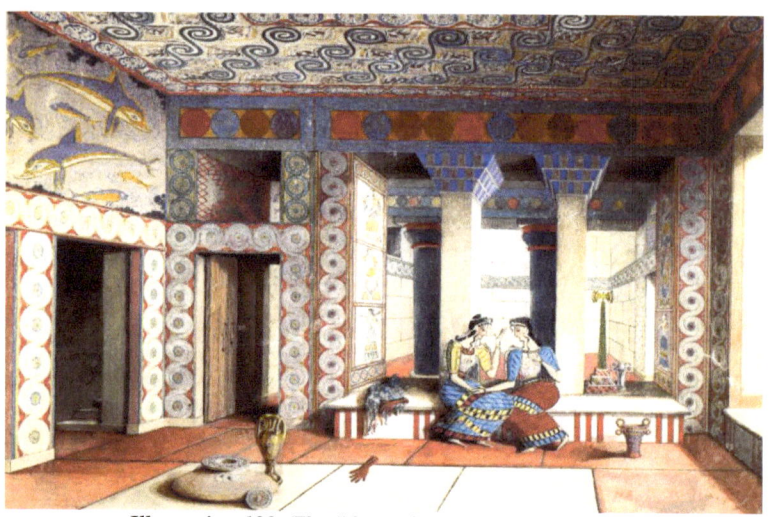

Illustration 128: The "Queen's Megaron" at Knossos

The "Queen's Megaron" at Knossos. Emile Gilliéron the younger, ca. 1922-1926, based on Sir Arthur Evan's excavation papers. Source: CCA 4.0 MartinPoulter/Vail via Wikimedia Commons

VII. D. 7. **Circle-Dancing**

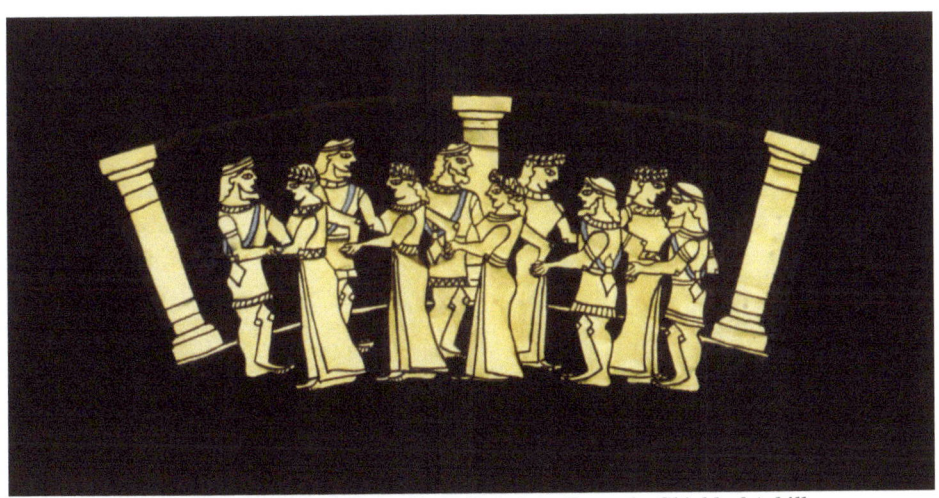

Illustration 129: Outer Ring: Circle-Dancing. From the Shield of Achilles
by Kathleen Vail © All Rights Reserved

"He fashioned there, also, a wide dancing floor..."

The palace at Knossos on Crete is an archaeological wonder; a witness to the wealthy Minoan civilization, as well as the authenticity of Homer's knowledge. The legendary King Minos charges Daidalos to build the Labyrinth, a maze-filled structure housing the terrible Minotaur. His daughter, Ariadne, gives Theseus the ball of string he uses to find his way back out of the Labyrinth after slaying the Minotaur.

Later, Minos' granddaughter, Aerope, marries the son of Atreus, carrying the glories of the Minoan civilization with her to Mycenae, where she gives birth to Agamemnon. Thus it is understandable to find dance floors described by Homer "like the one in Knossos' palace that Daidalos made for King Minos' daughter, the beautiful Ariadne."

Regarding the tunics of the young men dancing in this scene, the clay tablets discovered at Pylos provide an interesting clue. At an AIA lecture, entitled *Life in a Mycenaean Kingdom*, Professor Cynthia Shelmerdine of University of Texas at Austin explained the shining effect of oil-infused

Historical Motifs - Circle-Dancing, Cont'd

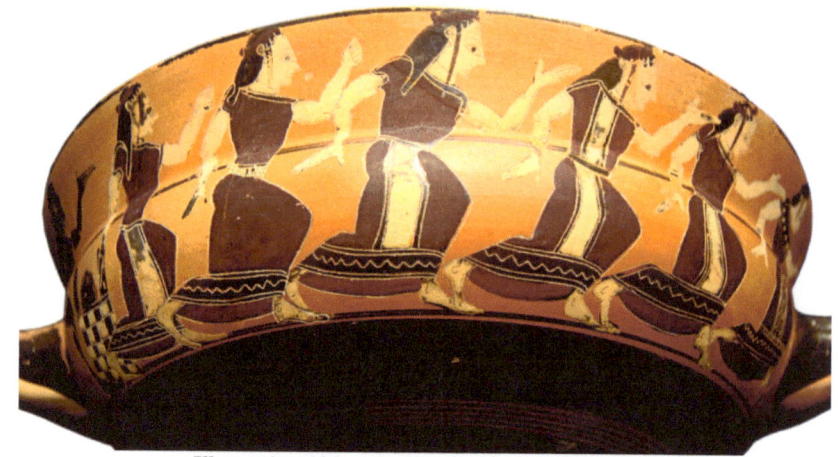

Illustration 130: Attic Black-figure Kylix (detail)

*Women dancing. Detail depicting Thetis' sisters, the Nereids, or sea nymphs,
dancing at the wedding of Thetis and Peleus -
from an Attic Black-figure Kylix by the C Painter, ca. 560 BCE.
Source: CC0 image by Bibi Saint-Pol/Vail via Wikimedia Commons*

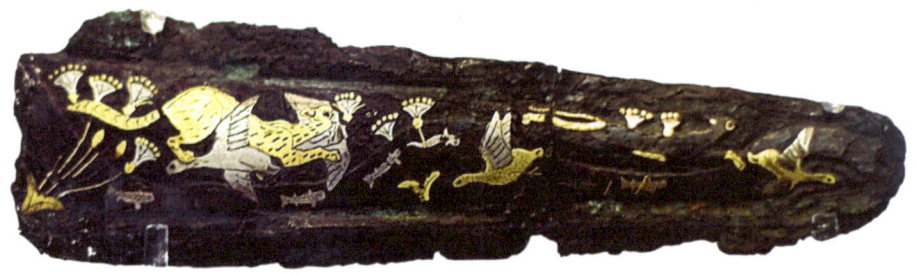

Illustration 131: Mycenaean Royal Dagger

*Mycenaean Royal Dagger. Bronze, inlaid with gold and silver,
ca. 16th century BCE.
Source: CCSA 3.0 Zde/Vail via Wikimedia Commons*

fabric. She noted that, among the Linear B inscriptions deciphered from the Pylos tablets, a quantity of oil for this purpose is designated. And, since then, experiments with infusing oil into fabric have been successful. The result is a beautiful, luminous material from which men's tunics may have been made. [1]

Regarding the socially privileged maidens dancing in this scene, Homer's word, *alphesiboiai*, literally means, "oxen-dowry." Robinson feels this name reveals the father's high regard for his daughter's dowry, denoting that he is looking forward "to his daughter's marriage-day when she would bring him some return for the cost of her upbringing." [2]

Documented sources for the motifs in this image include:

Daggers:
– Mycenaean Royal Dagger, bronze with inlaid gold and silver, ca. 16th Century BCE. At the National Archaeological Museum of Athens, No 765.

Men in Short Garments: (please see references, above)

Women: (please see references, above)

Women and/or Men Dancing:
– Attic Black-figure Lekythos by the Amasis Painter, ca. 550-530 BCE, at the Metropolitan Museum of Art; Richter, *A Handbook of Greek Art*, fig. 437.

– Attic Black-figure Kylix by the C Painter, ca. 560 BCE. On display at the Staatliche Antikensammlungen - Room 3.

– Attic Black-figure Volute Krater, "The Francois Vase," ca. 570 BCE; Mingazzini, *Greek Pottery Painting*, plate 7.

– Drawing of a Tondo from an Attic Black-Figure Kylix, ca. 550 BCE; Harrison and MacColl, *Greek Vase Paintings.* Plate V.

FOOTNOTES:

(1). Shelmerdine, Cynthia, PhD. AIA Lecture, *Life in a Mycenaean Kingdom,* Virginia Museum of Fine Arts, Richmond, VA, 2/28/91.

(2). Robinson, C. E. *Everyday Life in Ancient Greece,* pg. 18.

Historical Motifs - Line-Dancing

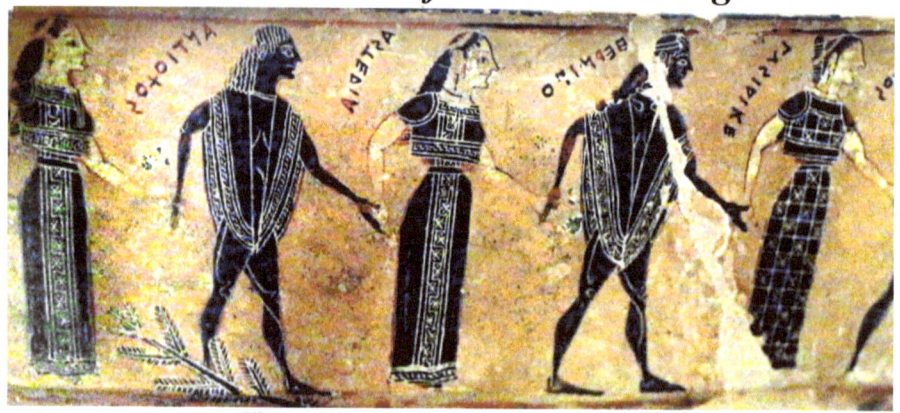

Illustration 132: The Francois Vase (detail)

Women and men holding hands and dancing in lines. Detail from an Attic Black-figure Volute Krater "The Francois Vase," by the Amasis Painter, ca. 560-530 BCE. Source: CCSA 3.0 Sailko/Vail via Wikimedia Commons

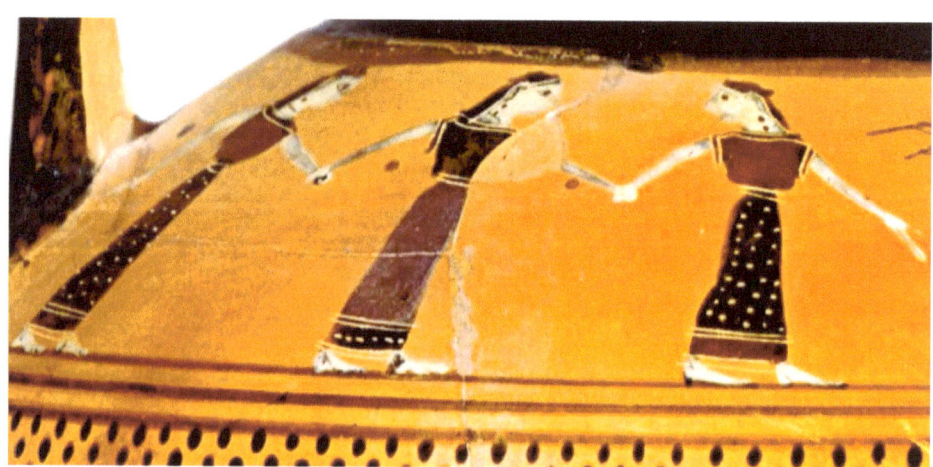

Illustration 133: Attic Black-figure Lekythos (detail)

Women dancing in lines between musicians. Detail from an Attic Black-figure Lekythos by the Amasis Painter, ca. 560-530 BCE. Source: CC0 Metropolitan Museum of Art via Wikimedia Commons

VII. D. 8. Line-Dancing

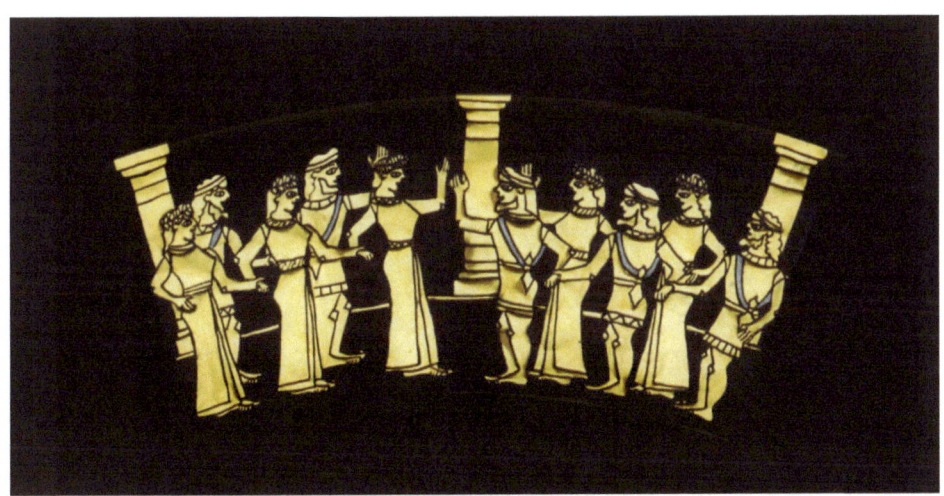

Illustration 134: Outer Ring: Line-Dancing. From the Shield of Achilles
by Kathleen Vail © All Rights Reserved

"And also in lines, they appeared as in ranks..."

Documented sources for the motifs in this image include:

<u>Daggers :</u> (please see references, above)

<u>Men in Short Garments:</u> (please see references, above)

<u>Women:</u> (please see references, above)

<u>Women and/or Men Dancing:</u> (please see references, above)

Historical Motifs - Acrobats Join the Action

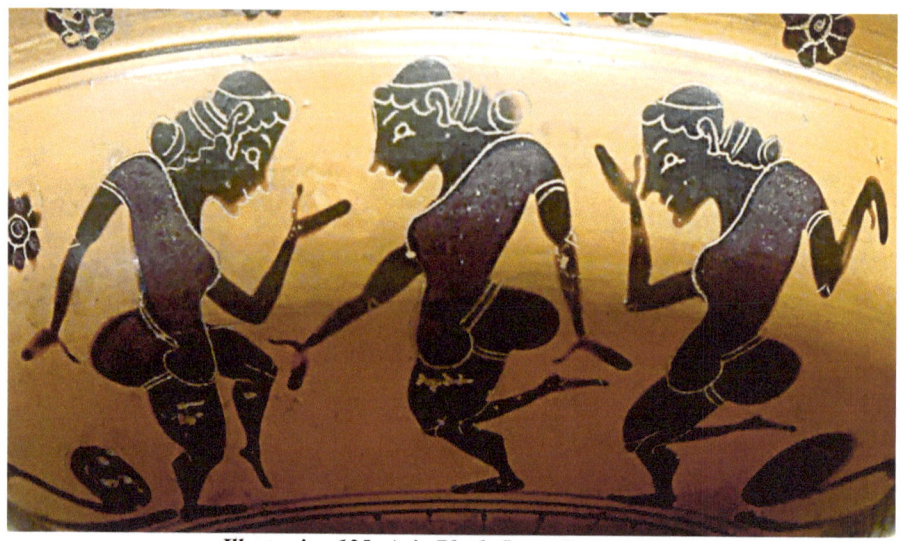

Illustration 135: Attic Black-figure Komast Cup

Three komasts (padded dancers) wearing padded clothing for comedic dancing.
Attic Black-figure Komast Cup, ca. 575-565 BCE.
Source: CC0 Marie-Lan Naguyen via Wikimedia Commons

Two young men performing acrobatic stunts.

Attic Red-figure Skyphos, ca. 470-460 BCE.

Source: CCSA 3.0 Marcus Cyron/Vail via Wikimedia Commons

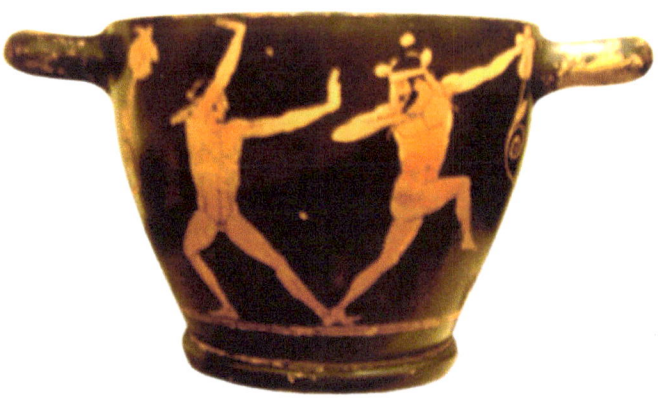

Illustration 136: Attic Red-figure Skyphos

VII. D. 9. **Acrobats Join the Action**

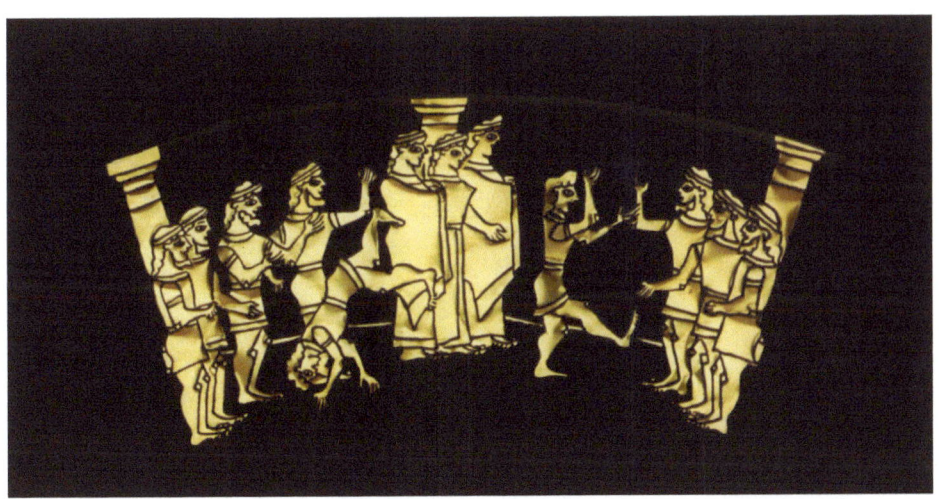

Illustration 137: Outer Ring: Acrobats Join the Action. From the Shield of Achilles by Kathleen Vail © All Rights Reserved

"Then with effortless spins and dexterous handsprings, two tumblers..."

This scene of acrobats, or tumblers, entertaining the guests at a festive celebration on the divine shield **of** Achilles has a remarkable parallel in Book 4 of Homer's *Odyssey*.

Telemakos, arriving at night with Nestor's son by chariot to the palace of Helen and Menelaus, hopes to hear news of his father, Odysseus. The palace is brightly lit and buzzing with guests, festivities, and excitement. Hermione, the daughter of Helen and Menelaos, is enjoying a feast in her honor before being sent off to marry Neoptolemos, the heroic son of Achilles.

Homer has built here a fascinating bridge in this last scene on the ageless shield of Achilles – not only between the *Iliad* and the *Odyssey*, but also between Achilles and his son:

> *So they were feasting in the great high-roofed hall, the neighbors and kinsfolk of glorious Menelaus, and making merry; and among*

Historical Motifs - Acrobats Join the Action, Cont'd

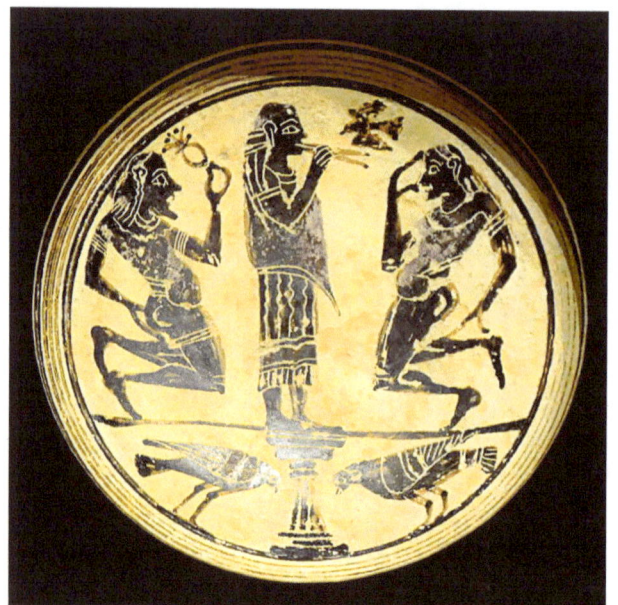

*Two men dancing
vigorously as another
man plays a double pipe.*

*Detail from a Laconian
Black-figure Kylix Tondo
by the Hunt Painter,
ca. 550-530 BCE.*

*Source: CCSA 4.0
Jerónimo Roure
Pérez/Vail via Wikimedia
Commons*

Illustration 138: Laconian Black-figure Kylix Tondo

*Two men performing comedic
komast dances.*

*Detail from an Early Corinthian
Black-figure Aryballos by the
New York Comast Painter,
ca. 620-590 BCE.*

*Source: CC0 image
Metropolitan Museum of
Art/Vail via Wikimedia
Commons*

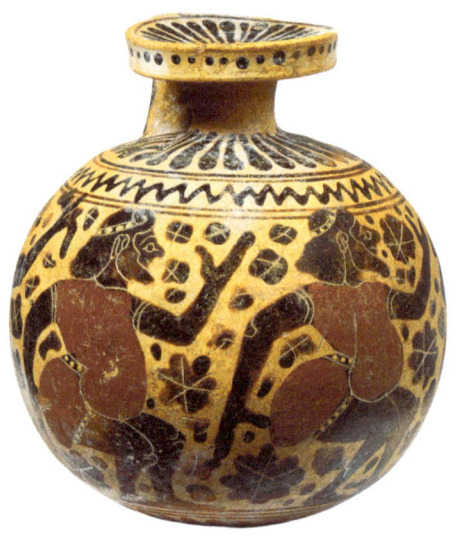

Illustration 139: Corinthian Black-figure Aryballos

them a divine minstrel was singing to the lyre, and two tumblers whirled up and down through the midst of them, as he began his song. [1]

Documented sources for the motifs in this image include:

Acrobats :

– Attic Black-figure Komast Cup by the KY Painter, ca. 576-565 BCE. At the Louvre Museum, Department of Greek, Etruscan and Roman Antiquities, Sully, first floor, room 41, case 8. Beazley, *Attic Black-Figure Vase Painters,* 32,9; add 2 8.

– Attic Red-Figure Skyphos, ca. 470-460 BCE. At the Antikensammlung, Berlin / Altes Museum. CCSA 3.0 image by Marcus Cyron/Vail via Wikimedia Commons.

– Early Corinthian Black-figure Aryballos by the New York Comast Painter, ca. 620-590 BCE, at the Metropolitan Museum of Art. Mertens, Joan R., *How to Read Greek Vases.* p. 62, fig. 29.

– Laconian Black-figure Kylix by the Hunt Painter, ca. 550-530 BCE. At the National Archaeological Museum of Spain (MAN), Inv. number 1999/99/45. CCSA 4.0 image by Jerónimo Roure Pérez/Vail via Wikimedia Commons.

– Red-figure Krater, ca. 500-490 BCE. On display at the National Museum, Warsaw. Dobrowolski, W., *Sisyphe et le komos* in: *Bulletin du Musée National de Varsovie.* Vol. 17, pp. K, 97, 100.

Daggers : (please see references, above)

Men in Short Garments: (please see references, above)

Women: (please see references, above)

Women and/or Men Dancing: (please see references, above)

FOOTNOTES:

(1). Butler's translation of Homer's *Odyssey*, Book 4, Lines 15-19.

Historical Motifs - Mighty Ocean Current

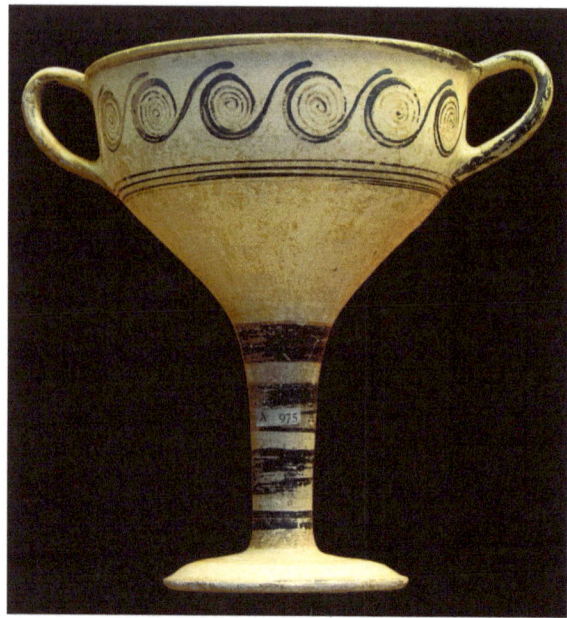

Connecting spirals form a decorative line of waves around the top of this cup from the Trojan War-era of Homer's Iliad.

Mycenaean Kylix, ca. 1300-1250 BCE

Source: CCSA 4.0 Zde/Vail via Wikimedia Commons

Illustration 140: Mycenaean Kylix

A beautiful wave pattern flows around the middle of this ancient Greek vessel.

Kamares Ware – Terracotta Vessel from Knossos, ca. 1800-1700 BCE

Source: CCSA 4.0 Zde/Vail via Wikimedia Commons

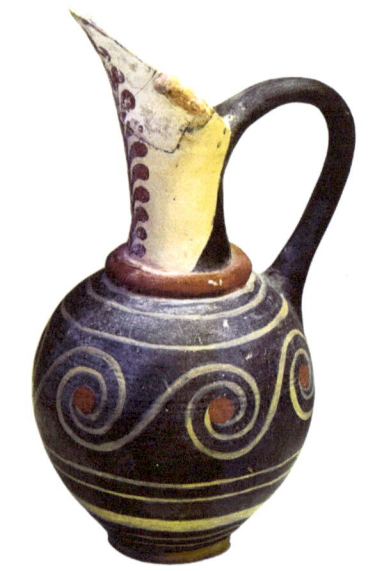

Illustration 141: Kamares Ware Vessel

VII. E. Reference Notes - Outer Rim: MIGHTY OCEAN CURRENT

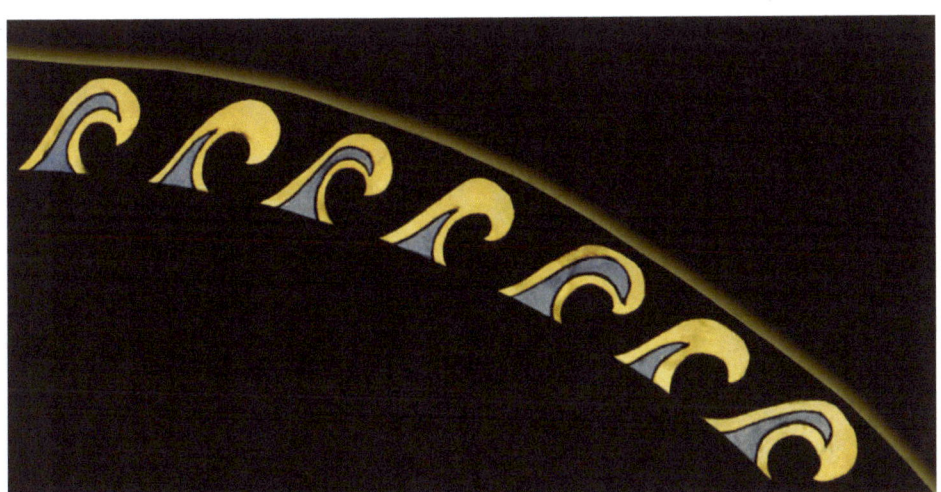

Illustration 142: Outer Rim: Mighty Ocean Current. From the Shield of Achilles by Kathleen Vail © All Rights Reserved

"Lastly, encircling the solid shield's rim, power brightly shined..."

The powerful symbol of the spiral as a motif representing ocean waves has clear associations stretching deeply into human history. This relationship is especially evident in the beautiful designs decorating artifacts from the islands and mainland of Ancient Greece.

As noted in the first scene at the center of the shield of Achilles, a motif of four fish swimming between four connecting spirals undeniably represents the ocean on a terracotta object, ca. 2700-2500 BCE, found on Naxos Island (see illus. 48, above). From the island of Knossos, ca. 1800-1700 BCE, this intimate relationship with the sea is seen in the lovely flowing waves decorating elegantly painted Minoan Kamares ware.

Bridging the Mediterranean Sea between the Minoan and the Mycenaean civilizations, we find connecting wave spirals colorfully featured in the frescoes adorning the palaces of both empires.

Historical Motifs - Mighty Ocean Current, Cont'd

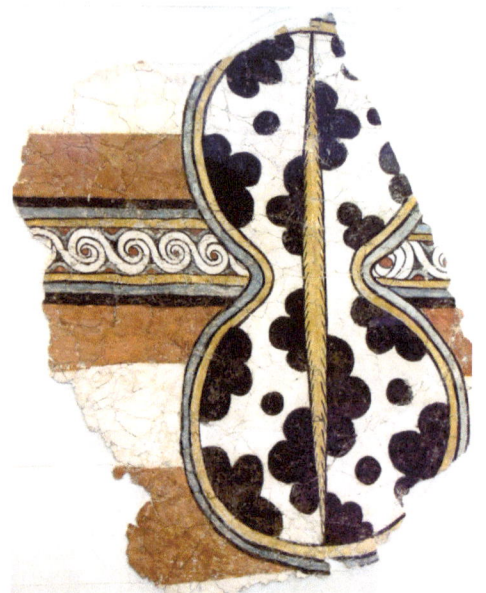

Figure Eight-shaped Shields depicted on a wall decorated with a line of connecting spiral waves.

Mycenaean Palace Wall Fresco, ca. 13th century BCE.

Source: CCSA 3.0 Marsyas/Vail via Wikimedia Commons

Illustration 143: Mycenaean Palace Wall Fresco

A beautiful line of waves decorates this elegant water jug.

Greek Black-figure Hydria, or Hadra Vase from Alexandria, Egypt, ca. 213 BCE.

Source: CC0 Metropolitan Museum of Art/Vail via Wikimedia Commons

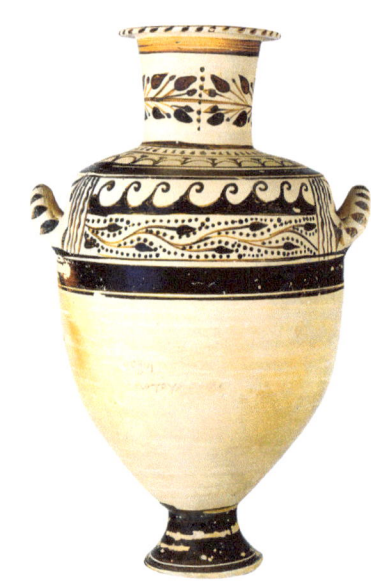

Illustration 144: Greek Black-figure Hydria – Hadra Vase

Continuing into the Classical era, connecting spirals representing ocean waves are frequently depicted on the brilliantly decorated vases produced throughout the developmental days of Western Civilization.

From the earliest ages of Ancient Greece and, indeed, even into our modern times, simple spiral wave motifs persistently communicate an eloquent appreciation for the "wine-dark sea."

Luring us like sirens to the shining shore of Homer's "mighty ocean current," we find ourselves timelessly entranced by the waves encircling our earth, just as the waves encircle the shining rim of the timeless shield of Achilles.

Documented sources for the motifs in this image include:

Ocean Waves:

– Corinthian Black-figure Hydria attributed to the Damon Painter, ca. 560 BCE. At the Louvre Museum, Paris.

– Early Cycladic Terracotta "Frying Pan," from Naxos, ca. 2700-2500 BCE. At the National Archaeological Museum of Athens, Inv. No. 6140A. CCSA 3.0 image by Zde/Vail via Wikimedia Commons.

– Greek Black-figure Hydria, or Hadra Vase from Alexandria, Egypt, ca. 213 BCE. At the Metropolitan Museum of Art. Casagrande-Kim, R., *When the Greeks Ruled Egypt: From Alexander to Cleopatra,* cat. 123, p. 104.

– Kamares Ware Terracotta Vessel from Knossos, ca. 1800-1700 BCE. At the Archaeological Museum of Heraklion. CCSA 4.0 image by Zde/Vail via Wikimedia Commons.

– Mycenaean Palace Wall Fresco, ca. 13th century BCE. At the National Archaeological Museum of Athens, Inv. No. 11671 and 11672. CCSA 3.0 image by Marsyas/Vail via Wikimedia Commons.

The Great Library of Alexandria

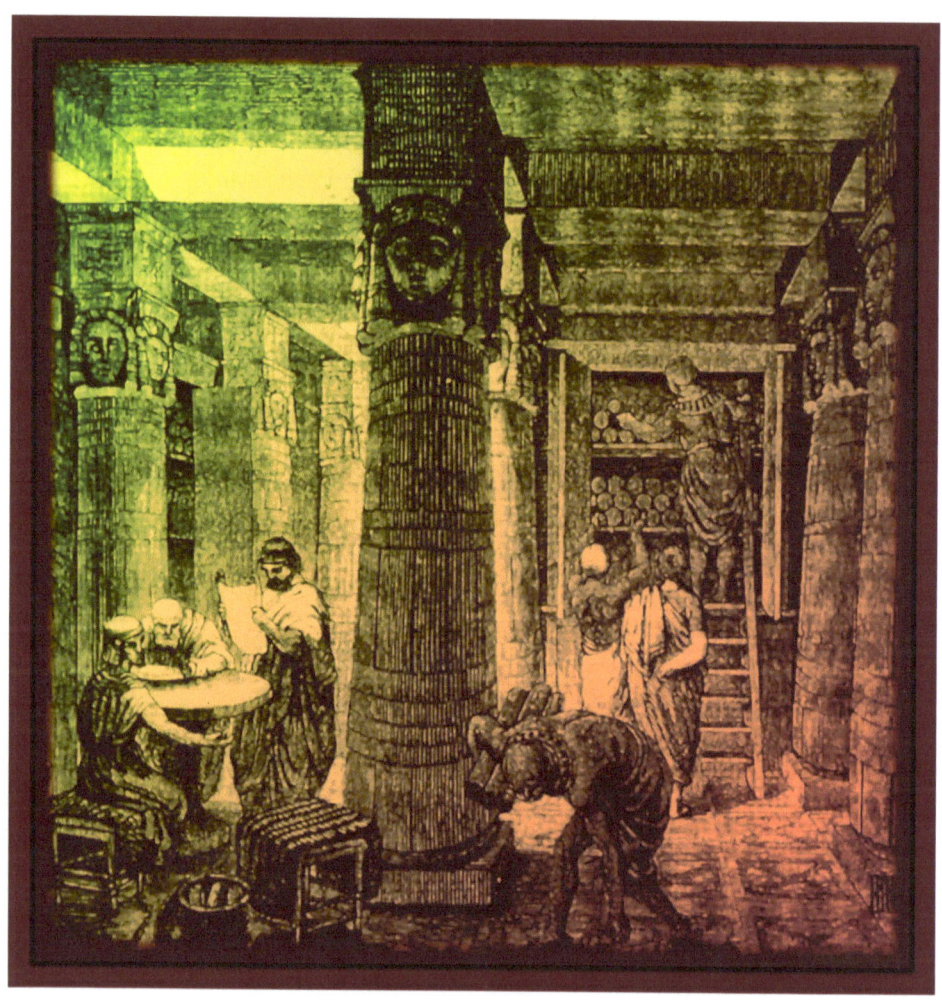

Illustration 145: "The Great Library of Alexandria." Digitally enhanced and colorized renovation by K. Vail of a 19th-century B&W engraving by O. Von Corven. Source: CC0 image by Von Corven/Vail via Wikimedia Commons

Bibliography

Altschuler, Eric Lewin. *Linguistic evidence supports date for Homeric epics,* BioEssays, Wiley Online Library., 2013.

Arieti, James A. *Achilles' Guilt, Classical Journal* Vol. 80/No. 3. Classical Association of the Middle West and South, Inc., 1985.

Atchity, Kenneth J. *Homer's Iliad: The Shield of Memory,* Carbondale: Southern Illinois University Press, 1978.

Beazley, J. D. *Attic Black-figure Vase Painters,* 1956 and *Paralipomena: Additions to Attic Black-Figure Vase-Painters and to Attic Red-Figure Vase-Painters [2nd edition].* Oxford: Clarendon Press, 1971.

Beazley, J. D. *The Development of Attic Black-figure*. Berkeley: The University of California Press, 1986

Beazley, J. and Ashmole, B. *Greek Sculpture and Painting.* Cambridge: The University Press, 1966.

Beijing Capital Museum *AGON The spirit of Competition in Ancient Greece,* Capital Museum, Beijing, 2008.

Boardman, John. *Athenian Black Figure Vases*. New York: Oxford University Press, 1974.

Boardman, John. *The History of Greek Vases*. London: Thames and Hudson, 2001.

Boivin, Jean. *Apologie d'Homere et bouclier d'Achille.* Paris: Chez François Jouenne, 1715.

Brilliant, Richard. *Arts of the Ancient Greeks*. New York: McGraw Hill. 1973.

Buschor, Ernst. *Greek Vase Painting*. London: Chatto and Windus, 1921.

Butler, S. rev'd by Power, Nagy. *Homer's Odyssey*. London: A. C. Fifield, 1900.

Carpenter, Thomas. *Dionysian Imagery in Archaic Greek Art*. Oxford: Clarendon Press, 1986.

Casagrande-Kim, Roberta. *When the Greeks Ruled Egypt: From Alexander to Cleopatra,* Princeton and Oxford: New York University, 2014.

Chadwick, John. *Linear B and Related Scripts*. Berkeley: University of California Press, 1987.

Clark, Andrew J. *Corpus Vasorum Antiquorum. The J. Paul Getty Museum 2 (USA 25)*. Malibu: Getty Publications, 1990.

Clarke, Howard. *Homer's Readers*. Newark: University of Delaware Press, 1981

Cook, Brian F. *Metropolitan Museum of Art Papers – Inscribed Hadra Vases*. New York: Metropolitan Museum of Art, 1966.

Cook, R. M. *Greek Art – Its Development, Character and Influence*. London : Weidenfeld and Nicolson, 1972.

Crawford, M. and Whitehead, D. *Archaic and Classical Greece*. Cambridge: University Press, 1983.

Dobrowolski, W. *Sisyphe et le komos* in *Bulletin du Musée National de Varsovie* . Vol. 17, 1976.

Dubnoff, J. *Translation: Poetry of Sappho*. (online, Center for Hellenic Studies)

Durant, Will. *The Life of Greece*. New York: Simon and Schuster, Inc, 1939.

Edwards, M. *Homer: Poet of the Iliad*. Baltimore: The Johns Hopkins University Press, 1987.

Fagles, Robert. *The Iliad/Homer; translated by Robert Fagles; introduction by Bernard Knox*. New York: Penguin Books, 1991.

Ferrucci, Franco. *The Poetics of Disguise*. Ithaca: Cornell Univ. Press, 1980.

Finley, M. I. *Economy and Society in Ancient Greece*. New York: Viking Press, 1981.

Fitzgerald, Robert. *Translation of the Iliad by Homer.* 1975 and *Translation of the Odyssey by Homer.* Garden City: Anchor Books, 1963.

Folsom, Robert. *Attic Black-figured Pottery*. New Jersey: Noyes Press, 1975.

Fowler, H. and Wheeler, J. *A Handbook of Greek Archaeology*. New York: American Book Co., 1909.

Gardner, Ernest A. *Poet and Artist in Greece*. London: Duckworth, 1933.

Gernet, Louis. *The Anthropology of Ancient Greece*. Baltimore: The Johns Hopkins University Press, 1981.

Hannah, Robert. *The Constellations on Achilles' Shield (Iliad 18. 485-489)*. Vol. 2, No. 4 Electronic Antiquity: Communicating the Classics. 1994.

Harrison, J. E., MacColl, D.S. *Greek Vase Paintings*. London: T.F. Unwin, 1894.

Hogan, James C. *A Guide to the Iliad*. New York: Anchor Books, 1979.

Homan-Wedeking, E. *The Art of Archaic Greece*. New York: Crown Publishers, 1966.

Hôtel Drouot. *Antiquités Grecques et Romaines*. Collection de M.E. Vente Drouot, 1904.

Jaeger, Cf. *Paideia: The Ideals of Greek Culture*. New York: Oxford University Press, 1945.

Jebb, Sir Richard Claverhouse. *The Complete Plays of Sophocles*. New York: Bantam Books, Inc., 1967.

Karouzou, Dr. Semni. *National Museum – Illustrated Guide to the Museum*. Athens: Ekdotike Athenon S.A., 1985.

Kiesling, B., *Conon, Fifty Narrations - Summaries in the Bibliotheca of Photius, Patriach of Constantinople, ca. 810-893. Codices 186-222*, Paris: Les Belles Lettres.

Kotin, Joshua. *Shields of Contradiction and Direction*. Hirundo: The McGill Journal of Classical Studies, Volume 1:11-16, 2001.

Lattimore, Richmond. *The Iliad of Homer*. Chicago: The University of Chicago Press, 1951.

Marg, W. *Homer uber die Dichtung*. Munster: Aschendorff, 1957.

Mertens, Joan R. *How to Read Greek Vases*. New York: Metropolitan Museum of Art, 2010.

Metropolitan Museum of Art. *Greek Art of the Aegean Islands*. New York: Museum catalog of exhibition, 1979-1980.

Mingazzini, Paolino. *Greek Pottery Painting*. London: P. Hamlyn, 1969.

Mireaux, Emile. *Daily Life in the Time of Homer*. New York: MacMillan and Company, 1959.

Murray, A.T., PhD. *Homer's Iliad with Translation*. Cambridge, MA, Harvard University Press; London: William Heinemann 1924.

Murray, A.T., PhD. *Homer's Odyssey with Translation*. Cambridge, MA, Harvard University Press; London: William Heinemann 1924.

Nagy, Greg. *Translation: Hesiod's Works and Days*. Center for Hellenic Studies.

Nagy, Greg. *Homer the Preclassic*, esp. Chapter 2, *I 2*Ⓢ*2. The making of Homeric verse in the Life of Homer traditions*. Berkeley and Los Angeles: University of California Press, 2010.

Nagy, Greg. *Homeric Responses*, esp. Chap. 4, *The Shield of Achilles: Ends of the Iliad and Beginnings of the Polis*. Austin: University of Texas Press, 2003.

New Orleans Museum of Art. *Greek Vases from Southern Collections*. New Orleans: Franklin Printing Co., Inc., 1981.

NOSTOS. *Brief History of the Olympic Games*, NOSTOS Hellenic Information Society.

Owen, S. T. *The Story of the Iliad*. Ann Arbor: University of Michigan Press, 1966.

Pache, Corinne Ondine. *Baby and Child Heroes in Ancient Greece.* Urbana and Chicago: University of Illinois Press, 2004.

Papakonstantinou, Z. *Prizes in Early Archaic Greek Sport.* Oregon, Nikephoros 15, 2002.

Payne, Robert. *Ancient Greece.* New York: W. W. Norton and Co., 1964.

Perseus Digital Library at Tufts. *Pausanias' Description of Greece (English - Online).* University of Chicago.

Pfuhl, Ernst. *Masterpieces of Greek Drawing and Painting.* New York: Hacker Art Books, 1979.

Picón, Carlos A. *Art of the Classical World in the Metropolitan Museum of Art: Greece, Cyprus, Etruria, Rome.* New York: The Metropolitan Museum of Art. 2007.

Rees, Ennis. *The Iliad of Homer.* New York: The Modern Library, 1963.

Renfrew, C. *The Minoan-Mycenaean Origins of the Panhellenic Games* in Raschke, W.J. (Ed.), *The Archaeology of the Olympics: The Olympics and Other Festivals in Antiquity,* Wisconsin: University of Wisconsin Press, 1988.

Richter, Gisela M. A. *A Handbook of Greek Art.* London: The Phaidon Press, 1963.

Rieu, R. V. *Translation of the Iliad by Homer.* Baltimore: Penguin Books, 1966.

Robinson, C. E. *Everyday Life in Ancient Greece.* Oxford: The Clarendon Press, 1933.

Spivey, N. and Squire, M., *Panorama of the Classical World,* Los Angeles: Getty Publications, 2004.

Stobart, J. C. *The Glory that was Greece.* New York: Frederick A. Praeger, 1969.

Trypanis, Constantine A. *The Penguin Book of Greek Verse.* Middlesex: Penguin Books, Ltd., 1971.

Valavanis, Panos. *The Olympics: From Ancient Greece to the World* (online - Greece Is) 2016.

Vidal-Naquet, Pierre. *Le monde d'Homère (The World of Homer),* Perrin, 2000.

VonBothmer, Dietrich. *The Amasis Painter and His World.* New York: Thames and Hudson, Ltd., 1985.

Webster, T. B. L. *From Mycenae to Homer.* London: Methuen and Company, Ltd., 1977.

Wescoat, Bonna D., ed. *Poets and Heroes: Scenes of the Trojan War.* Exh. cat, Emory University Museum of Art and Archaeology. Atlanta: 1986.

About the Author

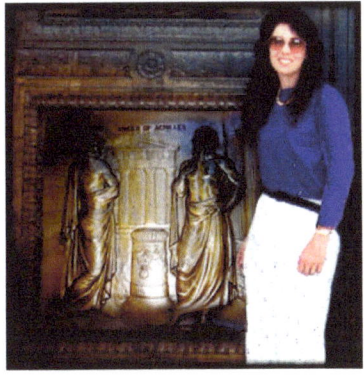

Kathleen Vail is a member of the Maker Movement taking on the Classics. Combining career skills as a computer engineer and graphic artist for the US Department of Defense with research skills as a lifetime student of Homer's Ancient Greece, Kathleen has created a physical, artistically relevant, life-size reconstruction of the divine shield of Achilles based literally and solely on Homer's specifications in Book 18 of the *Iliad*.

Enjoying great success since its creation, Vail's reconstruction of Achilles' shield appears on the cover of Dr. Kenneth Atchity's 2014 Kindle version of *Homer's Iliad: The Shield of Memory*, and Carolina López-Ruiz' *Gods, Heroes, and Monsters* (2nd Edition, Oxford University Press, 2018). She has also given presentations of her work to various groups and organizations, including Virginia chapters of the Classical Association and Mediterranean Society.

Visit Kathleen's website and blog, **http://theshieldofachilles.net** for an in depth exploration of all things Achilles, including his spectacular armor, and Homer's amazing power to excite our imaginations and inspire great creations by artists and artisans, aka Makers, throughout the ages and across all art forms.

Image credit: Vail exploring the litigation scene from Homer's Shield of Achilles on the massive front door of the US Supreme Court in Washington, DC.
© Kathleen Vail, all rights reserved.